Studies in Rhetorics and Feminisms

Series Editors, Cheryl Glenn and Shirley Wilson Logan

Domestic Occupations

SPATIAL RHETORICS AND WOMEN'S WORK

JESSICA ENOCH

Southern Illinois University Press
Carbondale

Southern Illinois University Press
www.siupress.com

Copyright © 2019 by the Board of Trustees,
Southern Illinois University
All rights reserved
Printed in the United States of America

22 21 20 19   4 3 2 1

Cover illustrations: foods laboratory in home economics building, Cornell University, 1917 (Human Ecology Historical Photographs, collection 23-2-749, item DD-FN-24, Division of Rare and Manuscript Collections, Cornell University Library); and floor plan from Beecher and Stowe's *The American Woman's Home* (1869), p. 26.

Library of Congress Cataloging-in-Publication Data
Names: Enoch, Jessica, author.
Title: Domestic occupations : spatial rhetorics and women's work / Jessica Enoch.
Description: Carbondale : Southern Illinois University Press, [2019] | Series: Studies in rhetorics and feminisms | Includes bibliographical references and index.
Identifiers: LCCN 2018053572 | ISBN 9780809337163 (pbk. : alk. paper) | ISBN 9780809337170 (e-book)
Subjects: LCSH: Sex role—History. | Women—Social conditions. | Women—Employment—Social aspects. | Home economics—Social aspects. | Feminism. | Rhetoric.
Classification: LCC HQ1075 .E6736 2019 | DDC 305.309—dc23 LC record available at https://lccn.loc.gov/2018053572

Printed on recycled paper ♻

For Jack, Nancy, and Teddy Wible

Contents

List of Figures   ix

Acknowledgments   xi

1. Contending with Home: Spatial Rhetorics and Women's Work   1
2. From Prison to Home: Spatial Rhetorics Regender the Nineteenth-Century School   31
3. The Domestic Scientist's Home Experiment: Spatial Rhetorics and Professional Ethos   72
4. The Motherless Home: Working Mothers, Emotive Spatial Rhetorics, and the World War II Childcare Center   120
5. Home Work: Spatial Rhetorics and Feminist Rhetorical Scholarship   171

Notes   195

Works Cited   201

Index   229

Figures

1.1. Title page of *The American Woman's Home*   3
1.2. Floor plan in *The American Woman's Home*   4
2.1. "Small Bracketed Cottage"   38
2.2. "The Sphere of Woman"   40
2.3. "Model Cottage"   41
2.4. School at the crossroads   50
2.5. *The Village School in an Uproar*   52
2.6. "Front Projection of Schoolhouse"   55
2.7. "Interior of School"   56
2.8. "The District School Teacher"   63
3.1. "Housekeeper's Laboratory"   95
3.2. "New England Kitchen"   101
3.3. "The Rumford Kitchen, Columbian Exposition, 1893"   107
3.4. "Interior Rumford Kitchen, Columbian Exposition, 1893"   108
4.1. Rosie the Riveter with child in backpack   121
4.2. Childcare center children at table   140
4.3. A child's day in the center   141
4.4. Outdoor playground at the Kaiser Centers   142
4.5. Tucking in at naptime   144
4.6. Pony Express at the childcare center   145
4.7. Group play   147
4.8. "'The Kitchen'—Women's Big Post-War Goal"   156
4.9. "We Can Do It!" poster   167

Acknowledgments

In part, this book is about what it means to find space for career and family. It has been an opportunity for me to meditate on the incredibly powerful pulls that women, especially, often feel to be both at home and at work. And indeed, as I reread these pages, I can track my own struggles with balancing the two over the past ten years. It has not been an easy book to write, but it's been a rewarding one. I want to thank those who have made it possible and who've helped me try to strike this uneasy balance and ultimately get this book *out*.

First, Kristine Priddy at Southern Illinois University Press expertly guided the book to production. To Shirley Logan and Cheryl Glenn, editors of the Studies in Rhetorics and Feminisms series, I am so grateful for your thoughtful feedback and generous support. You exemplify all that is good about feminist mentorship. Cheryl, neither this book nor my career would have happened without you. My gratitude for you abounds.

So many friends within rhetorical studies have read drafts, listened to ideas (good and bad), and presented with me at conferences as I composed this book. Jordynn Jack, Heather Adams, Carly Woods, Marika Seigel, Michelle Smith, Abby Knoblauch, Sarah Hallenbeck, Risa Applegarth, Jack Selzer, Jon Olson, K. J. Rawson, Ryan Skinnell, Jen Borda, Jean Bessette, Dahliani Reynolds, Pamela VanHaitma, Steph Ceraso, Stacey Sheriff, Elizabeth Miller, Heather Lindenman, Ruth Osorio, Danielle Griffin, Katie Bramlett, Scott Eklund, Nathan Tillman, Nabila Hijazi, and David Gold (who read the manuscript at the final hours): your advice and commiseration were invaluable. To the B.I.M.R. (Badasses in Mid-Rank) Facebook group (you know who you are), I am thankful to write and teach alongside you and to see our careers progress together; you all make accountability (and even word counting) fun. At a critical moment during the writing of this manuscript, I joined the formidable Work-in-Progress (WIP!) writing group at the University of Maryland; Ashwini Tambe, Holly Brewer, Laura Rosenthal, and Kristy Maddux helped me right the ship and finish. While completing *Domestic Occupations*, I also coedited with David Gold the collection *Women at Work: Rhetorics of Gender and Labor*. The very smart contributors to that volume emboldened my dedication to thinking through the thorny connections among gender, rhetoric, and work. My colleagues in the English department at the University of Maryland, especially the Language, Writing, and Rhetoric area group—Chanon Adsanatham, Linda Coleman, Jane Donawerth, Michael Israel, Shirley Logan, Leigh Ryan, Vessela Valiavitcharska, Scott Wible, and Sara Wilder—have made UMD a great place to work and write. I am very lucky. In addition to a community of fantastic colleagues, the University of Maryland has supported me in various ways but especially through the College of Arts and Humanities DRIF subvention award.

I could not have written this book without two groups of people that often go unnoticed: archivists and babysitters. I greatly appreciate the exemplary work of archivists at the Massachusetts Institute of Technology and the Schlesinger Library, as well as those who maintain Harvard University's digital archive *Women Working, 1800–1930* and Cornell's *Home Economics Archive: Research, Tradition, and History* (HEARTH). My three children were born during the course of writing this book. Our amazing childcare providers over the past ten years, especially Samantha Brown DiSalvio, Karol Orme, and Caroline Coller Cibak, gave me time, space, and peace of mind.

My friends and family provided much-needed breaks from writing and research. Julie, Kay, Marla, Steph, Caroline, Kathleen, Lisa, Jenny, Kim, Sara, Betsy, Dawn, Anissa, Becky, Sympson, Casabe, and my new WES friends: the laughs (and the wine) helped *a lot*. Pj and Melanie, our workouts got me through the worst of it. And, of course, Nancy McLinden Carr was with me every day and supported me in spirit. To Rob, Carleen, Jonah, Lily, and Oliver as well as Liz, Bernie, Bridget, Andrew, Brad, Jillian, Jasper, and Ruby, thank you for your encouragement and support. My parents, Bob and Barb, always remind me what's most important; thank you for your love (and help) and for always being in my corner.

Few people are lucky enough to have a partner who so fully respects and supports them and their work. Scott Wible, you're a very good person; I could not have written a word without you, and I wouldn't have wanted to. And finally, I dedicate this book to the three people who've made me think really hard about what it means to be a mother, a teacher, and a writer and about why it's so difficult to (try to) balance home and work. Jack, Nancy, and Teddy: I've been writing this book since the days you were born. Thank you for being patient with me and for cheering me on. I love you, and I'm done!

Domestic Occupations

1. Contending with Home

SPATIAL RHETORICS AND WOMEN'S WORK

> To the female, is committed the important office of guiding the house; of managing the internal conditions of the family; of contriving, ordering, directing, improving, or producing, almost every thing, that constitutes and promotes the comforts, the delights, and the endearments of domestic life. The duties of this station, however, so essential to civilization and refinement, may be considered as included in those of wife and mother. And let it be remembered, let it never be forgotten, no pursuits are more appropriate, or more honorable, to a female than the duties of the domestic circle. "A wise woman buildeth her house." It is her study and delight to contrive and improve whatever may conduce to the welfare of her household.
> —Joseph Emerson, *Female Education*, 1822

Joseph Emerson's words articulate a familiar understanding of the white middle-class home and the woman's place in it. The woman should occupy the home, and her work is "directing, improving, or producing, almost every thing, that constitutes and promotes the comforts, the delights, and the endearments of domestic life" (9). This dominant description of woman's work resounded throughout the United States in the nineteenth and twentieth centuries through a variety of cultural formations, with books, magazines, art, and even architectural manuals reinforcing the idea that the home was indeed woman's place. The title page of Catharine E. Beecher and Harriet Beecher Stowe's 1869 *American Woman's Home* is just one example that elucidates this point (fig. 1.1). Its central image depicts the peaceful, bucolic American home, and the peripheral images showcase the white middle-class woman's work inside it, tending to her children, and just outside it, tending to her garden. These authors underscore the expectation that it is "woman's true profession" (13) to take up this domestic work, and they use their book to instruct women readers on how not only to guide their husband and children to "intelligence, virtue, and true happiness" (23) but also to manage the home by attending to such major concerns as its architectural plan (fig. 1.2), its heating and cooling systems, as well as the physical designs for each room. The instructions Beecher and Stowe provided, however, were just that—instructions—and like all instructions, they were not wholly followed by their anticipated women readers. While many nineteenth- and twentieth-century women certainly took their place in the home, others wanted to or had to look outside it for different kinds of work.

In 1897 Frances Willard wrestled with these dominant perceptions of women's relationship to work and the home. Her *Occupations for Women: A Book of Practical Suggestions for the Material Advancement, the Mental and Physical Development, and the Moral and Spiritual Uplift of Women* begins by encouraging her women readers to look beyond the home and to work outside it:

> To-day girls in almost every position in life are wondering what they shall do for a living. Shall a girl go into business, study for a profession, go on the stage, take up art, or strike out on some new line into paths hitherto untrod? Like their brothers, the girls of to-day want to be something, do something, accomplish something. (22)

But even with this overt encouragement to step outside the home and explore new occupations, Willard tempers her enthusiasm by the end of the book. Echoing the expectations articulated by figures like Beecher and Stowe, Willard explains to her readers, "The advancement, improvement, and safety of the nation depend upon the perfect home, and earth's noblest thing is the woman perfected in the wife, the mother who rules that home" (240). Although the woman should certainly aspire to "be something," she should also see that her greatest accomplishment is the making of a home.

Willard's conflicted position regarding woman's place in the home and her interest in or need to work outside it can be traced throughout the nineteenth, twentieth, and indeed into the twenty-first centuries. From Fanny Fern and Susan B. Anthony II to Charlotte Perkins Gilman and Betty Friedan, writers have contended with the pervasive assumption that the ideal American home (read: white middle-class home) necessitates a woman's presence, and they have considered how this assumption has inflected women's attempts to seek

Fig. 1.1. Title page of Catharine E. Beecher and Harriet Beecher Stowe's *The American Woman's Home* (1869).

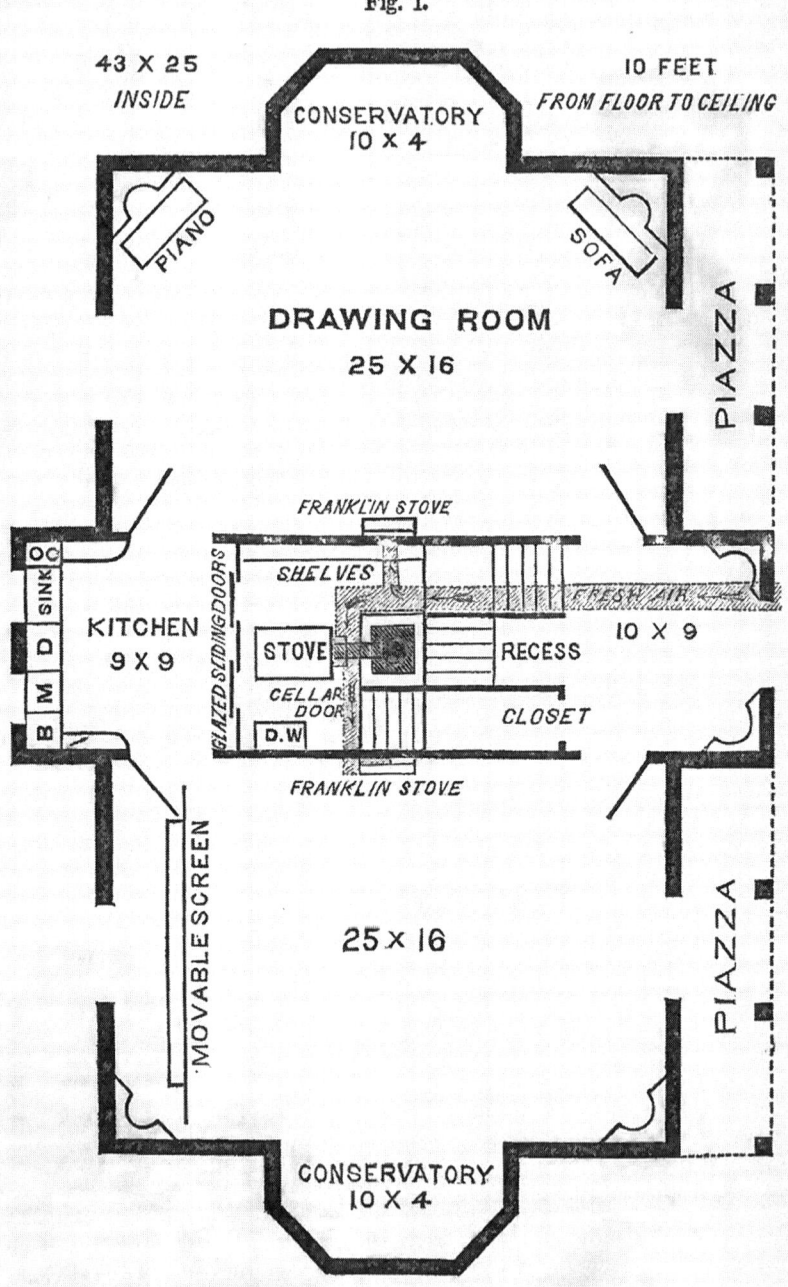

Fig. 1.2. Floor plan. Beecher and Stowe's *The American Woman's Home* (1869), p. 26.

professional development and new work opportunities. Even as recently as 2011, Facebook executive Sheryl Sandberg claimed, "The No. 1 impediment to women succeeding in the workforce is now in the home.... Most people assume that women are responsible for households and child care.... That fundamental assumption holds women back" (Auletta). As Sandberg's words suggest, when women attempt to move into the workplace, they often have to contend with the site of the home, articulating why and how they should leave this space to pursue other professional options.

Domestic Occupations: Spatial Rhetorics and Women's Work interrogates the historical connections among women, the home, and the workplace, focusing on the period from 1820 to 1950. The first step I take to pursue this project is to denaturalize these linkages, meaning that I see the relationship not as a given fact but rather as one that is constructed and reconstructed over time and circumstance. A major premise of the book, then, is that women's relationship to the home and to the workplace has not always been the same. It has shifted due to myriad exigencies and situations, and it has been conditioned by women's intersectional identities: their race, class, culture, sexuality, (dis)ability, and so on. Given this variety and mutability, I see this relationship as *rhetorical*. That is, this relationship is created, sustained, and reshaped through rhetorical operations that are crafted in response to particular constraints and that capitalize on specific opportunities.

My work in *Domestic Occupations* is to explore three distinct situations and the different rhetorical conditions that tied specific sets of women to the home and regulated their work outside it. More particularly, in the three chapters to follow, I examine the ways women came to dominate the teaching profession by leaving the home in the early nineteenth century (chapter 2), the material changes that women made to the home to claim expertise as domestic scientists at the turn of the twentieth century (chapter 3), and the rhetorical shifts that enabled mothers to find a secondary home for their children in the childcare center so these women could enter the war plant during World War II (chapter 4). To take up these examinations, I focus on particular domestic and professional circumstances as a way to investigate women's changing relationship to both the home and workplace as well as the complex rhetorical operations that at times tethered them to home and at others freed them to explore different professional paths.

Domestic Occupations is thus a feminist history of rhetoric. However, it takes up this historiographic project in a unique way. A more traditional feminist rhetorical study might examine the overt arguments women made for new work opportunities and their refusals to remain in the home. Such a project would engage the claims made by a host of historical figures who sought futures in nondomestic professional realms. While *Domestic Occupations* does at times include and analyze such overt arguments, its predominant trajectory moves in a different direction. As the title of the book indicates, this study explores the *spatial rhetorics* that shaped women's domestic ties and work-related opportunities. Rather than focusing on explicit arguments for women's professional advancement, I attend to the implicit, subtle, yet powerful spatial rhetorics of the home and the workplace that influenced expectations for women to remain in or move beyond the domestic scene.

As I discuss below and develop in the chapters that follow, spatial rhetorics are the multimodal ways through which spaces gain meaning. They are the material elements that create the space, as well as the pictorial, embodied, displayed, emotive, and discursive understandings that define what a space is and what it should be. Spatial rhetorics suggest the purpose of the space; the actions, behaviors, and practices that should happen inside that space; and the people who should occupy it. These rhetorics give significance and value to a space, affecting people's understanding of the space and their attachment to it. Spatial rhetorics also distinguish one kind of space from another, articulating differences between spaces as well as differences in people's (expected) investment in and experiences of them. Finally, these rhetorics have the power to divest spaces of their past identities and create new spatial meanings for the present and future.

Developing this definition of spatial rhetorics throughout this book, I look to three case studies to explore how the spaces of the home and the workplace were cast in ways that thwarted or enabled particular kinds of work opportunities for specific sets of women. Chapter 2 examines the spatial rhetorics that paved the way for women teachers in the early- to mid-nineteenth century. Analyzing the spatial rhetorics that composed both the home and the school, I argue that these rhetorics *regendered* the school from a masculine, prisonlike space of discipline and corporal punishment to a feminine, homelike space. Because this regendering process made the school into another kind of home, women were able to leave the family residence to claim their place at the head of classroom. Chapter 3 investigates the emergence of the domestic scientist on the professional scene at the turn of the twentieth century. Here I explore how domestic scientists leveraged spatial rhetorics to remake the home into a space fit for scientific examination, and I contend that by doing so, women carved out a new professional *ethos* for themselves. Chapter 4 moves to the

World War II period to consider mothers' opportunities to work outside the home and the concerns that emerged about the fate of the working mother and her children. To address these concerns and enable mothers to work, the government and industries built more than three thousand childcare centers so that mothers could leave the home and enter the war plant. After the war, however, these centers closed, but not without great protest from many mothers who desperately needed to continue working. This chapter focuses on the *emotive* spatial rhetorics that assuaged and amplified anxieties around what one figure called the "motherless home" (*Proceedings* [1942] 68). Chapter 4 studies how these spatial rhetorics pacified concerns during the war when women were needed to work and exacerbated them once the country saw the need for women to return to the home after the war.

A priority for the book is to reflect on how issues of race, culture, and class animate spatio-rhetorical discussions about women's work and their relationship to it. Certainly, not all women had or now have the same relationship to the home, given that women from various raced, cultured, or classed groups have negotiated the demands of work and their ties to the domestic sphere in different ways. The path I take to explore this contextual and historical complexity is to consider how *dominant* discourses at particular periods in time composed the ideal American home—that is, the white middle-class home—and to examine how such pervasive yet shifting spatial rhetorics inflected women's opportunities for particular kinds of work: teaching, domestic science, and World War II labor. Thus the goal is to investigate how these spatial rhetorics, which circulated powerfully through the public sphere, composed, preserved, and at times reconstituted the white middle-class home in ways that were significant to specific sets of working women.

Because of the perspective I take, the women who are the implicit and explicit concern of these dominant discourses are, not surprisingly, often white and middle class, and indeed a great deal of my focus is on how these women were affected by and negotiated such powerful spatial rhetorics. However, each chapter also complicates this view by acknowledging that studies of marginalized women's work "have been marked by the twin sins of silence and omission" ("Sisters" xvi). Throughout the main chapters I investigate the ways that dominant discourses about women's home life and work life—rhetorics that often assumed white middle-class status—were complicated when differently raced, cultured, and classed women encountered them. That is, I inspect in these moments how dominant rhetorics of the home and workplace reverberated for women who did not occupy this expected category, and I consider the complex negotiations these women made as they too contended with these discourses.

Individually, the three case studies of this book reveal unique moments of tension when women's expected place in the home was in flux and under debate. Collectively, the chapters offer critical insight into the subtle yet powerful enactments of spatial rhetorics that have differently defined the home and the workplace in ways that were consequential to women workers. The title of the book—*Domestic Occupations*—is, therefore, a play on words. The term "occupation" means *both* the taking possession of a space *and* a kind of work. Given this double meaning of "occupation," the guiding questions that propel this study are the following: (1) How have dominant rhetorics created understandings of the white middle-class home in ways that prescribed the (often white, middle-class) woman's presence in this space and shaped her work outside it? (2) How have spatial rhetorics defined certain professional occupations, workplaces, and sites of support (like childcare centers) so that women could (or could not) claim new types of work? In the remainder of this introduction, I begin thinking through these questions by pinpointing the major theoretical and methodological concerns that inform this study and by identifying the interventions it makes to feminist rhetorical studies in particular as well as rhetorical studies, feminist historiography, and humanities scholarship in general.

Spatial Rhetorics

In her 2005 presidential address to the American Studies Association, Karen Halttunen proclaimed that the humanities have made a "spatial turn," meaning that "space and place have never been more analytically important in humanities scholarship" (2). Rhetoricians Carole Blair, Greg Dickinson, and Brian Ott agree, writing in 2010 that "[p]lace and its most frequent companion term, space, seem to be on everyone's lips in recent years" (22). Within rhetorical studies, scholars such as Gregory Clark, Danielle Endres, Samantha Senda-Cook, David Fleming, Joan Faber McAlister, Roxanne Mountford, and Nedra Reynolds have joined Blair, Dickinson, and Ott in analyzing sites, ranging from national parks (G. Clark) to religious pulpits (Mountford), and seeing them as "rhetorical phenomen[a]" and "performanc[es]" (Endres and Senda-Cook 260, 263). For these rhetoricians, spaces are meaning-makers: spaces make statements about the world in which we live. Even so, while feminist rhetoricians such as Lindal Buchanan, Nan Johnson (*Gender*), Mountford, and Lisa Shaver are dedicating more scholarly energy to questions of space, McAlister is right to assert that there is much work yet to be done that uses gender as an analytic to study space (and vice versa) ("Ten Propositions"). *Domestic Occupations* addresses this need by developing a robust definition of spatial rhetorics, distinguishing what a spatio-rhetorical analytical method is, and demonstrating how this method offers a new way of doing *feminist* rhetorical history by examining, specifically, the spatio-rhetorical operations that tied women to the home or that (dis)enabled them from entering the workplace.

Before elaborating on the understanding of spatial rhetorics that guides my study, I first want to clarify my choice to use the term *space* rather than *place*. As Phil Hubbard, Rob Kitchin, and Gill Valentine admit, there is no broad agreement on what differentiates these terms. Indeed, the relationship between them is "a matter of some dispute" (3). One prevalent way of understanding the distinction between the terms is that of "particular to general," whereby place is particular and space is general (Endres and Senda-Cook 259). For geographers like Yi-Fu Tuan, space is "undifferentiated" territory, while place is defined (*Space* 6). Designated spaces are places, "particular locations (e.g., a city, a particular shopping mall, or a park) that are semi-bounded, a combination of material and symbolic qualities, and embodied" (Endres and Senda-Cook 259). Places as identifiable locations are thus "laden with meanings" and "full of human interpretation and significance" (G. Rose 43); a "place is space to which meaning has been ascribed" (Carter et al. xii). Given my definition of spatial rhetorics above, we might understand spatial rhetorics, then, as those discursive, embodied, displayed, emotive, pictorial, and material means that transform a space into a place.

While this relationship makes sense, I elected not to adopt this terminological distinction throughout the book. Rather than identify moments when a general space becomes a particular place, I call all the sites under inspection "spaces" and, by extension, the rhetorical work that composes and recomposes the sites "spatial rhetorics." I do so for three reasons. First, I choose "space" as a way to counter the claim that an area, location, or site is at any point bereft of value, that there is such thing as a meaningless space that turns into a meaningful place. Rather, my understanding is that all spaces hold some kind of rhetorical charge, even if it is one of seeming neutrality. There is no arhetorical space. Spaces are always interpreted and named, attended to at different times and in different ways—even disregard means something. Second, I choose "space" to disrupt the idea that sites like a school, a kitchen, or childcare center are permanent and unchangeable. As Michel de Certeau writes, "place implies an indication of stability" (117). Yet, a premise of this book is that sites are not stable. They are always open to revision and renovation. Instead of suggesting this stability by using the term "place," I choose "space" to mark the indeterminate nature of sites that may give the illusion of permanence. Third, I call the sites studied here "spaces" because, throughout the case studies of this book, I do not inspect one *specific* location—I do not study a particular schoolhouse, home, or childcare center. Rather, my concern is with how dominant discourses described these sites *in general* and how interlocutors attempted to revise such discourses. Of course, material renovation happened at specific locations, but my aim is to show how these renovations reflected overarching trends in rethinking what *the* home, *the* school, or *the* childcare center should be. The specific sites discussed in their respective chapters thus functioned synecdochically, whereby an individual home, school, or childcare center stood as an exemplar for what all were or should be like. In sum, I call the sites I study "spaces" to underscore their ability to change shape and meaning in the public imagination, to highlight their potential to affect women's spatial occupation and mobility, and to make clear that the spaces at the heart of this study are rhetorically important ones.

To elaborate further on the understanding of spatial rhetorics that drives this book, I set out below three premises that undergird my investigations, and I continue to define what spatial rhetorics are and how a spatio-rhetorical analysis operates. These premises stem from my preferred terminology of *space* and emphasize space's rhetoricity. That is, my claims below are based on the idea that spaces are not just "the scene" or the backdrop for lived events, "empty and neutral of our experiences" (Fleming 24). Rather, as rhetorics, spaces are "active" sites of meaning-making (Reynolds, *Geographies* 16) that are "charged and responsive to the movements of time, plot, and history" (Bakhtin 84). The premises below build on scholarship in human, cultural, social, and feminist geography as well as in rhetorical studies, and they provide the feminist theoretical framework that supports the investigations in the chapters that follow.

1. *Spatial (re)construction occurs through a variety of means and agencies.* One primary way for spaces to gain meaning is through purposeful human agency. As Fleming explains, "space is plastic, and we can mold it to our purposes" (24). Human actors create space not only through design and material composition but also through the rules and expectations for the space, the presence or absence of bodies and objects within the space, the activities that happen within the space, and the symbolic representation of it. Yet there is more. Beyond the initial setting out and establishing of what a space should

be, human *response* to, interpretation of, and creative use of space are other modes of spatio-rhetorical (re)composition. Furthermore, spatial rhetorics emerge because engagements with space are perspectival. That is, the same space can have different meanings for different people, and these interpretive differences derive from a constellation of factors: gender, race, class, culture, ability status, and sexuality primary among them.

One particular point regarding the (re)construction of a space is its emotional dimension. Actors create spaces through their feelings about them and attachment to them. Tuan even defines the deeply positive emotional response to a location—the love for a space—as "topophilia" (*Topophilia*). A key concern for the spatio-rhetorical analyses in my study is to explore the ways interlocutors create and contend with positive and negative bonds to places such as the school, the childcare center, and, especially, the highly emotive space of the home. In each chapter, and particularly in chapter 4, I interrogate how stakeholders reinforce, revise, or create new emotional relationships with these sites.

By (re)composing places, then, actors define, from the outset and through a variety of means, what a space is, what it does, and how it should operate. Actors also interpret, use, and remake spaces according to their own exigencies. Through this latter process of remaking, ideas about a space are confirmed, multiplied, rethought, or completely rejected. In this way, there is a reciprocal nature to space: human actors build spaces and suggest spatial actions, practices, and understandings, but then, through the inhabitation and "practicing" of space, new actors come up with different ideas about and meanings for that space (de Certeau 130). And we can push this point even further. Over time and through varieties of practices, a space's definition may also evolve *indirectly* through means that are not overtly purposeful. That is, a space may—through use, abandonment, or a variety of other unrelated circumstances such as funding, proximity to other locations, geographic and/or environmental change—gain new, unintended meanings. While these meanings may be inadvertent and even accidental, they are still consequential and contribute significantly to a site's spatio-rhetorical significance.

2. *Central to any effort to stabilize, redefine, claim, or occupy a space are questions of power.* To be sure, there are a number of ways people may understand a space. The meanings that interlocutors may make of it, however, do not always coexist peacefully; spaces are often sites of contest where power is realized and exercised in various ways (Massey). Spatial occupation, regulation, and restriction reveal the workings of power, for it is no surprise to state that whenever one names, lays claim to, is relegated to, or is excluded from a

space, that person exerts power or is subject to another's power. David Harvey articulates this familiar circumstance when he writes, "we all know ... what it means to be 'put in one's place' and that to challenge what that place might be, physically as well as socially, is to challenge something fundamental about the social order" ("Between" 419). Power is at the heart of space-making; spaces are laced with power.

A feminist spatio-rhetorical lens enables scholars to focus on how the "spatial trappings of power" circulate and function, and it invites scholars to explore how questions of gender, and indeed race, class, culture, sexuality, and ability status, animate this process (J. Allen 19). This invitation is seconded by Edward Soja's statement that "[w]e must be insistently aware of how space can be made to hide consequences from us, how relations of power and discipline are inscribed into the apparently innocent spatiality of social life" (6). The feminist spatio-rhetorical perspective that propels this study questions spatial classification, divisions, and expectations, and it interrogates what may seem to be "innocent spatiality" by exploring how such innocence refracts powerfully through particular women's lives.

3. *Bodies and objects within a space inflect and are inflected by the meaning of that space.* We cannot talk about space and power or the occupation and renovation of space without also thinking about the actual bodies that inhabit a site. Our embodied presence and the activities we take up within spaces help define what spaces are. In turn, however, our bodies are also affected by the definition, purpose, and design of those spaces. Foremost among these concerns are expectations for who is supposed to occupy a space and what one is supposed to do inside it. Choosing the terminology of "place" over "space," Reynolds confirms this point: "bodies and places impact upon each other, a body becomes marked with the residue of place, but places are also changed by the presence of bodies" (*Geographies* 143). Spatial rhetorics attend to what bodies do to spaces and what spaces do to bodies, distinguishing the ways that sites confine, constrain, or free bodies and the ways that bodies make and remake spaces through their presence and actions.

The same is true, in many ways, for the objects within a space. Certainly, spaces are created not just through architectural design and configuration. Spaces also gain meaning through the placement of objects within them that range from functional appliances to ornamental décor. A spatio-rhetorical analysis must attend to how objects sustain, shift, or bring new meaning to spaces (and vice versa). In this way, a spatio-rhetorical perspective aligns with and draws from scholarship on material rhetorics. Work by Scot Barnett and

Casey Boyle, Maureen Goggin and Beth Fowkes Tobin, Laurie Gries, Sarah Hallenbeck, Malea Powell, Jack Selzer, and Thomas Rickert builds on the premise that "material realities often (if not always) contain a rhetorical dimension that deserves attention" (Selzer 8). As Barnett and Boyle explain, material *things* function rhetorically: they "provoke thought, incite feeling, circulate affects, and arouse in us a sense of wonder" (1). Working from these scholars' ideas, I consider what objects within spaces *do* to shape experience. But a clarification is necessary: the project for any spatio-rhetorical analysis is not to examine material objects in isolation but instead to see them as part of their spatial environment. This kind of examination should attend to the confluence of materials and movements, bodies and buildings, words and silence. *Domestic Occupations* is therefore concerned with understanding what all of these moving parts have to say about the interanimation of gender, rhetoric, and space in general and, more particularly, how dominant perceptions of the home prescribed women's attachment to it and conditioned women's work outside it.

Women's Work

This study attends to how dominant spatio-rhetorical discourses of home affected the schoolteacher, the domestic scientist, and the wartime mother, and it explores the ways these women contended with such discourses as they attempted to enter new work environments. I have chosen these examples of women's career development for particular reasons. They are cases when specific women moved into new occupations in great numbers and when this movement exposed their strained relationship to the home. These women also had different agendas as they entered their careers: some sought to gain professional expertise and exercise their intellect, while others had no other choice but to work. The main chapters of this study reveal how variously motivated women came to dominate the teaching profession, how they claimed the professional ethos of domestic scientist, and how they moved into (and out of) the war plant as working mothers. Each of these new professional experiences required the women under study to negotiate and compose complex spatial rhetorics that shaped who they were as workers and as women.

The three examples at the heart of this study are, however, just part of a rich conversation about the ways women have managed their relationship to the home as they pursued occupations. From 1820 to 1950 in the United States, women's work opportunities shifted greatly due to the onset of the Industrial Revolution, the end of slavery, women's access to education, and the identification and development of new careers and professions, as well as shifts in the labor market owing to war, recovery, and economic depressions. And within all of these conversations about women and work, questions of race, culture, and class infused understandings of who worked, why, when, how, and for how much. While a fully nuanced picture of women's work is not possible here, it is important to gain a general sense of the situation and its complexity.

During the period from 1820 to 1950, women's work opportunities expanded to factory work, domestic service, nursing, business, clerical work, and teaching; women were journalists, doctors, laborers, astronomers, telephone girls, department store clerks, actresses, photographers, anthropologists, midwives, settlement workers, inventors, and more. While it is true that many of these occupations were more densely populated by women than were others (with domestic service, nursing, and teaching being top among them), by 1920 there were 232 occupations in which "1,000 or more women were employed" (Dempsey 3). In addition to the growing breadth of occupations, there was also depth: women in greater numbers were entering the workplace. Joanne Meyerowitz explains, "From 1880 to 1930, the female labor force increased from 2.6 million to 10.8 million. The number of women gainfully employed grew almost twice as fast as the adult female population" (xviii). By 1950 women made up 30 percent of all workers and were found in every census occupational classification, with "about half the employed women [being] clerical workers or operatives, a fifth . . . in various services, and over a tenth in professions" ("Changes" vii).

While these numbers indicate growth in vocational opportunity, women did not enjoy unrestricted employment opportunities during this period (or even at present, for that matter). Indeed, a priority for this study is to explore the barriers women faced as they attempted to move into these new roles. In addition to the spatio-rhetorical conditions explored here, limited access to education, racism, classism, and xenophobia barred many women's entrance into advanced professions and often confined them to domestic labor and factory work. Focusing on African American women after the Civil War, Rosalyn Baxandall, Linda Gordon, and Susan Reverby find that these women largely had no choice but to work: "Among African Americans, poverty and employment discrimination meant that men found it harder to get jobs, let alone jobs with a decent wage, so that women were far more likely to work outside the home, usually as servants or farm laborers" (xxii). Important to this point are the differing relationships that women from various backgrounds and cultural groups have had with the workplace and with the home. As Rebecca Sharpless explains in her study of black women's domestic service, the black woman's workplace was often the home—the white family's home. As such, "domestic work served as a middle ground between slavery and an open economy" (xi); the white home was the workplace within which black women had to make "'a way out of no way' . . . until better employment opportunities became available" (xii). When black women left "their own homes to go to white people's houses everyday," they "functioned within a world of extremely hard work, low wages, and omnipresent racial strife" (xiii). Thus, while the women studied here may have been attempting to leave the home or recast the work they did inside it, African American women's relationship to home and work was different. For the black woman domestic especially, the home was a workplace riddled with racial complexity and power dynamics not experienced by the working- and middle-class white woman.

Furthermore, if and when women from any variety of classed, cultured, and raced backgrounds entered work spaces ranging from other people's homes to sites beyond it, they were universally poorly compensated compared to their male counterparts. At the turn of the twentieth century, for example, women's wages averaged 50 percent of men's (Baxandall et al. xxiii). The spatio-rhetorical concerns at the heart of this book contributed to this inequity in earnings. As Alice Kessler-Harris writes, "the belief that women belonged at home permitted employers to exploit working women by treating them as though their earnings were merely supplemental" (103). Given the prospect of such low pay, it is critical to note the motivations for women to work. As suggested above, while some middle-class women may have wanted to work as a means of gaining a modicum of financial independence or personal freedom, many working-class women *had* to work out of sheer necessity. Women in this latter category were not only "the lowest paid workers" but also "performed the least-skilled jobs"; as such their living and working conditions were often untenable (Kessler-Harris 106). Unsurprisingly, the desire to work and the prospect of home and family were different for these women than for their middle-class counterparts. As Kessler-Harris explains, if it was possible, many women living through such difficult situations "left the workplace with relief when marriage and motherhood offered an acceptable escape" (106).

Given the barriers and opportunities that women from various backgrounds faced, and the exigencies that prompted them to enter and remain in the workforce, it makes sense that this period was alive with conversations about women's work, professional activity, preparatory education, and labor conditions. Figures such as Virginia Penny, Catherine Dall, and Ida Husted Harper argued for expanding women's work opportunities and called attention to issues such as wages. Elizabeth Blackwell, Liberty Hyde Bailey, and James Porter pointed to the education and training women needed to enter such fields as architecture, medicine, agriculture, and factory operations. Similar to Willard's 1897 *Occupations for Women,* capacious texts such as Annie Nathan Meyer's *Women's Work in America* (1891) and Catherine Filene's *Careers for Women* (1920) mapped the options for women in fields from government service and museum work to insurance and law. Authors such as Caroline A. Huling, Doris Fleischman, Jeannette Eaton, and Margaret Sumner offered career guidance and instruction through their respective texts: *Letters of a Business Woman to Her Niece* (1906), *An Outline of Careers for Women: A Practical Guide to Achievement* (1928), *Commercial Work and Training for Girls* (1915), and *Chats on Garment Salesmanship* (1917). Almond Davis, Annie Nelles Dumond, Jessie Field, and Rosalie Slaughter Morton leveraged the genre that Risa Applegarth calls "vocational autobiograph[y]" by reflecting on their experiences as preachers, book agents, teachers, and surgeons, respectively ("Personal Writing" 531). And fiction such as Fanny Fern's "The Working Girls of New York" (1868), Elizabeth Stuart Phelps's *Silent Partner* (1871), and Louisa May Alcott's *Work: A Story of Experience* (1873) focused on women's work and labor reform.

Recognizing the particular work-related challenges African American women faced, black writers and rhetors such as Anna Julia Cooper, Fannie Barrier Williams, and Mrs. N. F. Mossell extended and complicated this national conversation. Mossell's 1908 *The Work of the African American Woman* chronicled and named the many black women who were entering fields from journalism to dentistry and then advised readers on how they might follow these professional leaders. Cooper and Williams took on a more critical tone, as Williams in particular argued in 1893 that white society and especially white women were responsible for the black woman's lack of professional options. She asserted, "It is almost literally true that, except teaching in colored schools and menial work, colored women can find no employment in this free America. They are the only women in the country for whom real ability, virtue, and special talents count for nothing" (qtd. in Logan, "What" 157). Zeroing in on those responsible for this injustice, Williams makes it clear that her audience "should never forget that the exclusion of colored women and girls from nearly all places of respectable employment is due mostly to the meanness of American women" (157).

In addition to these individual efforts to understand and expand women's work opportunities, there were institutional responses as well. For example, the Women's Bureau was established within the Department of Labor in 1920, and it offered reports on issues relating to women's working conditions, wages, hours of employment, and the status of married women and mothers in the workforce. Bulletins from Boston's Vocation Office for Girls instructed women readers on career options such as telephone operating, manicuring, dressmaking, and bookbinding. Women's clubs like the New York–based Sorosis focused on more elite professions, while the Women's Educational and Industrial Union and the Working Women's Society attended to concerns relating to training, labor conditions, and legislation (Vapnek 76). Journals and newspapers such as the *Ladies' Home Journal* and *Women's Home Companion* published articles relating to women and work. And dedicating themselves solely to women's occupational opportunities and struggles were outlets such as *Woman's Work* (Brooklyn, New York), the *Operatives' Magazine* (Lowell, Massachusetts),[1] and *Independent Woman* of the National Federation of Business and Professional Women's Club. The question of work was also a prime concern within the feminist movement of the period, a priority emboldened in 1848 by the call in "Declaration of Sentiments" for women's "equal participation with men in the various trades and professions" (142) and affirmed in the words of leader Julia Ward Howe, who wrote that "the professions indeed supply the key-stone to the arch of woman's liberty" (2).

Complementing this vibrant conversation about woman's work *outside* the home was a rethinking of her work *inside* it. Certainly there was great conversation regarding domestic service. As noted above, black women often worked as domestics in white homes, but immigrant women, and especially Irish immigrant women, also entered these roles in great numbers (see Dudden). As Thomas Dublin reports, "in 1870, for instance, Boston had one servant for every three and one-half families; for New York City and Philadelphia, the comparable proportions were one servant for every four and five families" (157). Texts such as *Plain Talk and Friendly Advice to Domestics* (1855) offered guidance for how best to manage and train women for this in-home work, and unions such as the Household Workers' Association steered workers toward collective bargaining ("Household Workers' Association"). In addition to focusing attention on paid domestic employment, discussion also emerged regarding the unpaid work of wives and mothers. As Dolores Hayden writes, a line of feminist argument during this period identified the home as a space of work and thus called for "economic remuneration for women's unpaid household labor" (*Grand Domestic Revolution* 1).[2] Often defined as the material or maternalist strand of the feminist movement, groups such as the National Congress of Mothers and reformers like Jane Addams, Charlotte Perkins Gilman, and Inez Milholland argued that women should be compensated for their domestic labor and child-rearing (Ladd-Taylor 139).

An important strand of this conversation was one marked by concern. Interlocutors with widely differing investments voiced anxiety over the consequences of (some) women entering the workplace. Not surprisingly the focus was on the white, native-born, middle-class woman and the effects that her work outside the home would have on her virtue. Meyerowitz examines the turn-of-the-century phenomenon of women taking jobs that physically separated them from their families and their familial homes. She explains that a great deal of attention was paid to these women, so much so that observers understood this new gendered and spatial situation as "women adrift" and read it as a sign of their "moral decay" (xix). Historian Lynn Weiner elaborates on this idea by underscoring how concerns about race, culture, and class inflected these anxieties. She writes that the most serious concern was not directed at "immigrant and black women [because they] ha[d] always worked" (5). Rather, the concern grew when "native-born white women increased their propensity to work," and when they did, "the question of woman's proper place gathered strength in public debate" (5). The movement of the "respectable" woman into the workplace attracted national attention because once she went "adrift," so too, it seemed, would the middle-class Anglo-American home and family and, by extension, the dominant expectations for and practices of (white middle-class) American ways of life.

In this study, I engage these concerns by interrogating how they were differently articulated in three separate work-related circumstances: when the woman teacher took her place at the head of the classroom, when the woman science student set her sights on the laboratory, and when the mother entered the war plant in World War II. The central question for each chapter is to explore how spatial rhetorics quelled or enhanced these anxieties and made "respectable" women's movement into the workplace possible or improbable. As I take up this investigation, I also consider how such anxieties can be read as rhetorics of whiteness that sought to construct and preserve dominant gender and labor relations.

By thinking through these anxieties over women's spatial occupation, I see this project invigorating contemporary conversations and historical scholarship that engage questions of women and work. Twenty-first-century publications such as Tiffany Dufu's *Drop the Ball: Achieving More by Doing Less* (2017), Anne Marie Slaughter's *Unfinished Business: Women, Men, Work, Family* (2015), Arlie Russell Hochschild and Anne Machung's *The Second Shift: Working Families and the Revolution of Home* (2012), and Pamela Stone's *Opting Out: Why Women Really Quit Careers and Head Home* (2007) amplify Sandberg's 2013 book *Lean In: Women, Work, and the Will to Lead* and her claim, quoted above, that the home continues to be a considerable force affecting women's work and professional advancement. While *Domestic Occupations* is a historical study, I understand it as one that illuminates this contemporary conversation, as the main chapters reveal the critical influence that spatial composition, access, and mobility have had on women's financial security and personal independence as well as their attempts to gain professional expertise and enjoy intellectual rigor. *Domestic Occupations* not only adds historical depth to this conversation but also offers a spatio-rhetorical framework through which to read it.

Further and more specifically, by exploring the spatio-rhetorical constraints and opportunities that shaped women's work, *Domestic Occupations* contributes especially to an emerging yet important conversation within feminist rhetorical studies. While scholars outside feminist rhetoric such as Margery Davies, Thomas Dublin, Kessler-Harris, and Lara Vapnek have meditated on women's historical relationship to work, feminist rhetoricians have only just begun to consider the question of how their scholarly perspectives and investments might add substance and perspective to this conversation. Sarah Hallenbeck and Michelle Smith make this point in their 2015 essay "Mapping Topoi in the Rhetorical Regendering of Work," asserting that rhetorical scholarship dedicated to women's historical and present-day work is "under-theorized as a discrete area of study" (201). Hallenbeck and Smith prompt scholars to investigate "work-related rhetorics" by starting from the premise that work is "a historically situated, rhetorically constructed, materially contingent concept" (201). To be sure, feminist rhetoricians such the contributors to David Gold and Jessica Enoch's *Women at Work: Rhetorics of Gender and Labor* as well as Jordynn Jack, Liz Rohan, Carolyn Skinner, Heather Blain Vorhies, and Susan Wells have begun this pursuit, but in *Domestic Occupations* I respond to Hallenbeck and Smith's call in a distinctive way. This study introduces *spatial rhetoric* as a key factor in women's work opportunities and examines how the rhetorical pull of the home and the spatio-rhetorical composition of the workplace conditioned women's career options. Furthermore, by investigating the spatial rhetorics that informed the work of the women in this study,

Domestic Occupations shapes a range of discussions about the gendering and feminization of professions, access to career training, and the responsibility of childcare. Such conversations are rarely attended to within feminist rhetorical scholarship, and *Domestic Occupations* brings them to the fore.

Woman's Place Is in the Home

Two critical investigations that drive this book's project are how spatial rhetorics have animated dominant discourse regarding women's place in the home and how women have been affected by, negotiated, and even leveraged these rhetorics for their own work-related ends. Because this study asks such questions, one could say that this project takes up the concerns of "separate sphere" ideology by virtue of the fact that it interrogates women's movement away from the private domestic sphere and into the public sphere of work. Seen in this way, *Domestic Occupations* enters into a scholarly conversation that began almost sixty years ago and that studies the immense amount of literature produced during the nineteenth century that both celebrated and challenged woman's place in the American home. Alexis de Tocqueville's 1840 statement in *Democracy in America* often serves as a representative example of separate-sphere discussion in the United States. He observes:

> In no country has such constant care been taken as in America to trace two clearly distinct lines of action for the two sexes and to make them keep pace one with the other, but in two pathways that are always different. American women never manage the outward concerns of the family or conduct a business or take a part in political life; nor are they, on the other hand, ever compelled to perform the rough labor of the fields or to make any of those laborious efforts which demand the exertion of physical strength. No families are so poor as to form an exception to this rule. If, on the one hand, an American woman cannot escape from the quiet circle of domestic employments, she is never forced, on the other, to go beyond it. (225)

Though we can certainly question the validity of de Tocqueville's observation, his understanding of the American home and women's place in it certainly echoed through the century. Domestic advice literature, popular fiction, national newspapers, and magazines regularly called attention to woman's expected presence in the domestic sphere. Louisa Tuthill offers yet another emblematic statement in her 1848 text, *The Young Lady's Home*, in which she writes that women's "true and most powerful influence must be—*at home.* That their influence may be happy and permanent, women must be *keepers at home*; earnest that the sphere which Providence has allotted them should revolve with perfect order and harmony" (98).

Such discourse captured feminist scholars' attention during the 1960s, '70s, '80s, and '90s, with Nancy Cott, Aileen Kraditor, and Barbara Welter among those who offered what is now canonical scholarship that described the separate experiences of men and women and defined in the process such terms as *republican womanhood*, the *cult of domesticity*, and the *cult of true womanhood*. Their studies catalyzed waves of research that examined how women were expected to embrace what Welter defines as the "four cardinal virtues—piety, purity, submissiveness, and domesticity" (152)—and to see the home as their proper sphere. Focusing specifically on how this ideology framed women's work inside and outside the home, scholarship by figures such as Inga Bryden and Janet Floyd revealed the way popular literature of the period consistently prompted "female audiences to abandon 'the world' in favour of domestic seclusion, portraying in unflattering terms those who could not or would not abandon paid work or activity conducted outside the home" (4).

While this body of scholarship has been crucial for feminist theory and historiography, it has not escaped critique. For instance, Cathy Davidson and Jessamyn Hatcher use their aptly titled collection *No More Separate Spheres* to trouble the idea that *all* women had the same domestic experiences, as they work to "dismantle" the tradition of separate sphere scholarship since this intellectual tradition has often been riddled with assumptions of whiteness as well as "heteronormative biases, class biases, and nationalist positionings" (8). *Domestic Occupations* works alongside Davidson and Hatcher's collection by clarifying the misunderstanding that the home was ever a static spatial entity uniformly experienced by all women. But this study also helps to challenge another critique of separate sphere scholarship.

In her 1988 essay "Separate Spheres, Female Worlds, Woman's Place," Linda Kerber calls attention to the "loose" meanings scholars have given to separate spheres, asserting that the term has become "vulnerable to sloppy use" (17). Kerber explains, "When they used the metaphor of separate spheres, historians referred, often interchangeably, to an ideology *imposed on* women, a culture *created by* women, and a set of boundaries *expected to be observed* by women" (17). As a solution to this problem, Kerber argues for historiographic methods that treat sphere not as a metaphor or ideology but as an actual, physical site, encouraging scholars to inspect sphere as a "domain in the most obvious and explicit sense" (31). In Kerber's words, understanding spheres in this way makes the historian's work "simpler because the sphere can be understood to denote the physical space in which women lived, and more complex because even that apparently simple physical space was complexly constructed by an ideology of gender, as well as by class and race" (37).

In this study, I respond to Kerber's call and, by doing so, join scholars in feminist geography, history, and architecture who move well beyond the term *separate spheres* to gain a more detailed sense of the real, material spaces women have occupied and moved through. For while dominant discourse may have prescribed and dictated that women remain in the home, women did not and could not always heed this call. In fact, as Kerber argues and as the above section on women and work implies, "one plausible way to read nineteenth-century defenses of separate spheres . . . is to single out the theme of breakdown; the noise we hear about separate spheres may be the shattering of an old order and the realignment of its fragments" (22). In the chapters that follow, I listen for the noise Kerber identifies and explore how spatial rhetorics attempted to assuage or exacerbate anxieties regarding women's domestic emplacement or lack thereof.

By taking up this work, *Domestic Occupations* furthers the scholarly inquiry initiated by figures such as Sarah Deutsch, Glenna Matthews, Mary Ryan, and Daphne Spain, who have inspected how women moved from the actual, physical place of the home to traverse the world outside it. Examining what she calls the "gender geography" (*Women* 82) or "cartography of gender" (68) in cities such as New York and San Francisco, Ryan studies the monitoring and regulation that designated some places as acceptable and others as off-limits for women. She also explains how "the comings and goings of women in the walking city were marked by class and sexual distinctions more than by those of gender" (66): it was the "virtuous," middle-class white woman who was most carefully policed. Alternatively, Deutsch's scholarship investigates women's "active agency in shaping the city" of Boston (23). She explores "middle-class and elite white women creating safe space for themselves downtown and building launching pads for lobbying campaigns at the state legislature; black women creating residences, shops, and newspapers; and women workers creating child care and unions" (23). A great deal of this scholarship, then, challenges the idea that women remained in the home, and it considers instead the various ways that women from different backgrounds infiltrated public places, thinking specifically about the accommodations that were (or were not) made for them and the costs of these infiltrations.

While attention has been paid to women's movement into specific public spaces, scholars such as Polly Wynn Allen, Hayden, and Lynne Walker have also interrogated the physical and spatial dimensions of home as well as women's attempts to renovate it. Studying architectural plans for the nineteenth-century home, Walker, for instance, concedes that even though space was "feminized and endlessly depicted as woman's place, it was nevertheless heavily patriarchal in terms of territory, control, and meaning" (826). Manliness and social status, Walker continues, "were embodied and constituted, in part, through spatial boundaries that produced and upheld gender definitions and relations" (826). Approaching this question from a different angle, in *The Grand Domestic Revolution: A History of Feminist Designs for American Homes, Neighborhoods, and Cities,* Hayden explores how material feminists such as Charlotte Perkins Gilman and Melusina Fay Peirce—who, as discussed above, also called for mother's pensions—crafted innovative approaches to architecture and urban design with the goal of remaking the home and the asymmetrical relations of domestic labor perpetuated within it. These women offered "new ideals of equality through their proposals for community kitchens, laundries, dining halls, kitchenless houses, and feminist cities" (302). Hayden celebrates these women's understanding that "environmental changes are a necessary condition for ending the exploitation of women's labor" (302). Spain and others join Hayden in recognizing the importance of studying the material and spatial alterations women sought to make in their worlds, arguing that through this kind of historiographic investigation we come to know better the "tenacity of gender inequalities . . . by considering the architectural and geographic spatial contexts within which they occur" (3).

As alluded to above, feminist historiographers of rhetoric such as Buchanan, Johnson (*Gender*), Mountford, and Shaver have pursued the kind of inquiry Spain advocates, for they too consider how spatial realities have exacerbated gender inequalities. Bringing concerns of gender, rhetoric, and space together, their most prominent intervention has been interrogating women's access to and occupation of what Mountford calls *rhetorical* spaces, or the "geography of a communicative event" (17). As Cheryl Glenn notes in *Rhetoric Retold*, "Men have acted in the polis, in the public light of rhetorical discourse. . . . Meanwhile, women have been circumscribed within the seldom-examined *idios*, the private domain; women have been designated *idiots* who sustain family, friendships, and their public-discoursing men from within the *oikos*, the household" (1). Because women's expected place was in the *oikos*, it seemed logically impossible for them to be rhetors, for they were barred from the very places where rhetorical activity occurs: they had no access to the esteemed and privileged rhetorical spaces of the podium, platform, and pulpit. To gain a richer sense of women's rhetorical contributions, these scholars have refused the idea that women's systematic exclusion from such prized rhetorical spaces rendered them silent, and they have examined how women throughout history gained access to traditionally masculine rhetorical spaces or created new sites for their rhetorical activity.

My purpose in *Domestic Occupations* is not to analyze women's entrance into various rhetorical spaces to speak. The priority instead is to consider the rhetoricity of space and examine how various spaces have exerted influence on women's lives—not only those engineered explicitly for human rhetorical production in the form of writing or speaking. This study, in other words, sees all spaces as rhetorical and posits that the production, inhabitation, and representation of spaces, from the home to the school, should be key feminist rhetorical concerns, for they offer critical insight into the often-overlooked forces that articulate gendered norms and shape women's experiences.

Methods and Methodology

Due to the fact that spatial rhetorics are created through material, embodied, pictorial, emotive, and discursive elements working with and, at times, against one another, this study makes use of a multimodal historiographic research method. In pursuing this method, *Domestic Occupations* takes advantage of an array of archival and primary materials: architectural plans, photographs, paintings, magazine articles, educational tracts, school board minutes, and government bulletins, to name just a few. I accessed these materials through a range of resources, but primary among them were the physical archives such as the Massachusetts Institute of Technology in Cambridge, Massachusetts, and the robust digital archives of Harvard Library's *Women Working, 1800–1930* and Cornell University Library's *Home Economics Archive: Research, Tradition, History* (*HEARTH*).

The work of this book is to read these primary artifacts in a way that captures their spatio-rhetorical significance. To do so, I draw on the theoretical scholarship of cultural and social geographers such as Harvey and Tuan who see space as constructed and contested and explore how it is animated by power, privilege, and even emotion. *Domestic Occupations* is thus guided by "theories of spatiality" that are invested not only in "how larger structures act on people to assign them to spaces or to deny them resources within spaces, but [also in] how people make sense of and act in spaces" (Moje 18). Most critically, though, I build on the theoretical interventions of feminist scholars of geography and architecture such as Doreen Massey, Mona Domosh and Joni Seager, Linda McDowell, and Gillian Rose. The feminist perspective they cultivate is central to this study because it offers a lens through which "to investigate, make visible[,] and challenge the relationships between gender divisions and spatial divisions, to uncover their mutual constitution and problematize their apparent naturalness" (McDowell 12).

I infuse these theories of spatiality with the rhetorical theories of space and materiality discussed above and engaged by scholars such as Barnett and Boyle, Blair, Endres and Senda-Cook, Hallenbeck, Mountford, Powell, Reynolds, Rickert, and Selzer. I do so with the goal of crafting a spatio-rhetorical theoretical lens that enables me to read the materials culled for this study critically and carefully. This perspective is necessary to work toward the overarching goal for this recovery project and to assess the significance of many of the archival and primary sources studied herein. My aim is to gain a sense of three specific historical conversations about women, home, and work and to explore how spatial realities, interpretations, and expectations affected these conversations. To take on this analysis, I read materials that might at first glance seem insignificant to rhetoricians searching for overt argument about women's work options (or lack thereof). While a number of the artifacts examined here supply evidence of interlocutors overtly arguing for (or against) women's movement out of the home and into particular work spaces, much of the material I inspect offers more subtle evidence of the spatial tensions at play. That is, the bulk of this study's artifacts do the seemingly innocuous (yet, I argue, rhetorical) work of defining or describing a space, explaining the space's function, setting out its practical or expected use, or calling for renovation for reasons other than women's vocational pursuits. These artifacts often do not explicitly engage in discussions about woman's place in the home or her movement into work spaces, but they do implicitly shape these conversations. The combined theoretical investments I bring together enable me to realize the consequential nature of these supposedly pedestrian artifacts and to explore, for instance, how texts such as a schoolhouse architectural plan troubled expected gender divisions and in so doing helped to open up vocational options for the woman teacher.

A methodological premise, then, that guides this book is that reading these ostensibly mundane primary materials through a feminist spatio-rhetorical lens offers insight into dominant conversations about women, home, and work.

As noted above, these discussions were not absent of race, culture, and class but instead were infused with these concerns, so much so that I contend we should read these dominant spatial rhetorics as *rhetorics of whiteness* that crafted perceptions of the white middle-class American home and woman's work within and outside it. Thus, another key concern throughout this study is to identify how these spatial rhetorics of middle-class whiteness were operating. Scholar AnnLouise Keating writes, "the most commonly mentioned attribute of 'whiteness' seems to be its pervasive nonpresence, its invisibility" (904). She, along with Tammie Kennedy, Joyce Irene Middleton, Krista Ratcliffe, Kristan Poirot, Shevaun Watson, and many others, urges scholars to make whiteness visible by interrogating and explicating its rhetorical construction. *Domestic Occupations* contributes to this project by emphasizing how expectations of whiteness and middle-class culture infiltrated the spatio-rhetorical debates at the heart of this book's case studies. Explicit attention in each chapter is given to the ways that the white middle-class home was made and remade ideologically, discursively, and materially and how constructions of the home, school, and childcare center provided opportunities for interlocutors to think about what this home should be, how it should operate, and what the woman's roles were within it. Even as this study focuses on dominant discourses of home and women's work, it also attends to the ways rhetorics of middle-class whiteness resonated for women who were not their central concern. Focusing the conversation as they did, such discourses drew attention away from the complexity of marginalized women's home and work experiences, but given the pervasiveness and power of dominant rhetorics, marginalized women had to contend with them. A principal goal for each of the main chapters then is to remind readers of how these spatial rhetorics operated for those outside the white middle-class community.

While all of the chapters engage these larger questions about dominant spatial rhetorics, each of the three case studies takes up a particular spatio-rhetorical concern and leverages a specific theoretical concept. Chapter 2 draws on the work of gender theorists and feminist geographers such as Judith Butler, Domosh and Seager, Massey, and Spain to explore the ways spatial rhetorics *engender* and *regender* space. This chapter traces how the school shifted from a masculine site of discipline and corporal punishment to a feminine site of love and comfort that resembled the space of the home. I contend that by gaining these domestic characteristics the school became a feminine and feminized place that the woman teacher was able to enter. This investigation of the regendered classroom leads me to discern the conditions that led to women dominating the classroom as well as the factors that aided in the feminization of the teaching profession and the maternalization of the teacher.

Chapter 3 centers on the ways that women claimed the ethos of a scientist at the turn of the twentieth century, and in so doing it draws on scholarship from rhetorical studies that develops understandings of ethos as spatially situated. Broadening the idea that ethos is simply one's cultivation of credibility, I consider how spatial occupation and transformation enables ethos construction. In its original Greek etymology, *ethos* is connected to space: it depends on the sites one inhabits and the habits one takes up within those physical locales. As Reynolds writes, ethos is "the haunt where a person's character is formed" ("*Ethos*" 328). In chapter 3, I build on scholarship by Applegarth, Michael Hyde, Reynolds, Shaver, and Skinner to examine how domestic scientists remade the home as a means of remaking their ethos.

Chapter 4 centers attention on emotive spatial rhetorics and the ways they shaped discussions around working motherhood, the home, and the childcare center during World War II. Rather than seeing emotions as deeply personal and individually experienced, this chapter understands emotions as both rhetorical and collective, starting from the premise that the generation of public and shared emotion can indeed be, in the words of Daniel Gross, "strategic" (19). Thus, this chapter builds on the work of Sara Ahmed, Jenell Johnson, Brent Malin, Laura Micciche, and Robert Hariman and John Louis Lucaites to investigate how anxieties around the "motherless home" were produced and assuaged due to particular interests and exigencies. This chapter examines how the spatial rhetorics that defined the childcare center and the home generated emotions of anxiety, stress, peace, and assurance and considers the effect of these emotive spatial rhetorics on working mothers' (and their families') lives.

Collectively, these three major investigations respond to a call made by Michel Foucault over forty years ago. He writes, "A whole history remains to be written of spaces—which would at the same time be the history of powers . . . from the great strategies of geo-politics to the little tactics of the habitat" (149). This study is my attempt to write *a* (not *the*) rhetorical history of the home, as well as the school and the childcare center, and I do so by exploring how power animated these "habitats" in ways that opened up and closed down possibilities for the woman teacher, the domestic scientist, and the working mother. These spaces held (and continue to hold) different meanings at different moments for different people, and the power relations that have tethered people to these spaces have also changed. In fact, the diversity and complexity of spatio-rhetorical experience is exactly the point of taking up this work. *Domestic Occupations* highlights the importance of considering what a rhetorical history of a particular space might look like by prompting rhetoricians to ask and answer questions such as these: How do we capture the rhetorical complexity of a space's history? How do we understand a space's (changing) rhetorical power? For whom and in what contexts are particular spatio-rhetorical histories consequential? *Domestic Occupations* cannot and does not say it all, but it does invite others to consider how spaces like the home, school, and childcare center, in addition to myriad other possibilities, deserve our close rhetorical attention.

Politics of *My* Location

Before moving on to the major examinations of this study, it seems important to articulate my exigence for and investment in this study, to state where I'm coming from and how I arrived here. In other words, it seems important, borrowing from Adrienne Rich, to explain my own "politics of location." In my first book, *Reclaiming Rhetorical Education: Women Teaching African American, Native American, and Chicano/a Students, 1865–1911*, I sought to challenge the pervasive idea that the nineteenth- and early twentieth-century schoolteacher was an innocuous mother figure to her students. I argued that teachers such as Lydia Maria Child, Zitkala-Ša, and Jovita Idar politicized themselves and their pedagogies to compose rhetorical educations for their marginalized students that tested the status quo and prompted them to change the worlds in which they lived. While composing that book, I came across a speech that has stayed with me and compelled me to think about issues of space and women's work, and a quotation from this speech—Joseph Emerson's 1822 *Female Education: A Discourse Delivered at the Dedication of the Seminary Hall*—serves as the epigraph that opens this chapter.

A principal of the seminary, Emerson used this speech to envision what women students would do with their educations. As the epigraph makes clear, foremost in Emerson's mind was that women use education to enrich their lives as wives and mothers in the home. However, after detailing the importance of this domestic work, Emerson makes another suggestion to his students: he calls on women students to consider the teaching profession, and his suggestion rests on a spatial association. "Next to the domestic circle," Emerson asserts, "the schoolroom is unquestionably the most important sphere of female activity" (8). Of course. It makes perfect sense. Women could be teachers because the space of the school was similar to the space of the home. While writing my first book, this spatial association between the home and school helped me understand why historical narratives have often cast the teacher as mother and offered limiting understandings of her work as that of simple care and depoliticized comfort.

After the publication of *Refiguring Rhetorical Education*, Emerson's speech tugged at me. Why, I wondered, were the profession of teaching and the work of mothering so closely connected? How did the spaces of home and school enable or cultivate this association? Did Emerson's spatial parallel go beyond the imagined and ideological? That is, were there *really* material resonances and repetitions within these physical spaces? If so, what would all this mean? These questions intrigued me and catalyzed my thinking about women's spatial relationship to the home and the ways this relationship conditioned opportunities for their work. I soon moved on to consider other examples that would let me play these questions out by exploring, next, domestic scientists and their renovations of the home and, then, working mothers and their reliance on the childcare center in World War II. As I pursued these examples and as a vision for *Domestic Occupations* began to take shape, purely intellectual investments were not my only motivation.

Part of the exigency for my first book was my own discomfort with the feminization of the teaching profession and the idea that, as a teacher, I "mothered" my students. My work in chapter 2 of this book enabled me to continue to meditate on this discomfort and reflect on whether the spatial "palimpsest" of the school—the layered memories of a space's meanings—still resonates in classrooms today, subtly guiding us to see the school as a home, the teacher as a mother, and the students as her children (Reynolds, *Geographies* 2). But my investment in exploring the complicated triadic relationship between women, work, and home became even more poignant when I became a working mother, having and caring for three children throughout the period of writing this book. In many ways, the questions driving *Domestic Occupations* were also ones happening in my own life, only 75, 100, and 150 years later. As a scholar, teacher, and mother, I've often asked myself, what are my ties to the home and workplace? How do I negotiate them? What material, emotional, financial, and spatial supports do I need as I attempt to work and mother? How does one, at once, mother and work from home? In what ways does my spatial relationship to the home and my young children shape my professional ethos? How do constraints of childcare (or lack thereof) allow me to (not) do my job?

At times the distance between me and the women I study here seemed almost too close for comfort. I identified with them. Their concerns and anxieties often felt like my own. Indeed, many scholars might see this identification between me and my subjects as problematic: there was not enough critical distance. As Joan Wallach Scott argues, however, this is not a new phenomenon. Historians have always identified with those they study, hearing what Scott calls a "fantasy echo" or an "imagined repetition" between the stories of the past and the experiences of the present (48). But as Scott advises, the key for scholars like me is neither to be daunted by this association nor to take the "relationship between the past and present . . . for granted" (22). Instead the work is to see this fantasy echo as a "problem to be explored" (22). This problem is one that propels my work throughout this book. The identifications I've made have provided me with, and I hope will provide others with, a moment to think about how the creative composition of space has inflected and continues to inflect women's lives in materially and rhetorically significant ways.

2. From Prison to Home
SPATIAL RHETORICS REGENDER THE NINETEENTH-CENTURY SCHOOL

> But the daughter and sister in the quietness of the parental home, the faithful teacher in the village school-house, the mother in her secluded nursery, are all forming others after their own model, writing upon that which is never to die.
> —Lydia Sigourney, "Superficial Attainments," 1840

Lydia Sigourney's 1840 statement from *Godey's Lady's Book* equates the work of the woman teacher in the school with that of the daughter and sister in the home and the mother in the nursery. For women in each of these roles, the work is the same: to educate the young by employing their feminine qualities of nurturance and care. Given twenty-first-century understandings of nineteenth-century life, this list and the equations within it likely seem unremarkable. Sigourney is simply making a celebratory statement of fact regarding women's work and women's place: just as the woman as mother belongs in the home, the woman as teacher belongs in the school.

The project of this chapter is to challenge such an easy acceptance of Sigourney's epigraph and to call into question the seemingly unremarkable equation it sets forth. Here, I argue that Sigourney's words were not articulating an obvious and taken-for-granted association, but rather they were participating in a rhetorically complex moment that established women in a new space—the school—and introduced them into a new profession—teaching. Forty years prior to Sigourney's statement, teaching in the school was not seen as similar to mothering in the home, and women did not occupy the classroom in great numbers. In fact, in the late eighteenth and early nineteenth centuries, the school was defined as an uncomfortable, uncaring, prisonlike space where the male teacher ruled the classroom with discipline and corporal punishment. By midcentury, though, equating the school with the home had begun to take hold, and as it did, women gained new and unprecedented access to the classroom as teachers, so much so that by the end of the century one observer deemed the teaching profession an "Adamless Eden" (Bardeen 18).

This transition for the school and the woman teacher is the subject of this chapter. I contend that the transition was due in great part to a diverse set of spatial rhetorics that both renovated the school and remade the teaching profession, making both fit for the respectable white middle-class woman. To examine this transition, I study the spatial rhetorics that defined and described the physical space of the school, and I consider how these material, pictorial, embodied, emotive, and discursive alterations set the conditions for women's entrance into this educational space and the teaching profession writ large. More specifically, though, my work in this chapter is to analyze how spatial rhetorics *regendered* the school. I ask, how did spatial rhetorics transform the school from a space that was public, raucous, dirty, and violent (masculine) into one that was private, comforting, clean, and loving (feminine)? This chapter's investigations reveal the part spatial rhetorics played in this regendering process, renovating the school from a menacing educational prison—one off-limits to the respectable white middle-class woman—into the quintessential feminine space, the home—a space this woman was expected to inhabit and direct.

My analysis builds both on the definition of spatial rhetorics articulated in chapter 1 and on the work of gender theorists and feminist geographers such as Liz Bondi and Joyce Davidson, Judith Butler, Doreen Massey, Gwendolyn Wright, and Daphne Spain. Here, I explore how spaces, like bodies, *perform* their gendered identity. Spaces enact gendered performances through spatial rhetorics that include material construction and decoration as well as discursive definitions of the space, expectations about it, the inhabitation of the space, and the activities that occur within it. This examination rests on the idea that even though spaces are often made of brick and mortar, they are not static or stable. To borrow from Butler, spaces perform their gendered identity through "reiterative and citational practice" (*Bodies* 2), through the "stylized repetition of acts through time" ("Performative Acts" 520). Spaces are *en*gendered, then, when they are identified with masculine or feminine attributes and when they invite certain practices understood as feminine or masculine to happen inside them. Spaces are *regendered* when they shift their performance from masculine to feminine or vice versa.

Such performances of space, not surprisingly, affect and are affected by the bodies that occupy a space and the activities these bodies take up. As Bondi and Davidson state, "gender relations and identities are constructed in and through space" (20). Thus when a space takes on new gendered meanings, the bodies expected to inhabit it and the identities constructed within it also change. This chapter explores how the regendering of the school affected perceptions of the person best suited to manage this educational space. To be sure, as the space of the school changed, so too did understandings about the figure and work of the teacher. The relationship between the changing space of the school and the changing identity of the teacher is key because it is partly by virtue of alterations to the school that women gained a new professional opportunity: when the school became a feminine and even a domestic space, women were able to enter it and become teachers. Importantly and unsurprisingly, this transition was not wholly liberating for women. Questions of power always animate gendered distinctions, and the conclusion to this chapter considers how the spatial changes to the school contributed to the feminizing and devaluing of the teaching profession.

To explore these concerns, I first set out the dominant spatio-rhetorical discourse that defined the white middle-class "American" home and women's expected ties to it. While likely familiar to twenty-first-century readers as "separate sphere" ideology, I see this discourse as a spatial rhetoric that deeply affected the actual site of the home. It not only constructed idyllic understandings of domestic life, but it also prescribed physical and decorative features for the home and specific practices for those who occupied it. Second, I discuss the late-eighteenth-century and early-nineteenth-century educational scene in the United States, focusing attention on the school and the work of the schoolmaster to obtain a more detailed understanding of how the school was engendered as a masculine, public, prisonlike space. Third, I turn to discussions gaining exigence and momentum in the 1820s that called for radical renovation to the school. I analyze here the spatial rhetorics deployed by educational leaders such as William Alcott, Henry Barnard, and Horace Mann to assess the poor state of the school and how they worked from these assessments to renovate it. I show how the changes they advocated revised the school from a masculine space to a feminine one, with the end result paralleling, in many ways, idealized visions for the home. Fourth, I map these conversations about school renovation onto discussions about women teachers and their fitness for the classroom. I make clear how the spatial rhetorics that regendered the school set the conditions for women to leave the home and enter the classroom. Fifth, I move on to explore a contentious debate, or what we might call a "turf war," over school space. Even though women quickly came to dominate the classroom as the century progressed, many male teachers were not willing to yield control of the school. Disgruntled male teachers leveraged spatial rhetorics to try to regender the school (once again) so that it no longer was a feminine site that necessitated women's abilities but instead regained the definition of a masculine space that required a man's presence. The chapter's analytical sections reveal the complex role spatial rhetorics played in both renovations to the school and the consequent changes to the teaching profession, with the final examination presenting male teachers' attempts to undo what previous spatial rhetorics had accomplished and return the school to the masculine space it once was. I conclude by considering the implications of these spatial rhetorics and this regendering process on women's professionalization as teachers.

As I embark on this analysis, I want to be clear about concerns of temporality, causality, and intentionality. My temporal focus is on the period from 1820 to 1870: the period when educational leaders paid great attention to renovations to the physical site of the school and when new opportunities opened up for women as teachers. These two discussions happened concurrently, but they were not immediately seen or overtly articulated as aligned or in conversation with one another. That is, with few exceptions did educational leaders argue that the physical site of the school should change *so that* women could be teachers. Rather, the discussion was much more subtle and complicated; the conversations were connected but not directly. In part, then, a great number of the spatial rhetorics I explore in this chapter should be seen as, to use Sarah Hallenbeck's term, "nondeliberate" rhetorics—rhetorics that were engineered to achieve one end but became consequential for another (12). As Hallenbeck argues, nondeliberate rhetorics are important for feminist rhetoricians to study because they shift our attention from "deliberate, strategic rhetorical practice toward a wider range of rhetorical activities that impact gender and power relations more broadly" (11). In the case of this chapter, while the spatio-rhetorical revisions to the school were not specifically meant to pave the way for the woman teacher, they did regender the school space as feminine, and through this process, the paving was (unintentionally) accomplished.

Finally, it is important to note how race, culture, and class animate the chapter's analyses. The dominant discourses studied here projected understandings of *the* American home and *the* American school, and of course the assumption was that the teacher and the students were both white and middle class. Certainly, given the fact that much of this dominant discourse emerged from the northeastern corner of the United States, this was the population in mind. Furthermore, as Nancy Cott has argued, "New England had the most influential regional culture in the country's early history"; thus these discourses regarding the home and the school and their imagined inhabitants circulated prominently and powerfully throughout the nation (10). A central concern for this chapter is to consider how these dominant discourses functioned to define the home and the school and then to explore the consequences of these discourses for *actual* women—women who entered the classroom as teachers. More particularly, my aim is to investigate how the shifts in school space created new professional opportunities mainly for middle-class white women and how these shifts specifically enabled this contingent to gain entrance to the classroom and to adopt a new professional identity. The conclusion to this chapter, though, looks beyond this category to consider the ways this new vision of the school and the teacher refracted within other raced, cultured, and classed communities.

Domestic Spatial Rhetorics at the Turn of the Nineteenth Century

Scholars such as Cott, Glenna Matthews, and Linda Kerber explain that, around the turn of the nineteenth century, between the years 1780 and 1830, there was great instability in American culture. The establishment of the nation-state initiated moves toward democracy and undermined previous class patterns. Immigration brought new people, languages, customs, and religions to the United States. Westward expansion strained kin networks for Anglo-Americans, extended the bounds of U.S. territory, and decimated Native American communities and culture. Significant economic growth and industrialization spurred the emergence of factories and businesses, which in turn created urban centers as well as new professions and work patterns, especially for men. This latter shift had particular effects on understandings of the home as well as women's and men's roles within it. While in the mid-eighteenth century, white middle-class women and men had worked together to produce food and goods to sustain the family, by the turn of century, men were increasingly leaving the home to earn wages in offices, factories, and other workplaces. For men, such a shift divided their daily experience into "work" time and "home" time spent, respectively, in work space or home space. For women, these innovations did relieve them of some of their former tasks; however, they were still expected to take on numerous duties within the home, such as preparing meals, sewing, and tending to children (Cott 59).

On account of these changes, concerted attention was drawn to the home. As Spain observes, "since the home was no longer the major economic unit of production, Americans felt that family life was threatened by the transfer of its traditional functions outside the home" (122). In response, American thinkers explored ideas about what *else* the home could be, and a dominant understanding soon emerged that attributed to the home a new sense of importance: it was the stable and peaceful counterpart to the ever-shifting industrial, economic, professional, cultural, and political world beyond it. This spatio-rhetorical process engendered the home in a new way by establishing what Barbara Welter and many other twentieth-century scholars recognized as separate sphere ideology and the cult of domesticity. As Massey writes, spaces "are not only gendered themselves, but in their being so, they both reflect and affect the ways in which gender is constructed and understood" (179). At this time of transition, efforts were made not only to turn the home into a feminine space but also to refine understandings of what femininity was and indeed how women were to carry out this gendered expectation. In contrast, public spaces were identified with masculine characteristics: rough, competitive, and combative, these sites were made for men.

Describing the white middle-class home during this period became a "national mission" (Wright 75). Essays, sermons, advice books, periodicals, and novels permeated public discourse with spatial rhetorics that defined the home ideologically, emotionally, and materially. Ideologically and emotionally, the home was identified as a "haven of stability" (Matthews 10) and a "place of beauty, refuge, and Christian virtue" (Wright 75). As one writer notes in the poignantly titled periodical *Happy Home and Parlor Magazine*,

> Home enjoyments, home affections, home courtesies . . . form the sunshine of the heart; they bless and sanctify our private circle; they become a source of calm delight to the man of business after a day of toil; they teach the merchant, the trader, the working-man, that there is something purer, more precious even than the gains of industry. ("Cultivate" 56)

The home was the feminized opposite of and counter-space to the tumultuous public and masculine world of hurried exertion and competition.

The emotional and ideological element of the home was reinforced by the "manual mania" that identified what the physical home should be (Hayden, *Building Suburbia* 42). Hugely popular plan books by figures such as Andrew Downing and Samuel Sloan defined this new white middle-class American home's look and feel. Downing believed the home should be distinguished by its American-ness. He thus called for modest "republican homes" that were "comfortable and beautiful yet never so ostentatious as to belittle the neighbors or aggrandize the children's manners" (Wright 84). In addition to this understanding of the home, architects also made sure this residential site was removed from the bustle and strains of city life and that it stood in contrast to the other domestic formations emerging in this period and designed for working-class individuals and families such as row homes, boardinghouses, and tenements. As Wright explains, there was a distinct "anti-urban sentiment" throughout these manuals and a concerted attempt to set the white middle-class home and family outside the city and away from a working-class existence (85). Wright observes, "the most conspicuous theme in American model cottages, as in actual homes of the mid-nineteenth century, was privatism. Each pattern-book drawing showed a single, isolated dwelling surrounded by a carefully tended garden" (88). Figure 2.1 from Downing's *Architecture of Country Houses: Designs for Cottages, Farm-Houses, and Villas* adds substance to this claim, as the home pictured (and promoted) here is decidedly private and pastoral, not in eyeshot of an urban center.

A distinctive part of these designs is the way writers of these texts wove ideological and emotional elements together with the physical plans for the home. As Henry William Cleaveland, William Backus, and Samuel Backus write in their 1856 *Village and Farm Cottages*, "physical enjoyment [of the home] should not be the only aim. In building, as in everything else, the intelligent and rightly disposed man will remember and consult his higher nature, and will try to make his house, however unpretending, a teacher and promoter of virtue, by its evident regard for order, neatness, truth, and beauty" (44). Downing contributes to this idea, explaining that every residence should have a "home feeling" (79). But this emotional component of the home does not just occur naturally; rather, it is orchestrated through design elements such as gables, eaves, porches, and other types of ornament—elements showcased in figure 2.1 (79). Explaining how the simple addition of vines adds the important element he advocates for, Downing writes:

> Now, every cottage may not display *science* or knowledge, because science demands architectural education in its builder or designer, as well as, in many cases, some additional expense. But *feeling* may be evinced by every one possessing it, and there is no more striking or successful way of manifesting it in a cottage than by the employment of permanent vines to embellish it. (79)

Fig. 2.1. "Small Bracketed Cottage." Downing, *The Architecture of Country Houses* (1850), p. 78.

Inhabitants of Downing's ideal home were to cultivate, what Yi-Fu Tuan calls, "topophilia" for the home: a deep attachment to and love for a space (*Topophilia*). In no uncertain terms the spatial rhetorics of this period pronounced this domestic topophilia, making the home a beloved haven of security, care, comfort, and safety.

It should come as no surprise that this emerging depiction of a newly feminized home was incomplete without discussion of the person who should guide and manage it. Texts such as John Mather Austin's *A Voice to the Married* (1847), Catharine E. Beecher and Harriet Beecher Stowe's *The American Woman's Home* (1869), and Sarah Josepha Hale's *Manners: Happy Homes and Good Society All the Year Round* (1868) were just a few among many that celebrated the woman as wife, mother, and daughter, and identified her as the sole force that could make the home into what it should be. To create this idyllic space, women were prompted to divide their efforts in two distinct yet intertwined ways—one emotional and ideological, the other material. Not surprisingly, these dual efforts mapped onto the ideal vision for the home itself.

Regarding the first way, women were expected to conduct the home with gentleness, order, modesty, cheerfulness, selflessness, and peace. As relayed in George B. Emerson's popular 1832 lecture, which was republished in *Ladies' Magazine and Literary Gazette* (later retitled *Godey's Lady's Book*), and texts such as William and Anna Russell's *Introduction to the Young Ladies' Elocutionary Reader*, when one enters the "humblest dwelling under the prudent management of a discreet and well educated female," one should observe the "simplicity and good taste which pervade it" (G. Emerson 19). Emerson continues: "her own best ornaments are cheerfulness and contentment, and those of her house are neatness, good order, and cleanliness" (19). The home is peaceful and calm because the woman ensures there are no "harsh sounds"; rather her "gentleness communicates itself to all around her" (20). The 1850 publication in *Godey's Lady's Book* of the illustration captioned "The Sphere of Woman" (fig. 2.2) offers the visual argument for Emerson's discursive depiction. Here we see the emblematic image of the woman in her home, and it is clear how the ideal qualities of the wife and mother generate the ideal qualities of the home: the temperate, calm, neat, and ordered woman creates the temperate, calm, neat, and ordered home.

Woman's ideological and emotional responsibility evidenced in visuals such as "The Sphere of Woman" did not encapsulate the entirety of her work, however. Women's emotional duties were coupled with the physical management of the home. As discussed in chapter 1, Beecher and Stowe's text realizes this dual objective, but so too does the 1852 issue of *Godey's Lady's Book*. For instance, the periodical published the piece "Woman's Sphere in Modern Life" and promoted the point that "woman's true sphere is in her family, in her home duties," underscoring the emotional work she must undertake to perfect this space (171). Directly below this piece, as displayed in figure 2.3, readers encountered women's material responsibility, as the magazine instructed women on actual home designs. Architectural plans for versions of the "model cottage" pervaded this periodical, as *Godey's* initiated between 1846 and 1898 an "own-your-own-home" movement propelled by the publication of over 450 model house designs (Wright 82). Merging the ideological and emotional with the material and architectural, *Godey's* clearly outlined woman's full domestic responsibility, by consistently coupling the two imperatives together within its pages.

While women's magazines placed home designs next to ideological discussions of women's sphere, architectural plan books such as Downing's also envisioned the woman as the prime cultivator of "home feeling" and made

Fig. 2.2. "The Sphere of Woman." *Godey's Lady's Book* 40 (Mar. 1850), p. 209.

implicit suggestions of such gender roles through architectural drawings. Note, for instance, in figure 2.1 that the husband is leaving the model home ostensibly to go to work, while the wife sits securely within the domestic domain. Downing's suggestions regarding gendered spatial practice are subtle and purely visual here, but in other places he was much more overt. In fact, after identifying vines as a critical design element in the cultivation of home feeling, Downing points to the person responsible for this design feature:

> [V]ines are never planted by architects, masons, carpenters, or those who build the cottage, but always by those who live in it, and make it truly a home, and generally by the mother or daughter, whose very planting of vines is a labor of love offered up on the domestic altar, it follows, by the most direct and natural associations, that vines on a rural cottage always express domesticity and the presence of heart. (79)

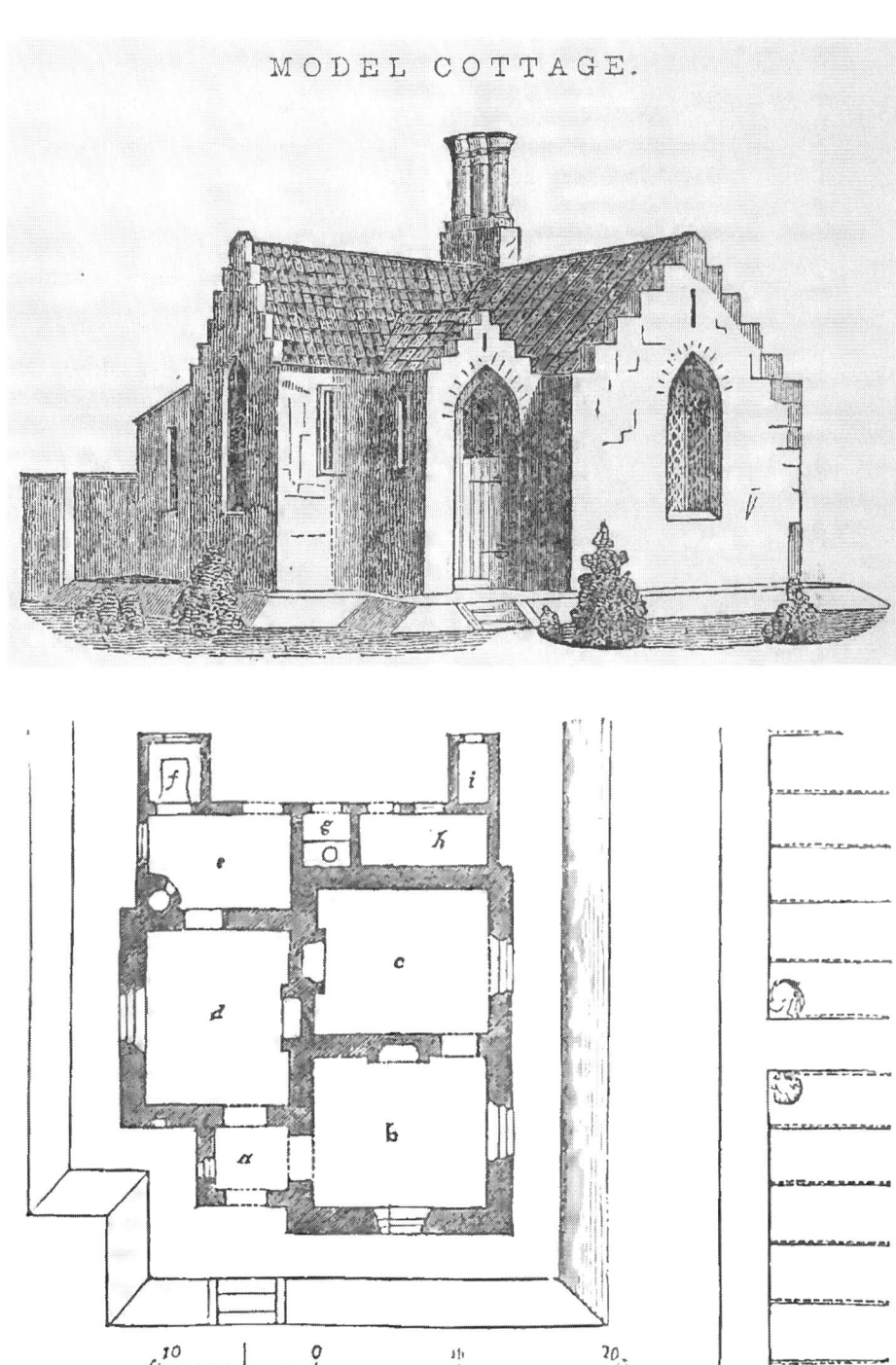

Fig. 2.3. "Model Cottage." *Godey's Lady's Book* 45 (July–Dec. 1852), pp. 172–73.

For Downing, it was the woman's work to grow and tend to vines; this act was the "labor of love" that made the home special and revered.

Not surprisingly, just as the exterior of the home was to be embellished by a woman's touch, the interior decoration was also her responsibility. Manual writer John H. Young offers evidence on this point: "Home is the woman's kingdom, and there she reigns supreme. To embellish that home, to make happy the lives of her husband and the dear ones committed to her trust, is the honored task which it is the wife's province to perform" (206). Catharine Beecher concurs, writing in 1835 that the woman "is the presiding genius" who "must regulate all those thousand minutiae of domestick business, that demand habits of industry, order, neatness, punctuality, and constant care" ("Essay" 62). The domestic tasks were thus clear: the woman governed the home not only through love and care but also through decoration and design as well as general order and upkeep.

These dominant spatio-rhetorical discourses defined the white middle-class home by outlining the woman's role in creating this space. By doing so, these rhetorics supported a larger-in-scale "gender geography" that not only identified the home as a feminine space for women, and public sites outside it as masculine sites for men, but also prompted women to avoid public engagement or at least to take great care if and when they did leave the home (M. Ryan, *Women* 82). For example, in her 1833 *Female Education*, Almira Lincoln Phelps writes, "The sphere of woman's duty is to be looked for in private and domestic life; and although she may and ought to do all in her power to elevate, refine, and embellish all that comes within her own circle, she should be cautious of suffering her desires to extend beyond it" (305). But even with this instruction, white middle-class women did not situate themselves solely in the home. As scholars Mary Ryan and Matthews have made clear, and as discussed in chapter 1, women's mobility actually increased during this period—a fact that suggests rhetorics like Phelps's might have been signaling anxiety regarding this new socio-spatial development more so than simple instruction (see also Kerber 22).

Indeed, white middle-class women gained opportunities for mobility during the early nineteenth century as a result of changes in work options outside the home, domestic purchasing patterns, and innovations in transportation. Such possibilities ignited concern that the purity a woman was supposed to cultivate for herself and others in the home would be ruined by encounters with the rough public world. The fear was that she would be tainted by the "untidy" experience of the world beyond the home and thereby gain the epithet of "public woman" (M. Ryan, *Women* 73). To be deemed such meant that a woman had exhibited improper behavior at best or sexually promiscuous, "vile," and "unclean" actions at worst (Matthews 4). To guard women from this possibility, there emerged numerous spatial arrangements, regulations, and expected modes of conduct that amounted to what Massey calls a "control of spatiality" (179). These directives aimed to police women's activity outside the home and preserve their revered feminine qualities by safeguarding them from witnessing or participating in uncouth public behaviors. So, for instance, respectable women were expected not to enter spaces such as bars and voting booths because these sites licensed swearing, fighting, spitting, and drinking. The argument followed that if they did, they would compromise their "inherent" purity.

The white middle-class woman's presence in and travels through public spaces were certainly policed. There was, however, one way that dominant discourse expected and encouraged her to extend her influence beyond the home and that was through what came to be known as republican motherhood. As Cott explains, "Motherhood was proposed as the central lever with which women could budge the world and, in practice, it offered the best opportunity to women to heighten their domestic power" (84). A mother's work was to rear her children (particularly her sons) into good citizens, and through this indirect action, she would shape the world. One anonymous writer articulates this spatial expectation regarding republican motherhood, writing in 1857, "Oh, mothers . . . look to it that your influence is toward the highest good the child's soul can attain. Your fireside may be away from the hum of the busy world, and your influence, in the simplicity of your heart, you may deem of little value; but remember, that influence, be it what it may, *never dies out!*" ("Startling Question" xxii). Words such as these contributed to the rich spatial rhetorics that differentiated and engendered both the home and public space. As Candace West and Don H. Zimmerman explain, "doing gender involves a complex set of socially guided perceptual, interactional, and micropolitical activities that cast particular pursuits as expressions of masculine and feminine 'natures'" (126). Through various spatio-rhetorical endeavors, the home became a feminine site of care, comfort, privacy, and tranquility—qualities that were made real through the efforts and steadfast presence of the woman. Alternatively, public spaces like voting booths, civic arenas, and, as we will see, schoolrooms were understood as masculine spaces—sites marked by aggression, competition, publicity, and hustle. They were sites intended for men and regulated so that "good" women did not enter them.

Early American Schools and Education

During the seventeenth and eighteenth centuries, establishing schoolhouses in newly settled New England was a distinct priority. Law mandated that a schoolhouse be built in every town with a population of five hundred families, and as Lawrence Cremin explains, establishing the school was seen as secondary in importance only to establishing a church (88). But even while instituting the school was an important objective, schooling itself and regular instruction were not consistent. School hours and school sessions depended greatly on agricultural and weather-related constraints, with many schools holding shorter hours in the summer so that boy students could continue to work in their family's fields. Students often passed in and out of school according to familial and work demands, attending school "irregularly, intermittently, and indeterminately" (Cremin xvi). To the question of who should teach in these schools, the answer was, of course, a schoolmaster. Men dominated the teaching profession largely because they had received enough education of their own to instruct others and also because their pedagogical style matched expectations for what education should be.

In the seventeenth- and eighteenth-century classroom, the schoolmaster offered classical education to his male students by teaching literature and language proficiency in Greek and Latin, and he instructed them in advanced English literacy skills and mathematics as well as Calvinist theology and catechism. Given these educational priorities, the schoolmaster was often a man who himself had received a classical education and had deep Calvinist investments. In fact, many schoolmasters were also ministers during this period, and if they were not, many men saw teaching as an occupation preliminary to taking up their lifelong profession of preaching (Martin 629). Whether the schoolmaster had dedicated himself to teaching or was preparing for another occupation, his objective was to educate students for either a career or college and, ultimately, for professional life and public service (Small 5, 6). To accomplish this goal, the schoolmaster practiced a pedagogy of inculcation and testing. George H. Martin explains, in his 1902 essay "Boston Schools One Hundred Years Ago," that "the business of the teacher was to set lessons to be learned. The business of the pupil was to learn them; this was study. The next business of the teacher was to examine to see if they had been learned; this was recitation" (641).

While inculcating specific subject matters was indeed the purpose of school and the work of the teacher, the most memorable classroom activity for students of this era seems to have been the corporal punishment they received. The school was a space where the teacher enacted his authority through regular demonstrations of physical punishment. As Martin states, if a student did not adhere to the "business" of the school and schooling, it was seen as the student's "failure," and "failure to study was rebelliousness against constituted authority and must be punished as such" (641). The roles of the teacher and student were clear: the student was the culprit and convict, and the teacher was the "judge and executioner" (641). Such expectations of punishment were consistent and pervasive. Just as Martin recounts his experience with a schoolmaster who was a "wholesale dealer in tortuous leather and torturing blows," George Minns sketches a similar pedagogical picture in his 1873 "Reminiscences of Boston Schools—Forty-Five Years Ago." Here, Minns remembers how "stern" teachers punished "culprit" students with rattan beatings or made them "ru[n] the ga[u]ntlet," a punishment in which students were forced to beat their peers (375). Minns even recalls one of "Mr. Stickney's peculiarities" in meting out punishment: "whenever a fight took place between two boys, he always flogged the one who was defeated" (374). "The rod," states Minns, "was continually used" (374).[1]

Descriptions like these reflect the dominant and harrowing educational scene at the turn of the nineteenth century in New England, but changes were beginning to take place that would substantively revise the understanding and experience of school. Significant among these changes was the gradual introduction of girls into New England schools. Due in large part to the growing conversation concerned with republican motherhood, the public realized that for mothers to raise good citizens, they would have to be educated themselves. As Sarah Josepha Hale writes in her 1834 essay "Female Education," a girl must be educated because she might later have the responsibility as a mother of "training up *another Washington*, who shall save his country" (502).[2] This logical connection in which educated mothers would rear educated children led to girls' increased attendance in school by the end of the eighteenth century, so much so that women's literacy had improved from a rate of 30–40 percent in the 1760s to approximately 80 percent by the 1790s (Perlmann et al. 123).

While girls were entering the school as students, women were also engaging more directly in the work of education in the late eighteenth and early nineteenth century. Importantly, however, this education did not yet fully extend to the physical space of the school.[3] Rather, increased attention was paid to how women educated their own children within the confines of the home. Given the tenets of republican motherhood as well as women's increased literacy, mothers were now seen as responsible for preparing their children, not just for eventual citizenship, but also for entering school by teaching them basic elements of literacy and morality. To guide mothers' work, scores of books on the topic of home-based instruction were published, with prime examples being Lydia Maria Child's 1831 *Mother's Book* and Samuel Goodrich's 1838 *Fireside Education*, a text whose title reinforced the point of exactly *where* this education should take place.[4]

As the nineteenth century progressed, conversations about education assumed more urgency and complexity. Horace Mann and Henry Barnard, secretaries of boards of education in Massachusetts and Connecticut, respectively, emerged on the scene and began to see the vital need to reform the New England school system. Both leaders wanted to make significant changes to the pedagogical theory and practice that structured the school. Before they could implement these new ideas, however, they had to attend to a related, yet pragmatic, problem: the physical state of the school. The schoolhouse itself was in an extreme state of disrepair, and Mann, Barnard, and other educators believed that if the schools remained as they were, their degraded condition would only undermine the theoretical changes the reformers wanted to make to classroom practice.

School as Prison

The conversation concerning the interior and exterior structure of schools began in 1829 when *School Magazine* published an article concerning their poor physical state. One year later, W. J. Adams delivered his speech "On School Houses and School Apparatus" before the American Institute of Instruction. In response to this speech, the institute initiated a contest with a twenty-dollar prize for the best essay on rehabilitating schools. Dr. William Alcott won the prize with his 1831 "Essay on the Construction of School-Houses," and his work was published both in pamphlet form and in the second annual volume of lectures delivered before the institute. Alcott's assessment of the schools and his proposals for change generated great interest in this topic and soon prompted Mann, Barnard, and other educational leaders to address the condition of schools in the northeast region of the country.

After conducting interviews with schoolteachers, soliciting reviews of school buildings from regional leaders, and assessing the state of schools themselves, Barnard and Mann published a series of reports.[5] In 1838 Mann made his statement on the subject in "Report of the Secretary of the Board of Education on the Subject of Schoolhouses," which was printed in pamphlet form and republished in the *Massachusetts Common School Journal*, the *Connecticut Common School Journal*, and the *New York District School Journal*. That same year, Barnard composed his "Essay on School Architecture" and delivered this speech in towns across Connecticut. Barnard continued to refine and expand this piece, and by 1842 his pattern book *School Architecture; or, Contributions to the Improvement of School-Houses in the United States* became a major manual and guide for building schools. This groundswell of interest in school space only gained momentum in the ensuing years, as portions of these reports were often reprinted and elaborated on in educational journals, pamphlets, and books.[6]

In these reports, one point is clear: the physical state of the school was of utmost importance to these educational leaders and their communities. Mann sets out that "school-house architecture [is] one of the cardinal points in the system" (*School Houses* 1). His colleagues agreed, as they underscored the critical rhetorical relationship between the building itself and the learning that goes on inside it. Alcott, for instance, makes the claim that "it will hardly be questioned" that "the general arrangement and appearance of even inanimate things around us, have an extensive influence in forming our character" (241). He continues, "the future health, vigor, taste, and moral principles of the pupil depend upon the position, arrangement, and construction of the school-house" (542).

These leaders' understanding of the relationship between the school and the student only compounded the gravity of the situation before them: New England schools were in a deplorable condition. Barnard writes that "the district School-house, stand[s] in disgraceful contrast with every other structure designed for public or domestic use. Its location, construction, furniture, and arrangements, seemed intended to hinder, and not promote, to defeat and not perfect, the work which was to be carried on within and without its walls" (*Practical Illustrations* 9). The board of the American Institute of Instruction agreed, setting out that "the most prominent defec[t]" in the country's educational system is "the want of spacious and convenient schools," and it is this defect that "retard[s] the progress of public education, and which loudly calls for a prompt and thorough reform" (qtd. in May 220).

In their descriptions of the schools, educators leveled five major complaints concerning their condition, and each reveals how the school was not only in a state of disrepair but also associated with masculine characteristics of public space. Both the physical state of the school and the conversation about it amounted to a spatial rhetoric that aligned the school with contemporary (and negative) understandings of public space: the school was raucous, dangerous, uncomfortable, profane, and even violent. The spatial rhetorics that gendered the school in this way created boundaries that, to borrow from McDowell, were both "spatial and social"—boundaries that "defined who belongs to a place and who may be excluded" (4). Through its material constitution, the school was engendered as a site of public masculinity, one where men governed and one that respectable women should not care to enter.

A first and common complaint charged the school with disrepair and lack of upkeep. The following description offers a detailed picture of a school's interior:

> [A]t one end [of the school, there is] a narrow and dingy entry, the floor covered with wood, chips, stones, hats, caps, odd mittens, old books, bonnets, shawls, cloaks, dirt, dinner baskets, old brooms, ashes &c., all thrown together in the order as here catalogued,—the principal room retaining its huge stone chimney, which for generations boasted its ghastly fire-place, affording a ready oblivion to annual piles of green and snow-soaked wood,—the burnt, smoked, scratched and scrawled wainscoting,—the battered and mutilated plastering,—the patched windows,—the crippled and ragged benches,—the desks which have endured a short eternity of whittling,—the masses of pulverized earth in constant agitation, filling the throats, eyes, and nostrils of the inmates[.] (Barnard, *Practical Illustrations* 20)

As this depiction makes all too clear, dirt and disarray marked the school's interior.

Corroborating these descriptions were reports that characterized the school as an uncomfortable, unhealthy, and even dangerous space for students. Poor ventilation and "foul air" infected the school atmosphere (Mann, *School Houses* 12). School furniture also posed a significant problem, with reports indicating that classroom seats were so ill suited for young children that teachers witnessed student "uneasiness, if not suffering" (Barnard, *School Architecture* 20). One teacher recounts, "Most of [the schools] have only slab seats, with the legs sticking through, upwards, like hatchel-teeth, and high enough to keep the legs of the occupants swinging" (28). And another complains that the seats often had "no rest for the back and were of uniform height," making it so that the "smaller children were suspended between earth and heaven, as if doing penance for some heinous crime" (Dressler 123). These particular complaints bolstered Mann's more general claims that beyond being old and broken down, the furniture in school was so poorly designed that students often faced the possibility of bodily disfigurement:

> [M]any eminent physicians . . . assure me that it is within their own personal knowledge, that there is, annually, loss of life, destruction of health, and such anatomical distortion as renders life hardly worth possessing, growing out of the bad construction of our schoolhouses. Nor is this evil confined to a few of them only. It is a very general calamity. (*Lectures* 51)

The "evil" that reporters noted, though, did not stop at a dirty schoolroom, foul air, and uncomfortable furniture.

In their reports, educators also expressed their disgust at the immoral images that decorated the classroom's walls. Barnard incorporates into *School Architecture* this lament from the director of the Essex County Teachers' Association:

> It is a humbling fact, that in many of these houses, there are highly indecent, profane, and libidinous marks, images, and expressions, some of which are spread out in broad characters on the walls, where they unavoidably meet the eyes of all who come into the house, or, being on the outside, salute the traveler as he passes by, wounding the delicate, and annoying the moral sensibilities of the heart. (36)

Another educator corroborates this assessment, writing that school "walls, desks, &c., are cut and marked with all sorts of images, some of which would make heathens blush" (28). Such descriptions of school space were widespread, as many raised deep concerns about the "gross and obscene carvings of impure hands" (6) and the "marks of lust and profaneness" that defaced both the interior and exterior of the school (44).

Further compounding this concern over school defacement and student exposure to obscenity was the school's physical location. Numerous reports criticized the fact that schools were often located on or near a "public highway" (38), with such placement presenting a multitude of dangers. For instance, Barnard shows his readers the visual (fig. 2.4) of a dilapidated school at the crossroads of a highway (Barnard, "School Architecture" 521). He goes on to include others' assessments of the school's location that add detail to the concerns raised by the displayed image, with educators noting that schools are "almost universally, badly located, exposed to the noise, dust and danger of the highway" (491). These public dangers were even more concerning when teachers considered what and with whom students were coming into contact. One teacher explains, "If children are compelled to resort to the highway for their amusements, we ought not wonder that they should be contaminated by the vices, brawlings, and profanities, which belong to frequenters of highways" (545). Mann agreed, remarking that when the school is placed "where roads encircle it on all sides, without any place of seclusion from the public gaze[,] . . . the modesty of nature will be overlaid with habits of indecorum; and a want of decency, enforced upon boys and girls, will become physical and moral turpitude in men and women" (*Lectures* 466).

These four complaints identify specific concerns for cleanliness, health, obscenity, and location. There was, however, a fifth and even more cutting criticism about what the space of the school was *like*. The spatial metaphor most consistently found in the reports likened the school to a prison. The reports already cited intimated this spatial association with suggestions that the school's interior figured students as "inmates" and its furniture positioned them as though they were "doing penance for some heinous crime." Other critics, though, explicitly equated the school with a prison. Report after report described the school similarly: "We see many a school-house which looks more like a gloomy, dilapidated prison, designed for the detention and punishment of some desperate culprit, rather than a place designed for the intellectual

Fig. 2.4. School at the crossroads. Barnard, "School Architecture" (1860), p. 521.

training of the children of an enlightened and prosperous nation" (Barnard, "School Architecture" 494). Such equations coalesced behind one educator's plea: "Let as much be done as can be, to remove those miserable prison-houses for our children, and in their stead let there be good, large, and convenient school-houses" (494).

It is critical to note that this assessment of the school as prison was consonant with another aspect of early-nineteenth-century education discussed above, corporal punishment, a practice that would also soon come under the scrutiny of critics. While figures such as Mann lamented the fact that schools *looked* like prisons, the most prevalent activities within the space made them *feel* that way too. Where else but in a prison would student-culprits learn from teacher-executioners who instructed them through "tortuous leather and torturing blows"? The spatial activity within the school-as-prison further pronounced the space a masculine site where violence and punishment were to be expected.

An engraving made from Henry Richter's 1822 painting *The Village School in an Uproar* encapsulates this totalizing vision of the early-nineteenth-century school (fig. 2.5). This popular image, which circulated widely throughout the United States during this period, displays the chaos, dirt, and dilapidation of the classroom and, indeed, the promise of punishment.[7] Central to this depiction of the school is, of course, the dominant figure in the image: the schoolmaster. Whip in hand, he is the one to bring order to this unruly environment—order that will come through force and violence. *The Village School in an Uproar* thus perfectly displays how the school was figured as masculine in terms of its activity and atmosphere and as masculine, too, in terms of the male students and teachers who populated it.

This depiction of the school becomes even more poignant when contrasted with dominant understandings of the feminized space of the home, revealing how difficult it would have been for a "respectable" woman to make her way into the classroom at this juncture. The school's "ghastly," "mutilated," and "pulverized" interior arrangements that caused health problems for students did not make for an environment the white middle-class woman was expected to inhabit or direct. Moreover, the profanities on the wall implicitly categorized the space as offensive to her. And the fact that the school's location was "contaminated" by the "vices, brawlings, and profanities of the highway" positioned it as a place far afield from the virtues and peace that the woman was to cultivate in the home. Furthermore, the placement of the school at the highway's crossroads would have been especially problematic for women who

Fig. 2.5. *The Village School in an Uproar*. From a painting by Henry Richter, 1822, steel engraving in the United States, 1835. Granger, NYC.

wanted to avoid the epithet of "public woman," for as McDowell writes, "the very act of their appearance on the streets left the status of women open to interpretation and, often, to unwanted sexual attentions" (154). Finally, the spatial metaphor of the prison created connotations for the school that made it off-limits to the white middle-class woman who presided over the home. Her presence in this "prison" would suggest that she either had committed a crime or was in the position of punishing others for their offenses—two activities she would have been expected to avoid. As physical spaces, then, the school and the home were opposed, and because of their stark differences, woman's occupation of the school was a not an option. Her place was in the home.

School as Home

In the 1830s, educational leaders moved quickly from critiques of the schoolhouse to proposals for change, and when they did, they altered the space in a way that transformed it from a masculine space into a feminine one. Their renovations reveal how, in Butler's terms, the gendered performance of the school shifted dramatically in this period; the spatial rhetorics that had formerly "constituted" the school in one way, now, through revision and renovation, "constituted [it] differently" ("Performative Acts" 520). It is critical to note, however, that while a regendered classroom was certainly a consequence of the renovation, the changes were not overtly discussed as ones that would make the school hospitable to women teachers. Rather, Alcott, Barnard, Mann, and others called for renovation because they believed the physical environment of the school was not working in concert with their new pedagogical goals. As this section demonstrates, their new emphasis made it clear that the school's physical location, its exterior and interior condition, and its regular activity—corporal punishment—had to change. To create the educational atmosphere they now wished for, these leaders found it necessary to eradicate the (masculine) prison that housed pedagogies of pain and replace it with a new kind of (feminine) space that looked and felt much like the home. But even though these spatial rhetorics were largely designed for a specific end, they were consequential to another one. The material, emotional, and ideological changes that leaders made to the school became nondeliberate rhetorics that transformed it into a space fit for the woman teacher.

Mann's ideas on education reflected the general shift in pedagogical emphasis during this period. Whereas predominant teaching practices focused on testing, memorization, Calvinist catechism, and corporal punishment, Mann's influential pedagogical program, known as the common school movement, stressed moral education, curiosity, and care. For Mann, education should be a positive, enjoyable experience: "pleasure should be made to flow like a sweet atmosphere around the early learner" (*Lectures* 50). The concern should be less for intellectual rigor and more, Mann argued, for moral instruction, with concerted attention given to teaching students "humanity and a universal benevolence; sobriety, industry, and frugality; chastity, moderation, and temperance" (qtd. in Downs 37). There should be "no annoyance, discomfort, pain, upon a child, while engaged in study" (*Lectures* 50). For Mann contended that when students are taught with the threat of physical punishment, there are significant consequences: their minds "are withdrawn" from their lessons, and "the pain blends itself with the study, makes part of the remembrance of it, and thus curiosity and love of learning are deadened, or turned to vicious objects" (50). Thus, Mann's new and enormously popular pedagogical program set out to change the atmosphere and activity of the nineteenth-century classroom dramatically.

Given this revised pedagogical stance, there was no doubt that the classroom and the rest of the school needed total renovation. In agreement with Mann, Barnard and others worked together to eradicate school prisons and imagine a new kind of space. The numerous publications dedicated to renovating school architecture and design revealed careful thought about this new environment, with topics of discussion ranging from location, size, lighting, ventilation, and heating to seating and desk design, pedagogical apparatus, interior décor, exterior appearance, and landscape. Throughout the renovation process, the school was divested of its masculine characteristics and invested with feminine ones that closely resembled those of the idealized home: the school should be private, clean, comfortable, safe, and tastefully decorated. This regendering process had significant effects, for it set the stage for asking new questions about who would teach best in the school that now looked and felt much like a home.

The first major site for renovation was the exterior and environs of the school. Alcott, Barnard, Mann, and other educators overwhelmingly agreed that the school should be separated from the profanity, bustle, and dirt of the outside world. Rather than being public and exposed, the school should be private and safe. Educators in Barnard's report call for the school to be "retired, shaded, healthy, [and] attractive" (*School Architecture* 25). As a means to realize such a space, Barnard's plans included fenced-in yards to enclose and protect the school from the public goings-on of the highway. Barnard offers his vision for the school in figure 2.6. Here, the school sits behind a fence that separates it from the "public" world, and indeed its similarities with contemporaneous depictions of the home are clear. Situated in a bucolic setting and replicating the theme of privatism, Barnard's school looks much like Downing's home: it too is distanced from the unruliness of city life.

Mann elaborated on this idea for relocation and separation by explaining the positive effects this change would have. The school should be "remove[d]," he writes, "from the public highway and from buildings where noisy and clattering trades are carried on; and, above all, rescue it from sound or sight of all resorts for license and dissipation" (*Lectures* 466). Once this relocation is accomplished, he argues, "a sensibility to beauty, a purity of mind, a sentiment of decency and propriety will be developed and fostered, and the chances of elevated feelings and correct conduct in after-life, will be increased manifold" (466). The school, like the home, would be a place of peace.

In addition to the change of location, educators also made the case for exterior beautification. Many called for planting flowers, gardens, shrubs, and trees on the grounds, seeing that such efforts would enable students to experience and learn about nature's serenity. Importantly, though, the new landscape was not to run wild. Flowerbeds and trees were to look "always neat,"

Fig. 2.6. "Front Projection of Schoolhouse with Trees, Shrubbery, etc."
Barnard, *School Architecture* (1848), p. 68.

even as their placement worked to make the school as a whole appear "gay and beautiful" (Barnard, *School Architecture* 86). Ideas for playgrounds also reinforced the overall efforts of the school's new pedagogical program: play spaces were to approach "elegance in the[ir] dressing and decking," with the goal of "afford[ing] a lesson which may contribute to refinement and comfort for life" (86).

Yet, the school's renovations did not end with its exterior. The interior also had to change dramatically. Educators believed that in place of the "wretched perversions of architecture which almost universally characterize[d] the district school-houses of New England," the interior of the school should be fashioned "in good taste and fit proportion" (Barnard, "School Architecture" 48). Everything inside the school should do the work of "delighting the eye, gratifying the taste, and contributing to the physical comfort" of the student (Barnard, *School Architecture* 22). The first step in achieving this end was to ensure that the classroom was clean. Mann writes, for instance, that the "schoolroom should be kept clean, not simply swept, but often washed, and every day dusted" ("Report" 293). He reinforces this point by explaining the deleterious consequences of the dirty schoolhouse: "Ineffectual efforts to keep things neat, led to neglect, neglect to filthy habits, and filthy habits to low and degraded vice" (293).

More than basic cleanliness, however, the classroom was also to be tastefully decorated. According to Alcott, the school-prison's obscene images and scribblings must be replaced with windows outfitted with appealing curtains, artfully painted walls, and attractive furniture. Leaders also argued for ornamenting the classroom with paintings, sculptures, statues, and vases filled with flowers. Figure 2.7 illustrates the interior design Barnard suggests to readers in *Practical Illustrations of the Principles of School Architecture*. Such an image reveals how educators were at pains, in Barnard's words, "to expel coarseness, discomfort, dirt, and vice" in exchange for "a taste for decoration and beauty" (42).

Each of these changes overtly worked to undo the spatio-metaphorical relationship between school and prison and implicitly create a new one: the school should be seen as a white middle-class home. Like the home, the school was to be neat, orderly, safe, private, and removed from public life. And, like the home, the school was to be decorated with flowers and gardens, vases and window treatments. These new physical characteristics came together to suggest that the "home feeling" that marked the domestic sphere could be similarly felt in this revised academic space by replacing the material elements of school that created pain and disorder with those that enabled peace and comfort.

The discussions above suggest that the regendered school was no longer a prison but could now be seen as a version of home. However, many interlocutors were much more explicit about the school's new spatial parallel. They equated school not just with the home but, more specifically, with the domestic parlor. For example, editor and contributor to *Godey's Lady's Book* Lydia Sigourney asks these questions: "Why should not the interior of our school-houses aim at somewhat of the taste of our parlour? Might not the vase of flowers enrich the mantle-piece? And the walls display not only well executed maps, but historical engravings or pictures?" ("Perceptions" 9). It is clear how Barnard would have responded to Sigourney, as he writes thus in *School Architecture*: "The Schoolroom is the Teacher's parlor and drawing-room; and

Fig. 2.7. "Interior of School." Barnard, *School Architecture* (1848), p. 181.

should always, not only be neat and tidy, but exhibit evidences of good taste and useful ornament" (189).

The rhetors who propelled the spatio-rhetorical regendering of the school did it for a specific end. Educators needed to repair the dilapidated condition of the schools, and the school-as-prison could not accommodate Mann's new pedagogical ideas. The changes made to the school did more, though, than improve the educational environment for students. Though these rhetorics were not purposely crafted as arguments for the woman to take her place at the head of the classroom, this spatio-regendering process set the conditions, albeit inadvertently, for her entrance. Now that the school was more like a home than a prison, it only made sense that the genteel, white middle-class woman would direct this new kind of domestic space. The "separate sphere" literature and the architectural plan books clearly indicated that it was she who governed the home. She was the one who created "home feeling" not only through decoration and upkeep but also through caring for the space and its inhabitants. The nondeliberate spatial rhetorics that remade the school into a home thus enabled the respectable white middle-class woman to move from one iteration of domestic space to another. Because the school was now a home, the woman could now become a teacher.

Calling the school a *parlor* especially sharpened this spatial analogy and set the stage for arguments for women's new role as teacher. As Domosh, N. Johnson, Seager, and Spain have explained, the nineteenth-century parlor was seen as a distinctly feminine room within the already feminized home: it was *the* space created for and governed by women. Architect J. C. Loudon explained in 1853, for instance, that the "arrangement of the multitudinous furniture and ornaments [in the parlor] must be left to the taste of the lady of the house; none but a lady can do it" (qtd. in Garrett 56). When Sigourney questioned, then, why the school should not "aim at the taste of the parlor," she called for a redecoration that would not only make women feel comfortable in the classroom but also prompt them to see themselves as the rightful candidates to be in charge of it.

A Woman's Place Is in the School

The spatio-rhetorical arguments to renovate the school-prison did not fall on deaf ears. During the 1830s and 1840s, more than $516,000 was spent on building 405 new schoolhouses in the Northeast, while $118,000 helped to renovate 429 more (Barnard, "School Architecture" 64). As reformers transformed the physical condition of these sites, they regendered the school from a masculine space to a feminine one. This gendering process, however, pertained neither just to the school's materiality nor to its prime spatial activity, corporal punishment. Rather, the spatial rhetorics and new pedagogical practices also contributed to the regendered identity of the teacher. This section makes clear how processes of spatial designation and gendered identity are, in Bondi and Davidson's words, "interrelated and mutually constitutive processes" (16). Arguments about the school and about the teacher not only animated one another but also made available other opportunities, for the spatial rhetorics that renovated the school from prison to home and revised pedagogy from discipline to love also set the stage for a new kind of teacher to enter it.

Mann, Barnard, Beecher, and Mary Lyon were educational leaders who argued vociferously to open the school to the woman teacher. But while these discussions about the school and the teacher were contemporaneous to one another and were even engaged by the same figures, the conversations themselves were rarely linked in overt ways. That is, these rhetors did not claim that the renovations to the school were made for the purpose of installing the woman teacher at the head of the classroom. Instead, their arguments for women teachers often alluded to and capitalized on the spatial rhetorics that regendered the school. With the school now so similar to the home, white middle-class women could become teachers because taking on this professional role would not cause them to breach their gendered sphere.

Before discussing arguments concerning women's movement into the physical space of the classroom, it is important to note the primary argument for women teachers these advocates deployed. This argument rested on the premise that because the pedagogical emphasis had shifted from discipline and authority to care and morality, women were a better fit for the job. Argued Beecher in 1829,

> It will be long, if ever, before the female mind can boast of the accurate knowledge, the sound judgment, and ready discrimination which the other sex may claim. But if the mind is to be guided chiefly by means of the affections; if the regulation of the disposition, manners, the social habits and moral feelings are to be regarded before the mere acquisition of knowledge, is not *woman* best fitted to accomplish these important objects? (*Suggestions* 50)

Because good teaching was now defined by feminine affections and moral feelings (instead of accurate knowledge and sound judgment), women should be chosen as teachers over men. This popular argument was only reinforced by spatial rhetorics that regendered the school into a home and reminded the public that it was a place where the woman could exercise her "inherent" traits without really leaving the domestic sphere.

While few educational leaders overtly connected the physical changes of the school to arguments for women's rightful entry, Barnard did link the two discussions quite closely in *School Architecture*. As has been made clear in this chapter, Barnard uses this text to detail the changes that needed to be made to the physical space of the school. Toward the conclusion, though, he contemplates the figure who should occupy the space he has imagined and proposed. He writes,

> to train boys and girls to mild dispositions, graceful and respectful manners, and unquestioning obedience,—to preserve and quicken a tenderness and sensibility of conscience as the instinctive monitor of the approach of wrong ... to do all these things and more, require in the teacher a rare union of qualities, seldom found in one in a hundred of the male sex, and to be looked for with the greatest chance of success among females "in whose own hearts, love, hope, and patience have first kept school," and whose laps seem always full of the blossoms of knowledge, to be showered on the heads and hearts of infancy and childhood. (232)

After more than two hundred pages of discussion regarding the material renovation of the school from prison to home, Barnard argues that the woman teacher is the best candidate to "teach these schools properly and regulate the house of play and study" (232). She can oversee and conduct this new school space because the feminine and domestic qualities she possesses now match the new school atmosphere and material reality.

Other leaders did not as overtly place conversations about the woman teacher within texts about school architecture, but many did take advantage of the fact that a domesticated school could become a legitimate site of professional occupation for the respectable white middle-class woman. Beecher, for instance, anticipates this possibility in *Suggestions respecting Improvements in Education* (1829) when she leverages the emerging understanding of the school as a private, feminine space to assert the idea that women could enter the classroom as teachers. She writes, the "time is not far when [teaching] will become an honourable profession, and beneath its liberal portal, woman is gladly welcomed to lawful and unsullied honours" (51). Women can be teachers because the school as "portal" is a place of honor, not public incivility. Beecher reinforces this point, explaining that by entering the school as teacher, the woman "can discern before her the road to honorable independence, and extensive usefulness, where she need not outstep the proscribed boundaries of feminine modesty, nor diminish one of those retiring graces that must ever constitute her most attractive charms" (52). For Beecher, the space of the school falls within the gender geography accessible to women: they could occupy the classroom without making themselves "public."

Lyon, founder of Mount Holyoke Female Seminary, seconded Beecher's claim that entering the classroom was in no way a breach of woman's proper duties or spatial domain by arguing that teaching in the school was an extension of teaching in the home. In her 1837 speech "Principles and Design of the Mount Holyoke Female Seminary," Lyon defines the work of the teacher as decidedly private and feminine:

> All the duties [of the teacher], of whatever kind, are in an important sense social and domestic. They are retired and private, not public like those of the other sex. Whatever she does beyond her own family should be but another application and illustration of social and domestic excellence. She may occupy the place of an important teacher, but her most vigorous labors should be modest and unobtrusive. (290–91)

To Lyon, the work of the teacher in the classroom does not move her into public space or invite public scrutiny. The school is neither prison nor voting booth. Instead, the school is yet another kind of domestic arena, one that is secluded and private, in line with both Barnard's and Downing's prescriptions.

Similar to Lyon, Mann also made use of the spatial rhetorics of the regendered school to argue for woman's rightful place in the classroom. Throughout his advocacy for female teachers, Mann quieted any potential anxieties that women's passage into the classroom was even the most minuscule step into public space. In *A Few Thoughts on the Powers and Duties of Woman* (1853), he writes that women should not occupy the masculine spaces of the battlefield or courtroom by taking on professions of the soldier or lawyer (85–91). Mann argues instead that women should take charge of the classroom. He writes, "Education, then, I say emphatically, is woman's work;—the domain of her empire, the scepter of her power, the crown of her glory. At first, it is, and necessarily must be, almost exclusively hers" (84). Mann fine-tunes this point concerning the spaces women should enter and "rule" in his first lecture as secretary of the Massachusetts Board of Education. Here, he explains that when the woman becomes a teacher, she "does not forego, but, in the eye of prophetic vision, she anticipates and makes her own, all the immortal honors of the academy, the forum, and the senate, when she lays their deep foundations, by training up children in the way they should go" (*Lecture* 25). Echoing republican motherhood discourse, Mann explains how the woman teacher can achieve honors similar to those made by men in the academy, forum, and senate. Her achievement, though, is not accomplished through work done directly in public spaces of consequence. Like the mother in the home, the teacher makes her impression on the world *indirectly*: in the domesticated space of the school, she "trains up" children so that they might go out and enter the public spaces she cannot.

All of these arguments for women's movement into the classroom and the teaching profession lay at the foundation of the epigraph that opened this chapter: "But the daughter and sister in the quietness of the parental home, the faithful teacher in the village school-house, the mother in her secluded nursery, are all forming others after their own model, writing upon that which is never to die" (Sigourney, "Superficial Attainments" 29). This chapter's spatio-rhetorical analyses make clear that Sigourney's words were neither commonplace nor uninterested but instead signaled a complex rhetorical achievement that remade the school from prison into home. For Sigourney and her like-minded interlocutors, the school was an extension of the home and nursery. This parallel could not have been drawn without the robust nondeliberate spatial rhetorics that erased the school's masculine features and ascribed to it feminine characteristics. The regendered school set the stage for Sigourney to make the statement that the "faithful" woman teacher belonged in the schoolhouse.

These arguments for women's entrance into the classroom clarify how spatial rhetorics contributed to the regendered identity of the teacher. As Nedra Reynolds has argued, "identities take root from particular sociogeographical locations, reflecting where a person comes from and, to some extent, where she is allowed to go" (*Geographies* 11). The spatial rhetorics these educational leaders deployed reveal how the gendered identity of the teacher took root. When the classroom was defined as exposed, vulgar, dirty, and uncomfortable, it would seem that only a male teacher acting as judge and executioner could occupy it. Once the school began to mirror the home, though, once it became comfortable, private, clean, secluded, and decorated, the classroom transformed into a place where the identity of the teacher could change. It became possible for the teacher to be a woman.

In part, as a result of such arguments, women teachers began entering the classroom in great numbers. By 1900 there were 325,000 women teachers in U.S. classrooms, occupying 73.4 percent of teaching positions (Clifford, *Those Good Gertrudes* 35). But numbers alone are not the only evidence of women's newfound professional dominance. Popular discourse also acknowledged that one should expect to find a woman at the head of the classroom. Just one example is the cover illustration for the November 9, 1867, issue of *Harper's Weekly* captioned "The District School Teacher" (fig. 2.8). Here, readers are presented with an image of *the* teacher, not the "female" teacher or the "woman" teacher, but the "district school" teacher, who is, of course, a white woman. This image was consistent with the (now) normal educational scene. It also, though, both contrasts vividly with the pedagogical scenario depicted in the engraving of Richter's *Village School in an Uproar* (see fig. 2.5) and resonates powerfully with the image of the mother in the home as depicted in *Godey's* "Sphere of Woman" (see fig. 2.2). Much like *Godey's* mother figure, the *Harper's Weekly* teacher generates a classroom "feeling" of feminine peace, order, and care. And unlike Richter's classroom scene, there is no sense of punishment or chaos or even male presence within the school this district teacher inhabits. The message is clear: the woman was now in the classroom and the school and its students were better for it.

Turf Wars

The spatio-rhetorical progression from assessment of prison-schools, to domestic renovation and proposal of a new pedagogical focus, to the installation of the new woman teacher might seem like a smooth one. However, the woman's move into the classroom was not entirely without contest. Collective and widely publicized protests from groups such as the Male Teachers' Association of New York City and from individual critics decried this new pedagogical situation and school occupation, with article titles such as C. W. Bardeen's "The Monopolizing Female Teacher" and Alfred Cleveland's "The Predominance of Female Teachers" signaling this discontent. Spatial rhetorics once again animated these discussions, as this set of interlocutors attempted to return the classroom to a masculine site of intellectual rigor and disciplined order. Their harsh criticisms underscore the part that spatial rhetorics play in establishing and challenging both the gendered definition of spaces and the bodies that inhabit them. These protesters knew that to reinstitute the male teacher in the classroom, they had to challenge newly accepted perceptions

Fig. 2.8. "The District School Teacher." Cover of *Harper's Weekly*, Nov. 9, 1867.

of what the classroom space should be and who could effectively teach in and manage it.

The spatio-rhetorical critiques made during this period fall into two major categories. The first had to do with the kinds of classrooms men and women teachers cultivate and the educational environment they create, especially for their male students. In their most general form, these criticisms warned the public of the ways the woman teacher's classroom was, in the words of the *New York Times* article "Appeal for Men Teachers," "making boys effeminate" (12). That is, this line of argument asserted that the woman teacher and her classroom practices could not make boys into men. As the anonymous writer of the 1904 *Educational Review* article "Are There Too Many Women Teachers?" explains, "a boy should, during his school life, gain, above all, true, sterling, manly character," and such character can only be developed when the boy student comes under "the grip and control" of "a just, capable, and devoted man" (101). In contrast, women teachers, according to this writer, "feminize the course of study" through teaching that is "sof[t]" and "showy" (102). D. L. Leonard concurs in his 1872 essay "Women as Educators," offering a critique that encapsulates this disturbing line of argument by defining the woman teacher in this way:

> [T]he average woman of the period is deficient in true intellectual independence, . . . is a born conservative in all things, a worshipper, above her mate, of the dead ceremonial of method and routine. She is more apt than he to be a mere teacher of words, of rules, of textbooks, of dogmas, and so to discourage investigation and lend no stimulus to reason and imagination. (275–76)

Methodical and uninventive, the woman teacher creates a school environment that stunts the growth of all students but especially that of male students. These critics asserted, however, that when men are teachers, they generate a learning environment that is inspirational and ambitious, defined by notions of "right and justice" ("Are" 102). Under a male teacher's direction, school is a place where boys not only learn the "courag[e] and high purpose of a manly character" (104) but also are exposed to a productive pedagogy of "sternness, justice, self-reliance and originality" (Cleveland 292).

The second category of spatio-rhetorical critique moved from arguments contending that women, by their nature, could not create an effective learning environment to those claiming that women's *embodied* presence in the classroom prevented them from adequately keeping order and quelling disruption.

Cleveland sets out this concern in his article by highlighting how masculine physicality better manages the classroom. To Cleveland, men "have a more commanding appearance; have the physical force necessary to enforce obedience; . . . have better control of themselves; and secure more natural, more spontaneous obedience" (294). For these writers, women could not manage the classroom in this way. Leonard explains that women's "physical stature and bulk" is "comparatively diminutive, and furnishes them with smaller measures of physical force" (274). He goes on to cite that women's "constitutional timidity" and "physical cowardice" result in weak classroom management (274). Rather than employing the "irresistible 'thou shalt,'" women prefer the "despicable 'please do,' followed . . . by a flood of tears" (275). Such feeble teaching, he argues, prompts male students to "concoct treason and trample on the laws" (275).

These two categories of demeaning critiques illuminate the concern raised by those who wanted to reclaim the classroom. Echoing but reversing the spatio-rhetorical complaints leveled at the male teacher's classroom at the beginning of the century, these interlocutors contended it was now the woman teacher who could not keep order. The male teacher should resume his place in the school so that he could create the kind of classroom that male students, especially, require for learning.[8]

Conclusion

The resistance articulated by Bardeen, Leonard, and the Male Teachers' Association of New York City was certainly not the only alternative vision for the classroom in this period. Advocates of the Lancasterian system, for instance, offered a spatio-rhetorical educational design that focused on classroom efficiency, oversight, and management. With desks in long, ordered rows, where older students were asked to monitor younger ones, this system promoted a completely different vision of teachers and their work. And if we look past schooling programs for white students to one, for example, centered on Native American students at the Carlisle Indian Industrial School in Carlisle, Pennsylvania, we find a much different set of spatial rhetorics. Colonel Richard Henry Pratt built Carlisle on (or moved the school into) an old army barracks, and, as K. Tsianina Lomawaima writes, "Pratt ran Carlisle in military fashion, with issued uniforms, close order drill, and students organized by company and by rank" (229). In line with the military atmosphere of the school was the idea that neither the white nor the Native American women teachers in charge of most of Carlisle's classrooms were defined as mothers. White women entered the school's grounds as part of a "standing army of school teachers" whose job was to ensure that students adopted white American ways (qtd. in Adams 27). And Carlisle framed its Native American teachers, who were often women, as examples of Carlisle's educational success; they were proof that its pedagogical program worked. Pratt's mission for all teachers was not to nurture and guide students. As soldiers in this army, working in these barracks, these women were expected to "civilize" their students by ridding them of their language and heritage.[9]

But even with this diversity of educational programs and in spite of the arguments for male teachers, the domesticated school and its mother-teacher dominated the American scene. There were a number of reasons for why it did so. As Geraldine Clifford explains and as will be discussed in more detail below, "[c]ost was a factor": women were simply a much cheaper labor supply than their male counterparts (*Those Good Gertrudes* 37). Additionally, many women "'overchose' teaching, because relative to men, they lacked respectable remunerative options" (37). Finally, a major contributor to this trend was the fact that Mann's pedagogical vision for the "common school" became *the* "dominant model of schooling for America's children" (33). And because Mann's popular model regendered the school into a home, the newly minted mother-teacher "became the chief instrument by which [the common school] could grow into the *public's* school, spreading across the continent and into outposts of American presence and influence elsewhere in the world" (33). Due to these factors, alternative visions for the classroom were not as fully realized, and they help to explain why the teaching profession became an "Adamless Eden" by the turn of the century.

Certainly the spatial rhetorics discussed in this chapter offer insight as to why white middle-class women especially were able to enter the nineteenth-century classroom in such numbers, but we should take care to explore the implications and consequences of this renovation. As the *Harper's Weekly* cover suggests, the expectation was that a schoolteacher would be a white, seemingly middle-class woman, and the implication was that her pedagogical work in the school was quite similar to her domestic work in the home. This chapter's analysis confirms this visual resonance. Indeed, this vision for who the teacher should be did open professional doors for women in this category. White middle-class women flooded the teaching profession. It is also important to note, though, how women outside this category took advantage of this moment and entered the profession alongside the anticipated and targeted candidates.

As Clifford writes, not only did middle-class college graduates and "daughters of farmers and small businessmen" enter the classroom, but so too did mill and factory workers ("Lady Teachers" 5). For the working-class group in particular, this professional shift offered them a chance at class mobility and new work opportunities, as these women often saw teaching as "'cleaner' and more respectable employment" than their current options (6). By becoming teachers, working-class white women were able to support their families or even claim their own financial and personal independence. This latter possibility is particularly compelling, especially when reflecting on the parallels between the mother and the teacher, for when women chose to teach and gain the independence to live on their own, they were presented with the opportunity to *avoid* marriage and children. In fact, in most districts, women could not continue teaching once they wed, so remaining single was the only way to sustain a long-term teaching career. The well-known and much derided figure of the unmarried schoolmarm is a reminder that school teaching may have released women from the unwanted prospect of marriage and family. As Blount explains, many women teachers at this time enjoyed "unprecedented independence and autonomy from men in their personal lives and often in their working lives" (83). Thus, we might see here that when spatial rhetorics made the school into a home and the teacher into another kind of mother, there was a critical difference between these parallels: in the school, the husband and father was conspicuously (and for some women, happily) absent.[10]

As indicated with the Carlisle Indian Industrial School example discussed above, questions of race and culture troubled and challenged the assumed picture of the woman teacher. Surely, dominant discourse of the period, as well as twenty-first-century educational history, focuses attention on the white teacher, and the spatial rhetorics studied in this chapter suggest why this is so. However, when the professional demographic shifted from a male to a female majority and the regendered classroom opened its doors, women of varied cultured and raced categories entered. By 1910, for example, "native-born daughters of foreign-born parentage were 27% of all women teachers" (Clifford, "Daughters" 18), with German, Scandinavian, Irish, and Jewish women populating classrooms in cities such as Boston, Chicago, and New York (Clifford, "Lady Teachers" 5). Significant too is the fact that by 1920, "there were 30,000 black women teachers in the United States" who were teaching in segregated schools (5). Jacqueline Jones records that the great number of black women teachers in the South in particular made up a "teaching force" that "reflected the feminization of the profession that took place throughout the country in the nineteenth century" (*Labor* 124). But, as Jones notes, the "lot of the black teacher was a particularly difficult one, for she relied upon either hostile white administrators or poverty-stricken black parents for her livelihood. And she contended daily with the baneful effects of the maldistribution of southern county school funds that worked to the detriment of black pupils" (124). Even still, black women teachers often envisioned their work as a politicized kind of racial uplift. Shirley Wilson Logan asserts, they "optimistically viewed this necessary cultural work as a means of preparing black people to take their place in American society" ("When" 48).

Just a glimpse at the growing diversity within the teaching profession makes it clear that while the middle-class Anglo-American woman may have been the imagined and expected figure in the classroom, she was not the only teacher in the school. For women from varied classed, cultured, and raced backgrounds, teaching not only brought with it possibilities for personal and financial independence but also newfound options for mobility beyond the home. Of course teaching moved women from the home into the school, but by doing so it also became possible for many women to travel far from home to wherever their school might be. For instance, women were "half or more of all teachers" in western states, excluding Kansas and Indiana (Clifford, "Lady Teachers" 6), and during the Civil War, approximately four thousand Northern women traveled South to educate newly freed men, women, and children (Jones, *Soldiers* 9). In terms of the latter contingent, Jones explains that the "motivation" for many women choosing freedmen's teaching was a combination of wanting to contribute to the antislavery cause and of "liberat[ing] themselves from the comfort and complacency of a middle-class existence" (8). Thus, while the spatio-rhetorical renovation suggested the school was an extension of the home, many women stretched the distance between the two quite dramatically.

Class and geographic mobility, racial uplift, different career options, and newfound independence may be read as positive consequences of the regendered school. There were, however, at least two major and more negative effects of this regendering process. First, even though women from varied classes, cultures, and races were entering the classroom, the spatio-rhetorical renovations to the school sent particular messages not only about who the teacher should be but also, and importantly, about how she should teach. Assumptions of whiteness are critical to note here. As calls by Barnard, Mann, Beecher, Lyon, and Sigourney suggested and as the *Harper's Weekly* cover displayed, in this new academic counterpart to the home, the white middle-class woman teacher would nurture and guide her white students. She was a maternal figure whose work was simple and apolitical: she was to repeat in the classroom the white middle-class values celebrated in the home. This dominant understanding was bolstered by the spatial rhetorics explored in this chapter, and together they suggested that these women carried out a particular spatial, ideological, and educational function.

Such a vision of the nineteenth-century teacher and classroom ignores the very real and damaging implications of this expected educational function. As I explore in greater detail in *Refiguring Rhetorical Education*, numbers of women teachers resisted these pedagogical marching orders and politicized their teaching *because* they or their students were not white or middle class. The teachers I examine in that book, and certainly many others during this period, challenged dominant and domesticated pedagogical expectations that often prescribed ways for their students to "act white," and they devised other, more culturally relevant and politicized options (Fordham and Ogbu 117). This chapter's findings suggest reasons why history may not record such acts of pedagogical resistance: the domesticated classroom has been cast not only as a site of whiteness but also as one for feminized, docile, innocuous teaching. The malleability of spatial rhetorics should remind us, however, that just because figures such as Mann and Beecher remodeled the classroom into a space where such "mothering" should occur, it does not mean that *all* women teachers followed these rules or created pedagogies consistent with the dominant expectations for the spatial environment. Neither the discursive constructs nor the physical materials that compose places like the school are impenetrable. Inhabitants of spaces can resist old and invent new practices even within a variety of very real, powerful constraints.

Second and finally, it must be clear that even though some women may have resisted their role as maternal, innocuous figures who were tasked with perpetuating white middle-class values, the spatial rhetorics that regendered the school also aided in the process of devaluing the teaching profession. As indicated above, when the school became a home, the teacher's work was inscribed not only as apolitical but also as simple—so close to the supposedly natural practice of mothering that teaching was not really seen as work at all. Historians of education Allison Prentice and Marjorie R. Theobald confirm this point, explaining that because the woman teacher has been continually inscribed as "young, naïve, and malleable" (4), she has been cast as the "ideal, natural" teacher who was "easily dominated by [her] employers" (6). Edwina Walsh elaborates on this point in *Schoolmarms: Women in America's*

Schools, arguing that the very definition of "schoolmarm" diminishes the woman teacher's work. She writes that while "[e]arly American male teachers were called schoolmasters, a term *Webster's* defines as 'one who disciplines or directs[,]' [f]emale teachers were called schoolmarms, defined in *Webster's* as a person who exhibits strict adherence to arbitrary rules" (29).

Because teaching was (and in many ways still is) defined in this way, women were compensated for the "easy" work they performed. To be sure, teaching did offer women a modicum of financial independence, but compared to men, they were grossly underpaid, earning 40–50 percent of the male wage. Compounding this financial disparity was the reality that paths to professional advancement and promotion were often closed to them (Clifford, "Daughters" 20). Reasons for this bleak situation are evidenced even in arguments that advocated for women's move into the classroom. Catharine Beecher's call for the installation of women teachers provides a case in point:

> [W]hen we consider the aversion of most men to the sedentary, confining, and toilsome duties of teaching and governing young children; when we consider the scanty pittance that is allowed to the majority of teachers; and that few men will enter a business that will not support a family, when there are multitudes of other employments that will afford competence, and lead to wealth; it is chimerical to hope that the supply of such immense deficiencies in our national education is to come chiefly from that sex. It is woman, fitted by disposition, and habits, and circumstances, for such duties . . . ("Essay" 145)

With these words, Beecher asserts that the woman teacher's "disposition," "habits," and "circumstances" qualify her not only for the "sedentary, confining, and toilsome" work of teaching but also for the "scanty pittance" that will be her salary. Defining and rewarding teaching in this way, it is no surprise that this new profession occupied by women was placed far below newly emerging and male-dominated career options emerging on the scene at the end of the century—options that I discuss in more detail in chapter 3. Here, though, it is impossible to miss how the teaching profession became both feminized and devalued.

The school and the classroom have certainly gained new spatial meanings since this nineteenth-century moment. To borrow a notion from Nedra Reynolds, the school is a palimpsest, being seen at various points in time as a laboratory, a borderland, a city, a community, and most recently a war zone

(*Geographies* 2). It is a space "layered like sediment... with histories and stories and memories" (2). And, yet, the memory of the school as home and the teacher as mother persists. Nancy Hoffman articulates this point in her aptly titled text *Women's "True" Profession: Voices from the History of Teaching*, where she writes that the terms *woman* and *teacher* are so "natural a pairing" in our national consciousness that they are an "invisible part of the landscape" (4). Moreover, as Theresa Enos, Sue Ellen Holbrook, Susan Hunter, Susan Miller, and Eileen Schell have surveyed, the classroom continues to be deemed a place for "women's work" because the instruction inside it supposedly requires from its teachers those feminine qualities of nurturance, self-sacrifice, and service (Miller, "Feminization" 41–42). The analysis of this chapter offers insight regarding how and why the teacher, the school, and the teaching profession gained these gendered meanings. Through spatial rhetorics—rhetorics animated by materiality, ideology, embodiment, activity, and emotions—the school became a home and the teacher became a mother.

3. The Domestic Scientist's Home Experiment
SPATIAL RHETORICS AND PROFESSIONAL ETHOS

> We have been treated for some years to discussions from eminent men as to our mental ability, our moral and physical status, our predilection for matrimony, voting, or the presidency, etc.; but the kind of home we should make if we did make one . . . the influence we should have on that centre and source of political economy, the kitchen, seem to have been ignored. . . .
>
> The whole [home] situation must be studied from the bottom, the same patient and scientific method must be used as in interpreting an obscure fact in natural history, or in deciding a vexed question in the history of nations.
>
> —Ellen Richards, "The Relation of College Women to Progress in Domestic Science," 1890

In 1890 Ellen Richards made a seemingly conservative argument regarding women's role in society and the education that should support it. Turning attention away from more progressive conversations about women's mental, moral, and physical acuity; marital possibilities; and even their access to full citizenship, Richards asserted that women should focus their attention on the home and see it as the site where they hold the most "influence." Due to the significance of this domestic influence, Richards argued that women should study the home by examining it with "patient and scientific method"; it is this space—rather than sites of public and civic import—that should be pursued and scrutinized as though it is a "vexed question." The work of this chapter is to explore why and how Richards made this call and to consider what it meant for women to follow the educational—and, indeed, professional—path Richards and her colleagues identified for them. Ultimately, Richards's objective was to create for women the field of domestic science, a profession reliant on a spatio-rhetorical transformation of the home into a site for experimentation and of the housewife into a scientist.

As this chapter details, Richards and her colleagues faced a complex rhetorical situation when it came to carving out the educational program and professional work of domestic science. By the end of the nineteenth century, women were entering colleges and universities in growing numbers, but as they were making their way onto campuses, the culture of university life was changing. Rather than offering a liberal and general education, collegiate curricula were becoming more specialized and professionalized: the college man now went to the university with the expectation that he would specialize in a particular field of study and then apply that knowledge to a professional career. Not surprisingly, this new educational emphasis posed a problem for women students and concerned observers: Why would women take up studies, such as science, that would prepare them for professions that would draw them out of the home? What should women learn and where might this learning take them?

Certainly, more progressive-minded education activists such as Bryn Mawr College's M. Carey Thomas contested the idea that woman's education (or, indeed, her professional future) should be constrained in any way. Women could and should, Thomas argued, leave the home to explore different professional options. But Richards and her colleagues offered a different response. This cohort contended that women should study science and could become scientists, but—and this was the critical point—their scientific education would lead them back to the home, not take them from it. That is, domestic scientists would apply their newly gained scientific knowledge to the problems of the home.

While Richards's plans for women's education and their professional future were on the surface less controversial, she and her colleagues did encounter a significant challenge when they argued that women could claim the emerging and increasingly coveted title of *scientist*. To be seen as true scientists who had relevant expertise and important knowledge, domestic scientists had to remake, for themselves and the watching public, the home as a relevant site of investigation. Women could not be scientists if the home remained a site where they either applied their natural talents of love and care or performed the daily drudgery of housework. For women to do the work of a scientist, the home had to become a space for rigorous investigation and experimentation, a space to apply and generate newfound, intellectually stimulating scientific knowledge. Thus, one might read in Richards's epigraph a conservative, perhaps even regressive, professional and educational position because she is calling on women to (re)turn their attention to the home. But, as I contend in this chapter, to gain the expertise Richards was envisioning meant that women would pursue a rigorous scientific education and then leverage that knowledge within a new version of the home, one that needed to be "studied from the bottom" by way of the scientific method ("Relation" 2).

This chapter traces how domestic scientists changed the home in order to take on their new professional identity. To make this investigation, I study the relationship between spatial rhetorics and ethos. While a basic understanding of ethos defines it as the rhetor's ability to gain credibility in the eyes of an audience through establishing the Aristotelian trifecta of good will, good moral character, and good knowledge, I focus in this chapter on the spatial component of ethos construction. Along with rhetoricians Risa Applegarth, Michael Hyde, Nedra Reynolds, Lisa Shaver, Carolyn Skinner, and Craig Smith, I see a critical part of ethos as being the space from which one speaks. As Martin Heidegger writes, "*Ethos* means abode, dwelling place. The word means the region in which one dwells" (qtd. in Hyde xix). It is the "haun[t]" one occupies that inflects the public persona one crafts and consequently the authority one attempts to claim and embody (Hyde xvi). Smith explains, "*ethos* has an ontological dimension because it emerges from the way one makes decisions, the way one lives on a day-to-day basis, the way one dwells" (2). The act of dwelling in a particular space inflects who someone is, what kinds of knowledge one cultivates in that space, and how one is expected to operate in the world. Spatial occupation, practice, and revision help constitute ethos.

Critical to the examinations of this chapter, however, is that ethos construction is not only space-based but also collective. Ethos composition can be a collective endeavor that indicates the spatial occupations and allegiances of a group, as in the case of this chapter's domestic scientists. S. Michael Halloran writes, "To have *ethos* is to manifest the virtues most valued by the culture to and for which one speaks" (60). Applegarth elaborates on the part that space plays in this collective endeavor: "rhetors learn to enact culturally specific notions of 'good will, good sense, and good moral character' through their participation in particular communities and their habituation, within *places*, to shared norms that make *ethos* effective" ("Genre" 43). Ethos is deeply connected to one's relationship to a group and that group's location. As Applegarth explains, "*where* one participates in social life influences *what* one can understand as 'good sense' or 'good character'" (49). This chapter uncovers how domestic scientists identified space as a critical component in their collective and professional ethos construction.

Of course, a rhetor's use of space to craft collective ethos is not made without encountering constraints. As Kathleen Ryan, Nancy Myers, and Rebecca Jones set forth, history reveals the ways it has been "culturally and socially restrictive for women to develop authoritative ethē" (2). Gender, especially when it is animated by class, culture, race, sexuality, and ability, conditions where a person is able to go, the spaces that can be occupied, and the kinds of knowledge and credibility that can be cultivated within that space. As a group of mainly white middle-class educated women, domestic scientists faced a particular set of constraints when they worked to take on the professional identity of the scientist. Indeed, they had a space-based ethos problem, and this chapter explores how they attempted to solve it. For while domestic scientists may have satisfied onlookers by setting out that their version of scientific study aligned with dominant spatial expectations for women in their sociopolitical position (they would focus their attention on the home), they faced a great challenge by asserting that the home could be a space where a scientific ethos could emerge. Shaver makes clear that spatial occupation can be a "sourc[e] of authority," but she also asserts that it can be a source of perceived incapacity ("No Cross" 66). One's connection to or inhabitation of a space can *limit* expectations for the enactment of expertise. This was the case for domestic scientists. The idea that a scientist could work within the home seemed, to borrow from Skinner, like an "incompatible" professional position (183).

I argue that domestic scientists sought to reconcile this incompatible ethos position by deploying spatial rhetorics that remade the home into and displayed it as a site for science. Spaces, as this study sets forth, are not static. Because one is aligned with, inhabits, or is expected to be in or come from a space does not mean there is only one possibility for ethos construction. By changing the space one inhabits, one can change ethos. This chapter examines the spatial rhetorics that domestic scientists deployed to renovate the home into a site for science so that the space from which they were speaking and working—the home—could be seen as amenable to scientific investigation and capable of producing the ethos of a scientist. Through spatial rhetorics that remade the home—by enacting new habits and practices and by incorporating new material features into the home—domestic scientists worked to gain a new collective professional ethos.

Underlying this discussion of domestic scientists and the spatial rhetorics they employed to compose a professional ethos for themselves are questions of race, culture, and class. Indeed, an implicit part of the domestic scientists' argument was to offer a new definition of the "good" wife and mother: she now ran the home as an educated scientist, and any other mode of conduct was inferior and even irresponsible. Thus, domestic science was often inflected with tones of educated elitism. Furthermore, as a group of mostly white, middle-class women, domestic scientists often took it upon themselves to teach women from working-class and marginalized cultural positions how to adopt new scientific approaches to the home, especially through cooking and housekeeping. The cost of this adoption often meant the erasure of these women's cultural practices. Domestic scientists therefore created their ethos not just by remaking their own homes but also often by advocating new spatial practices for "other" women through teachings laced with cultural superiority and noblesse oblige.

In this chapter, I explore three specific ways domestic scientists leveraged spatial rhetorics to revise the home as a means to create a new professional ethos for themselves. I begin by considering how domestic scientists used spatial rhetorics to challenge two dominant (and contradictory) notions of the white middle-class home: (1) the home as a site of idyllic comfort, where the nurturing mother reigned with instinctive knowledge, and (2) the home a site of drudgery, where women conducted mind-numbing repetitive work. Challenging these two perceptions, domestic scientists recast the home as a site rife with complex problems that could only be solved by rigorous intellectual engagement and scientific experimentation. Next, I examine how domestic scientists used the spatio-rhetorical strategy of display to educate the public about the new home they were creating through their scientific experimentation. Focusing on two displays, the New England Kitchen and the Rumford Kitchen, I uncover how domestic scientists put the private space of the home on public display to showcase their new professional ethos within this renovated space. Finally, I analyze the ways that domestic scientists expanded the purview of their work *beyond* the family residence by proposing that spaces other than a brick-and-mortar family dwelling resembled the home. They claimed that spaces such as the city street, the hospital, and the municipal office were homelike spaces and thereby necessitated the skills and expertise of the newly trained domestic scientist. By doing so, domestic scientists argued they had the expertise and jurisdiction to oversee these spaces. The spatial rhetorics that remade the boundaries of the home and domestic scientists' ethos certified them to gain such positions as nutritionists, founders and managers of settlement houses, government officials, and social workers.

Before delving into the three spatio-rhetorical moves that redefined ideas of home and allowed for the construction of the domestic scientist's ethos, I first set out the rhetorical context in which these women were living and working. I explore the dominant spatial rhetorics of the white middle-class home and the expected domestic ethos of the wife and mother who presided over it, and I outline the new imperatives of collegiate education that focused on application and professionalization. Domestic scientists carefully intervened in both of these conversations.

Women's Domestic Ethos, Home Work, and the Industrial Revolution

When women such as Ellen Richards sought to create the new professional occupation of domestic scientist at the turn of the twentieth century, they were in many ways responding to a complex conversation already under way regarding women's domestic ethos. As Craig Smith writes, "everyone has *ethos* whether it be noble or ignoble" (2). A person's ethos, as well as the site from which that ethos emerges, precedes the rhetor, so the rhetor must either emphasize that already-in-place ethos or work to revise it. Domestic scientists were not, therefore, starting from scratch. When they set out to compose their new professional identity, they had to address both dominant expectations for women's domestic habituation and the ethos they gained through it, as well as new ideas regarding women's work in the home that put this ethos in flux. Indeed, by the end of the nineteenth century, there was great debate about a woman's place in the home and the work she performed within this space.

As discussed in chapter 2, dominant spatial rhetorics of the early nineteenth century inscribed the white middle-class home as the space where the woman took on the role of the loving mother who leveraged her peaceful demeanor to create a space of care and comfort for her family. But these spatial rhetorics also identified this woman's duty as that of manager of the home and the prime worker within it. She was the one who maintained the home and kept it running on a day-to-day basis. While domestic scientists sought to revise both of these depictions of woman's duty in the home, it was the latter understanding of woman's domestic ethos that came under particular scrutiny in the late nineteenth century, and it was also the one that aspiring domestic scientists paid special attention to.

The immensely popular genre of the antebellum-era domestic advice manual lends insight into this facet of women's domestic ethos, as it described the kind of daily work the white middle-class woman was expected to accomplish. Lydia Maria Child's 1828 *Frugal Housewife* was the first text of this kind in the United States. As Sarah Leavitt explains, authors of these texts were often, like Child, "white middle-class women who had some personal experience with homemaking," and their goal was to pass their knowledge on to similarly situated women who were newly taking on household duties (10). Child writes that her goal is to "offer . . . this cheap little book of economical hints" (5) to "young housekeepers" (6), and her focus in *The Frugal Housewife* is on instructing readers about how to run their homes without waste or unnecessary expense.

The expansive range of material in manuals like Child's is astonishing, as they covered topics such as administering home remedies and health care; making candles and soaps; dying fabrics; keeping a vegetable garden; tending to animals; cooking, baking, and butchering; sewing and linen-making; maintaining furniture; caring for children; and educating daughters. For the most part these manuals operated in a register of basic guidance. Serving as a representative example, Child's popular text, which went through twelve editions in just two years, instructs readers that "a little salt sprinkled in starch while it's boiling, tends to prevent it from sticking" (24) and that when "sweet oil is much used," readers will find "it is more economical to buy it in the bottle than by the flask" (23). As these instructions indicate, the domestic advice manual was a comprehensive guide that provided readers with simple directions on how to run a home and keep it in order. The goal for this genre was breadth, not depth, and the overarching spatio-rhetorical message was that the home required the woman to take on a great deal of work. This work could made lighter, though, if she followed the manual's quick tips and took in its bits of knowledge. The domestic ethos of the woman from this spatio-rhetorical perspective was that of a busy worker who had plenty to do and who was always alert to making smart decisions regarding home care.

The onset of the Industrial Revolution, however, brought great change to the white middle-class home and the kinds of work that women were expected to perform inside it, as much domestic production was gradually replaced by mass production in factories. Bertha Terrill discusses this situation in her 1907 text *Household Management*:

> In former times the home was practically the entire economic world. Most of what was produced to meet the needs of the people originated there, while all of it found ready consumption within the family circle or by limited exchange. To-day the shop and the factory

have taken most of the productions and developed them one by one, into large industries outside the home. (1–2)¹

Terrill concludes that not much of interest was left in the home for the woman to do: owing to developments of the Industrial Revolution, many women were finding that "all which adds zest and is worth while [in domestic work] is taken from them" (3). Historian Laura Shapiro confirms Terrill's assessment, writing that "with the exception of child-rearing, most of the work a woman did consisted of day-to-day maintenance: feeding and cleaning and mending and feeding and cleaning. Her tasks were fewer but they were distinctly monotonous and in a tangible sense unproductive" (13). Thus, the question of domestic drudgery became a prime concern for white middle-class women as many wondered how they might reduce or suffer through their monotonous domestic duties and even whether they needed to remain in the home at all.

Calling on women to escape from household drudgery, women's rights activists argued that women should leave the domestic sphere to gain educational experiences and professionalization. Charlotte Perkins Gilman, for example, assesses the situation in this way in her 1903 text *The Home: Its Work and Influence*: "the progress of industry has cut the lady off from even her embroidery"; her "few remaining industries" are taken "from her, away from the house, into the mill and shop where they belong" (222).² Given these industrial improvements that should seemingly free women from domestic duty, Gilman questions the dominant perception that women should remain tied to the home, writing that, now with "ever idler hands," women are expected to "stay behind" (222) and "work morbidly inside the painfully inadequate limits of the house" (223). Gilman celebrates those who test these limits and encourages others to find a new place for themselves in this changing world: "More and more the necessity for full and legitimate social activity makes itself felt; and more and more [woman] is coming out of the house to take her rightful place in the world" (224).³

If the composition of ethos includes the "ritual acts" that are rooted in space and that "manifest our group identity" (Halloran 63), it is clear that the domestic ethos for white middle-class women at century's end was in flux. Activists like Gilman identified industrial developments as exigencies to free women from domestic duty and prompted them to rethink who they wanted to be and what they wanted to become. Because the home was now often described and experienced as a space of drudgery, it seemed logical for women to turn their attention to new locales and to consider becoming someone else. Contemplating these new ethos possibilities, many women looked to increasingly available collegiate education as a way to imagine other futures. It was in the college setting that domestic scientists responded to these discussions regarding what women's ties to the home should be given recent industrial and technological changes. Here, domestic scientists designed their new field of study and professional ethos as scientists who would dwell within and study the problems of the home. But as they composed their ethos and their discipline in this way, they also contended with another quite powerful discussion regarding the purpose of higher education for both men and women.

Women's Higher Education and Professionalization in U.S. Colleges

A variety of factors paved the way for women to enter U.S. colleges and universities, not the least of which was the idea that the work of the home was changing and that women could now leave it to gain credentials as teachers, to invigorate the pedagogical duties of republican womanhood by teaching their own children to be good citizens, or even to consider other professional options besides that of wife and mother. In 1837 Mary Lyon established Mount Holyoke, the first women's college in the United States, and Oberlin initiated coeducation from its start in 1833. By 1875 women's colleges such as Vassar, Smith, and Wellesley had opened their doors, and schools such as the University of Michigan integrated women into their student body. As women were making their way onto college campuses, they also witnessed and participated in a major revision to the curriculum that brought with it pressing questions regarding the aims of their education.

During this time and keeping pace with the Industrial Revolution, higher education changed from a classical model of general instruction, which sought to shape the whole "college man," to one centered on application, specialized learning, and professionalization. Collegiate educators now asked a new question of themselves and their curriculum: How would students apply their learning to real-world, career-specific circumstances? As one response to this question, universities introduced an elective system that enabled students to take a suite of courses particular to a field of study so they could gain expertise applicable in that field. Rather than a universal college experience for all students, the ultimate goal of the elective system was to center students' attention on how to solve the distinct problems that concerned professionals within their chosen career. Education historian Laurence Veysey writes that such deep investment in specialization and application created a collegiate atmosphere that was "permeated with vocational ambition" (62). Indeed, one contemporary contributor to the journal *Education* argued that the university should not create "pedants steeped in useless lore" but rather should cultivate "true men, who are earnest, and practical, who know something of the problems of real life and are fitted to grapple with them" (qtd. in Veysey 62). Reading this shift in collegiate culture from the perspective of ethos construction, one could say that the university had become a place to form a student's professional identity. As Halloran writes, "schooling" is one of the "most subtle and powerful" sites for ethos construction because there students learn the knowledge, habits, behaviors, and practices of the group they want to join and, critical to the work of this chapter, there they also learn about the place they will inhabit and apply their expertise (63).

Yet another important consequence of this educational shift was the subject matter, intellectual practices, and career path it now emphasized. This new elective model emulated the German university, and as a result, many U.S. universities also came to see the study of science as a rigorous field of intellectual work, the practice of the scientific method as a mode of learning, and the cultivation of the scientist as a new professional option. During the nineteenth century, prominent figures such as Yale's Theodore Woolsey and Harvard's Charles Eliot visited German universities and examined their laboratories and attended their seminars. Through this process, U.S. educational leaders not only observed the focused curriculum of the German model but also witnessed how its emphasis on science enabled the Germans to "turn out trained scientists, text-books, and apparatus" as well as scholarly publications and original, useful research (Bernal 553). This new model became the master and guide for many U.S. university leaders (Royce 97), and they returned to the United States from Germany "with the phrase 'scientific research' on their lips" (Veysey 127).

Aspiring to replicate German success and ingenuity, U.S. educators identified science as an important field to develop. Such a move was significant because in the early part of the nineteenth century, science was not seen as a legitimate arena for professional work. Science was instead perceived as an extracurricular educational activity for lay practitioners—one open to both men and women (Kohlstedt; Milbourne and Hallenbeck). However, after witnessing the German model's focus on science and the way this intellectual pursuit enabled experts to solve real problems and create new knowledge, U.S. educators began to explore possibilities for their students to take on this same kind of work. The integration of the elective system into collegiate curricula was a key way for students to specialize in fields such as physics, biology, and chemistry (Bernal 554–55). Of particular spatio-rhetorical interest is the fact that laboratories emerged as new fixtures on college campuses during this period. Laboratories enabled students to sharpen their scientific acumen by providing them with a space and equipment for conducting the now-desired cutting-edge research. All of these practices collectively worked toward enabling students to build a prestigious scientific ethos for themselves that would assume importance outside college when they moved into their professional fields of work. Not surprisingly, as this professional identity gained distinction and value, it became gendered in certain ways.

Stakeholders invested in science education and women's education wondered why and how women would specialize in science, where this scientific learning might take them, and who women students would become in the process. For while it was clear that men could study physics to become engineers and physiology to become doctors, the application question became a problematic one for women students. Harvard president Charles Eliot, for instance, argued that since women primarily either "bear and rear children" as mothers or "do not bear, [but] bring them up" as teachers, their "one single occupation" is "rearing children" (103). To Eliot, a specialized education would mean that women develop the "capacities and powers which will fit them to make family life more intelligent, enjoyable, happier, more productive" (105). Figures such as Bryn Mawr's Thomas and Vassar's Abby Leach opposed proposals like Eliot's, asserting that specialization for women would track them into specific kinds of study. Such tracking would render some fields off-limits to women given a perceived inability for them to apply this new knowledge to their gendered circumstances and to professional futures deemed acceptable. Arguing against the emerging elective, specialized collegiate experience, Leach asserted instead that college "does its duty when it sends forth women who know how to use their minds" and offers them broad instruction that enables them to "look at the larger questions of life and be trained in large-mindedness" (20). A woman's education, Thomas insisted, could not be "too broad, too high, or too deep" ("Present Tendencies" 56).

While activists such as Thomas and Leach resisted specialization and application, others embraced the discourse of professionalization and claimed that application, and even science application, was a relevant consideration for women students. For example, figures such as M. W. Whitney contended that general education, without the guide of specialization or application, left women directionless: "Our young men find in their universal calling as providers the incentive which gives tone and concentration to their endeavors. Our girls, as a class, lack this incentive" (62). Whitney suggested that the woman student needs a "more definite purpose in her life" (62). Whitney thus saw great good in the new educational model and praised the German-bred elective system as a means of offering it. Isabel Bevier and Susannah Usher agreed with Whitney on this score. Reflecting on the recent history of women's and men's education in science in particular, these authors discerned a stark difference in the two, with men lucky enough to have an arena for application and women, unfortunately, lacking one:

> It is not, perhaps, too much to say that much of women's early work in chemistry was a more or less indefinite playing with test tubes in which one of the three results was expected—a beautiful color, a bad odor, or an explosion. She was not long in discovering that her brother took chemistry and bacteriology, not because some one had told him that it ought to form a part of a liberal education, but because he expected to use this knowledge later in his work with soil or in the dairy. (14)

According to these authors, women's scientific education without the possibility of application was mere play, while men's with it was meaningful and important.

When educators called for women's specialization and professionalization and argued that women should be able to pursue careers like their male counterparts, they often encountered considerable backlash. Figures such as A. Lapthorn Smith asserted that the new university culture was affecting women's investment in traditional American home life, for "too great a cultivation of the female intellect ... [is] result[ing] in [the educated woman's] scorning to perform those duties which are cheerfully performed, and even desired, by the uneducated wife" (467). Psychologist and educator G. Stanley Hall agreed, claiming that higher education was effectively "castrat[ing]" women, prompting them to "deplore the necessity of child-bearing" and to "abhor the limitations of married life" (634). The general complaint, then, as Mary Schenck Woolman explained, was that focused university education "not only will injure a God-given power, but also will tend to remove all lovable and womanly qualities that the subjects possess" (7). Collegiate educators thus faced quite a quandary: How could women students specialize in a particular academic arena without generating criticisms like Smith's and Hall's? Was it possible for these students to craft a professional ethos without "scorning" traditional duties?

Ellen Richards and her domestic science colleagues, Bevier and Usher among them, offered persuasive answers to these questions. These women created a field and a scientific ethos for themselves and their students by arguing that women could take on the rigorous work of science and the role of the scientist but would do so by applying their newly gained knowledge to the home. It was this argument that became the domestic scientist's saving grace and most critical problem. While onlookers may have been satisfied to see women (re)turning their attention to the home, domestic scientists knew that for their field and ethos to be taken seriously, they had to remake this space in the eyes of potential women students and the watching public. The home could not be a site for women's natural enactment of love and care or even a site of routine drudgery. It had to become a place for rigorous experimentation and serious investigation. To accomplish this revision and to craft their professional ethos, domestic scientists deployed a rich and diverse set of spatial rhetorics.

Yet the domestic scientist's work was made even more difficult due to the ways power and gender operated within the discourses of professionalism circulating so widely at this time (Des Jardins). As historian Sarah Stage explains, "professionalism was gendered with a vengeance, down to its language of objectivity, science, expertise, and disinterested inquiry" ("Home Economics" 3). Such discourse, of course, worked to exclude women, who were often defined by their supposed virtues of emotional attachment and their nonprofessional role of instinctive caretaker. In arguing for an application to the home, then, domestic scientists had a great deal of rhetorical work to do. Their first and most pressing concern was to revise the home so that women in particular and the public in general would see it as a site fit for science.

Before exploring the spatio-rhetorical tactics that enabled this transformation, however, it is important to offer a more detailed picture of the leading figure of the domestic science movement, Ellen Richards, for her career narrative is illustrative both of the popularity of the domestic science movement and of the careful negotiations that domestic scientists made as they carved out a place for themselves in the scientific and professional worlds.

Ellen Richards

An 1870 graduate of Vassar College and student of famed astronomer Maria Mitchell, Ellen Swallow Richards was the first woman admitted to the Massachusetts Institute of Technology (MIT), where she studied chemistry at the graduate level. In 1876 Richards became an assistant instructor (without pay) at MIT and soon helped to found a laboratory on its campus called the

Women's Laboratory that was intended specifically for women's scientific study. There, under Richards's direction, more than eighty-five women conducted experiments over the course of six years, with work in the Women's Laboratory ending in 1883 when MIT allowed for coeducation and admitted women to its regular labs. A distinguished and rigorous scientist in her own right, Richards studied, experimented, and published on topics such as water analysis, mass water supply, sanitary chemistry, and nutrition. Richards was best known, however, for leading a very public discussion about the value of scientific education for women, for forming the academic discipline of domestic science (also known as home economics), and for crafting the professional identity of the domestic scientist. As Shapiro explains, "most of the domestic scientists who set the movement on its course . . . either were trained by Ellen Richards or worked alongside her, or at the very least owned a copy of her first book, *The Chemistry of Cooking and Cleaning*, which remained in steady demand for close to thirty years" (38). Richards gained this attention and esteem through her untiring public advocacy, her academic and professional activism, and her prolific publishing career.

In addition to *The Chemistry of Cooking and Cleaning: A Manual for House-keepers* (1881), Richards published such texts as *Food Materials and Their Adulterations* (1885), *Air, Water, and Food from a Sanitary Standpoint* (1900), and *First Lessons in Food and Diet* (1904). Richards frequently presented at national conferences on education and published shorter articles in such periodicals as the *Journal of Home Economics*, *Good Housekeeping*, and the *American Kitchen Magazine*. She also took on significant leadership roles in national organizations. Richards served as the first president of the American Home Economics Association (AHEA); she, along with Marion Talbot, founded the Association of Collegiate Alumnae, which eventually became the American Association of University Women; and she initiated the famous Lake Placid Conference on Home Economics. As discussed in more detail below, Richards was also instrumental in creating a series of public demonstrations that informed general audiences about domestic science innovation.

Under Richards's direction, both the Lake Placid Conferences and the AHEA worked to legitimize the work of home economics generally and of domestic science more particularly, and a significant aspect of legitimation was selecting a name for this field of study. After appointing a committee on nomenclature, Richards and her colleagues finally decided to designate their work *home economics*. Yet, even once this decision was made, there remained conflict concerning what home economics encompassed. As Stage explains, some women viewed home economics as "primarily sociological and economic,"[4] while others were more concerned with women's return to their traditional domestic duties; still others identified with Richards's main concern—and the concern for this chapter—which was domestic science, or the application of scientific principles to home problems ("Home Economics" 6).

Certainly, the varied interests gathered under the umbrella of home economics brought with them differing levels of rigor and authentic scientific engagement, and, to be sure, Richards's domestic science strand represented the most serious intellectual work. But even though these tensions did exist, Richards and others chose to look past their differences and worked toward the overarching goal of professionalizing their area of study and organizing an educational path for women students. In addition to focusing on professionalization in traditional instructional settings, Richards and her cohort also advocated for women who had limited access to university life. The twelve-volume *Library of Home Economics* series, with Richards as an editorial board member, was billed as a "complete home-study" course, through which women who were interested in domestic science but not enrolled in collegiate courses could learn about this field from "teachers of recognized authority."[5] And, finally, domestic scientists also reached beyond the college campus by introducing courses at the high school and elementary levels, by bringing their work to women's clubs, and by offering classes in trade schools for women interested in obtaining work in domestic service. The cumulative message of these curricular and extracurricular efforts was that domestic scientists were cultivating a serious scholarly discipline that required dedicated study and resulted in professional expertise.

Thanks to the tireless work of Richards and her colleagues, home economics and domestic science became a major presence on college campuses around the turn of the twentieth century. While elite women's colleges like Thomas's Bryn Mawr questioned the significance of this discipline, larger coeducational institutions embraced and propelled it.[6] In part this support came from the 1862 Morrill Act, which created and funded "land-grant" universities across the nation, whose express purpose was to supply a practical, application-based collegiate curriculum for both men and women. Applying science to the home matched the priorities of the Morrill Act perfectly, and because of this alignment, home economics and domestic science thrived, with over 250 institutions offering the subject by 1915 (Shapiro 185). Notes Shapiro, "In agricultural colleges, in state universities, in technical institutes—in any school where there was coeducation, in fact—departments of home economics were flourishing" (185).[7] Home economics thus found its place in these large institutions by providing an application-based education for their women students. Yet, even while the discipline enjoyed this popularity, questions regarding its rigor and prestige persisted, as many wondered whether women within this emerging field were conducting real science and how this kind of study would affect women and their domestic investments.

In particular, Richards's arguments for women's scientific education and their professional identity were inflected not only by public warnings about what science and specialization might do to women but also by her own experience at MIT. Not surprisingly, Richards faced discrimination as a student there. Upon entering MIT, Richards was categorized as a "special" student, and while this designation saved her tuition, it also "allowed MIT to keep her name off its student roster and avoid the precedent of coeducation" (Stage, "Ellen Richards" 21). With this special designation, Richards completed graduate-level courses in chemistry but was refused a PhD because MIT did not want to award its first advanced degree in the subject to a woman (22). MIT's overt discrimination was compounded by more subtle exclusionary practices. Richards, for example, described segregation in the physical space of the laboratory, reporting that she was cordoned off from her male counterparts "very much as a dangerous animal might have been" (qtd. in Stage, "Ellen Richards" 21).

Setting the course for her later actions as a leader of the domestic science movement, Richards did not respond to these events by becoming a women's rights activist. Her reaction was quite the opposite. In the lab, Richards defused the perceived strangeness of the gendered situation by taking on traditional domestic duties, from mending her male classmates' clothes to sweeping the laboratory floor (22). Here, Richards articulates her attempts to negotiate her place as a woman scientist in the lab:

> I hope in a quiet way . . . I am winning a way which others will keep open. Perhaps the fact that I am not a Radical or a believer in the all powerful ballot for women to right her wrongs and that I do not scorn womanly duties, but claim it as a privilege to clean up and sort of supervise the room and sew things, etc., is winning me stronger allies than anything else. . . . [Y]ou see I am useful in a decidedly general way—so they can't say *study* spoils me for anything else. (qtd. in Hunt, *Life* 90–91)

As a student scientist, then, Richards worked to forge a path for other women to follow. By taking on a maternal role in relation to her male peers, Richards preempted public criticism and made clear that science did not "spoil" women for domestic duties.

Richards's acute concern for public critique continued as she worked with students in MIT's Women's Laboratory. During this period, she challenged the argument that the study of science compelled women to deplore married life, and instead she celebrated her students' domestic future. Richards set out, "But it is perhaps as wives and mothers that their greatest glory lies. They have proved as no other college could better do that the most severe training did not make them repulsive nor unfit for housewifely duties" (qtd. in Slaughter 15). In the Women's Laboratory throughout the 1880s, Richards conducted her own educational experiment, and as she reports, the results were positive. She found "severe" scientific study did not make her students unfit or repulsive but rather prepared them for their "greatest glory": the work of wife and mother. The careful balance that Richards struck between arguing that women should study science while also pointing women (back) to the home would continue throughout her career and the careers of many domestic scientists of this period. Crucial to this nuanced argument, though, was the premise that the home was not what it used to be. Domestic scientists were *real* scientists because their spatial rhetorics transformed the home into a viable site for applying science.

Spatial Rhetorics and the Domestic Science Ethos

From the mid-1880s to the first decades of the 1900s, Richards and her colleagues put forth a multipronged spatio-rhetorical effort that aimed to cultivate a professional ethos for themselves and their students by asserting that women could indeed be scientific experts. The remainder of this chapter details their moves to claim this expertise and examines how these moves relied on spatial rhetorics that reconstituted the home as the site where they would conduct scholarly inquiry and scientific experimentation. The following section in particular focuses on key spatio-rhetorical efforts domestic scientists deployed within the educational and domestic science community that sought to revise already-in-place perceptions of their ethos and, in so doing, address the ethos problem they faced. As Coretta Pittman explains, a rhetor's ethos often "precede[s]" her, meaning that rhetors come to a rhetorical situation having first to contend with an audience's preset ideas about who the rhetor is and where she comes from (47). A critical part of the domestic scientists' ethos problem was that their potential students and the watching public perceived the white middle-class home and the woman's work in it in limiting ways. Domestic scientists realized that one way to solve their ethos problem was by revising these spatial perceptions. If they could remake their haunt, they could remake their ethos.

In terms of the specific understandings of home that domestic scientists attempted to counter, leaders of the movement first challenged the idea that the home was a site of drudgery and boredom; second, they altered the perception that the home was the natural environment where women's maternal and domestic instincts were all that was necessary for its proper care. Through forums such as the *Journal of Home Economics*, the *Library of Home Economics*, and the Lake Placid Conferences, domestic scientists articulated spatial rhetorics that enabled them to achieve these ends by revising understandings of the home, by outfitting this space in new ways, and by reconceiving the activities that women would do inside it. These multiform renovations ultimately worked to transform women's domestic ethos.

Household Drudgery Becomes Household Science

As discussed above, since the advent of the Industrial Revolution, the tasks of the home had been greatly diminished, with activities such as candle- and dressmaking being outsourced to factories, often completed on machinery with piecework labor. For many white middle-class women in the late nineteenth century, domestic duty now mainly included monotonous tasks that were often seen as unrewarding. Such perceptions of household drudgery provided the basis for a number of educational activists to balk at the integration of domestic science into women's collegiate curriculum, seeing it as a regressive and repressive pursuit. Thomas of Bryn Mawr, for instance, argued that "college women" would not be "willing to do household drudgery" (79). Bryn Mawr's position was that "there [were] not enough elements of intellectual growth in cooking or housekeeping to nourish a very serious or profound course of training for really intelligent women" (qtd. in Stage, "Home Economics" 7).

A first step within the domestic science community was to challenge such understandings by cultivating spatial rhetorics that would exchange drudgery for scientific intrigue. Richards, for example, took the term *drudgery* head on at the 1890 meeting of the Association of Collegiate Alumnae, arguing that science is the answer to how women might re-envision their domestic work. She contends, "The woman who boils potatoes year after year, with no thought of the how or why, is a drudge; but the cook who can compute the calories of heat which a potato of a given weight will yield, is no drudge. Knowledge of principles always gives interest to work, and is an incentive to the acquisition of more knowledge" ("Relation" 2). Alice Norton, domestic scientist at the University of Chicago, seconded Richards's argument: "chemical problems which arise in the household arts are of much greater variety and complexity than is often imagined. Many of these problems have never been solved, while others are only in the process of solution" ("Home Economics" 39). Spatial rhetorics such as these reoriented dominant understandings of the home and women's work in it. The home could be understood as a place where drudgery reigns, but if domestic scientists reframed their approach to the home such that they found "variety and complexity" in the domestic environment, then this space would transform into an site full of intellectual challenge.

Domestic scientists based their new educational vision and professional identity on this spatio-rhetorical renovation of the home. Once these women had established that the home posed significant intellectual problems, they could make use of their rigorous curriculum and their newly gained expertise. Bevier and Usher make this claim when they write, "The teachers of domestic science are not content to follow a dull routine of household drudgery in their teaching. They are appealing to the scientist and specialist in lines which touch the home life to explain the principles on which home practices should rest" (39). The newly recast home required in-depth scientific study to manage it, and domestic scientists were keen on setting out the various scientific investigations that this space invited. In "Teaching Chemistry in Connection with Domestic Science," Mary Converse, for instance, offers the following opportunities for domestic study:

> Proteins are taken up with the study of eggs; and of milk with testing for composition, quality and adulterations. Determination of fat by the Babcock method and action of rennet on milk are given. Meat is studied with regard to the effect of heat and cold, hot and cold salted water and the extraction of food principles for soup making, etc. Gelatine, legumes, food adjuncts, etc., also have their place in the work. Tests on flours, breads, baking powders and other materials are made for adulterations as well as to find their composition. Tests with antiseptics, preservatives, and the action of alkalies and vegetable acids on metals are included. (197–98)

Such lists made it clear that by pursuing domestic science, women students were not signing on to a life of domestic boredom. As Mary Williams points out, activities previously understood as monotonous drudgery, such as "cooking, housekeeping, laundry and nursing lessons," were now intellectually stimulating and required that students gain expertise in "bacteriology, physiology, chemistry and physics" (79).

These arguments to exchange drudgery for scientific inquiry were not superficial gestures toward rigor. A quick glance over the material covered in the *Library of Home Economics* series reveals the seriousness of domestic science study and the real ways the home was being reconceived. For instance, *Food and Dietetics* teaches readers how to detect adulteration of foods by conducting experiments to identify oleomargarine as opposed to genuine butter (Norton 169), and *Personal Hygiene* offers a detailed explanation of the process of digestion by discussing the work of chemicals in the saliva such as mucin and ptyalin (Bosquet 52–54). Similarly, in *Household Bacteriology*, S. Maria Elliot argues even "dust, just common every-day dust, is a very important and complex substance, which promises much of interest in its study" (3). She then goes on to instruct readers to observe the ways that dust operates by inviting them to grow and inspect a "dust garden" within the home. Like the other texts in this series, *Household Bacteriology* demonstrates how commonplace household problems become curious when viewed through the lens of domestic science.

Domestic scientists bolstered their arguments for this new domestic activity and the scientific education it necessitated by creating spatial equations. Refusing to see drudgery in the home, these women deployed spatial rhetorics that compared the home to more easily identifiable sites demanding study. For instance, Bevier and Usher ask women students to understand that the "laws of heat could be illustrated by the kitchen range quite as adequately as by the steam engine" (14). Domestic scientist Mary Roberts Smith asserts, "demonstration in bacteriology might as well include cultures from the kitchen as well as the sick room" ("Shall" 10). By equating the kitchen range with the steam engine or the kitchen with the hospital, domestic scientists, in Gail Lippincott's words, "elevat[ed]" the home's status and women's activities within it, making it clear that the home could be "a serious site for the production of knowledge and application of science" (368). Through these equations, too, domestic scientists anchored their ethos in a domestic space known not for boredom but for stimulating study.

Home Is Where the Beaker Is
At the same time that domestic scientists argued for disciplinary and professional status by working to erase ideas of household drudgery, they also

contended with another quite different yet equally compelling popular perception of home and women's domestic work. They had to address the idea that the home was an idyllic site of solace and love where a woman's main activities were limited to comfort and care and guided by her maternal instincts. If this perception of the home persisted, domestic scientists would have no work to do and no one to teach, for the study of science with the goal of applying it to the home would be foreclosed. So that domestic scientists could create a space of intellectual challenge from which to craft their ethos, they needed to disrupt old and propose new understandings of woman's spatial activity: the good wife and mother could no longer manage the home by relying on maternal instinct. Her work in the home was now distinguished by scientific study and careful experimentation.

This part of the domestic scientist's spatio-rhetorical project was marked by de-sentimentalizing the home and deskilling the traditional version of the wife and mother. Linda Hull Larned articulates such arguments in her presentation for the Lake Placid Conference of 1902: "The treatment of the home has been sentimental rather than scientific and the general idea has prevailed that any woman could keep house satisfactorily provided she had a liking for it. Now we may all love our homes but it does not follow that we all know how to manage them, for the natural born housekeeper is rare" (86). In her 1897 speech "The Place of Science in Woman's Education," Richards anticipates Larned's point when she contends that women cannot be "warped by sentiment" but should instead be "held fast by the cable of scientific fact" (227). "Love is all right," Richards concedes elsewhere, "but it is not today enough to keep a house" ("Wanted" 10). These domestic scientists contended that previous criteria for good domestic spatial practice no longer made the grade: a new bar had been set for managing the complex, intellectually challenging home. Good sense as a criterion for the mother's ethos was something entirely new.

To advance their arguments about the inadequacy of natural feminine attributes to manage the home, domestic scientists often harshly critiqued women who did not embrace science for being irresponsible to their homes and families, and these critiques were inflected with tones of classed and cultural superiority. Anna Barrows, for instance, writes that instead of "cling[ing] to the traditions of the past," women should learn "to observe, to adapt, to experiment" (vi). Similarly Mrs. C. S. Buell argues that women are often "blindly confusing the 'sanctity of the home' with unwillingness to enter into a concerted effort toward improvement" (97). Criticisms such as these pointed the finger at traditional women's domestic irresponsibility, but they also paved the way for domestic scientists to exalt their new discipline and ethos by celebrating those who took up a scientific approach to the home. No longer the woman who clings to tradition, it was now, as Whitney sets forth, the "woman trained to scientific habits" who makes the "excellent mother" (69).

As domestic scientists celebrated the scientist mother who pursued the education they prescribed and made the home into a site for science, they mapped their rhetorics directly onto the language of professionalism that was circulating so prominently on college campuses at the time. In publications such as the *Journal of Home Economics*, contributors consistently asserted that they were training women for the "*vocation* of home making" ("Meeting" 12; emphasis added), and it was only an education in science that "*qualif[ied]* the future mothers" to do their work (Williams 79; emphasis added). One *Library of Home Economics* text makes this point clear. In the opening pages of the aptly titled *The Profession of Home Making: A Condensed Home-Study Course*, readers learn that

> home-making as now taught in many schools and colleges takes rank as a profession as truly as any occupation. It is the greatest of the professions—greatest in numbers and greatest in its effect on the individual and on society. The profession of home-making has added as much to every day housekeeping as scientific farming has to that of the past generations. (3)

Sentimental mothers no more, women could choose a legitimate profession and claim expertise in several scholarly domains when they learned to apply scientific principles to the home. Richards relays this exact point when she writes that through a domestic science education, the woman would become

> enough of a *sanitary engineer* to intelligently manage the electric-lighting plant, the steam-heating apparatus, the ventilating flues [in the home, and] to test the drains; enough of a *chemist* to know whether this or that new fad in regard to a food or diet has any foundation in fact, or it is merely unscrupulous advertising. ("Place" 227; emphasis added)

Thus by erasing the idea that the home was solely a place of love created through women's natural abilities, domestic scientists crafted a field for themselves and a new scientific ethos for the woman student. This woman was an expert who learned to conduct her work at home, beaker in hand.

Scientific Spaces and Domestic Experiments

A critical component of the domestic scientist's professional project was to use spatial rhetorics to undo ideas of drudgery and natural instinct attached to the home and to argue instead that women should study physics, chemistry, and bacteriology as they prepared to take on redefined forms of housework. As educational leaders relied on such discursive means to transform domestic space and women's professional ethos, they also deployed spatial rhetorics that demonstrated *exactly* how women students would become domestic scientists. These spatio-rhetorical tactics offered material and embodied changes to the home environment that would enable daily experimentation, making it possible for the woman to cultivate a scientific home environment and to take on the ethos of the scientist.

A first step in this process was for domestic scientists to help their students realize the spatial equation discussed above: the home could become a site for science. Thus laboratories needed to be set up within the home. M. W. Whitney, for instance, writes, "The woman in her home has the material at hand for innumerable researches that might result in benefit to herself and the community. This is again her peculiar province, and the only requisites are a good knowledge of chemistry and a small laboratory, which any woman might have side by side with her kitchen" (65). While Whitney argues that women could easily set up a laboratory *next to* the kitchen, Woolman asserts that the kitchen itself should actually *turn into* a laboratory. The woman's "kitchen is a science laboratory," she explains, for "from it proceed[s] chemical compounds on which depend the life, health and happiness of her household" (7). But advice for how to transform the home and kitchen into a laboratory became much more specific than this. In the *New England Kitchen Magazine*, Richards published an article titled "The Housekeeper's Laboratory" along with a corresponding visual (fig. 3.1) that detailed what this laboratory should look like, the specific items that should be included in it, and the kinds of work that women could take on because of it.[8] Encouraging women to conduct in-home experiments for acids, phosphates, lime, and chlorides, Richards supplied readers with the exact materials that would enable them to make their homes into laboratories and take up this work.

The newly established home laboratory outfitted women so they could apply their scientific knowledge to the domestic arena and leverage scientific principles to do such work as removing stains, taking out iron rust, and detecting flagrant adulterations in foods. Indeed, the integration of these scientific

The Domestic Scientist's Home Experiment   **95**

materials into the home was critical to the domestic scientist's ethos construction. As Pierre Bourdieu explains, identity "is found in all the properties—and property—with which individuals and groups surround themselves" (173). Ethos is therefore created not only through the space we occupy but through the objects that define that space's meaning. Stocking the home with chemicals and laboratory equipment changed how the home—and the woman inside

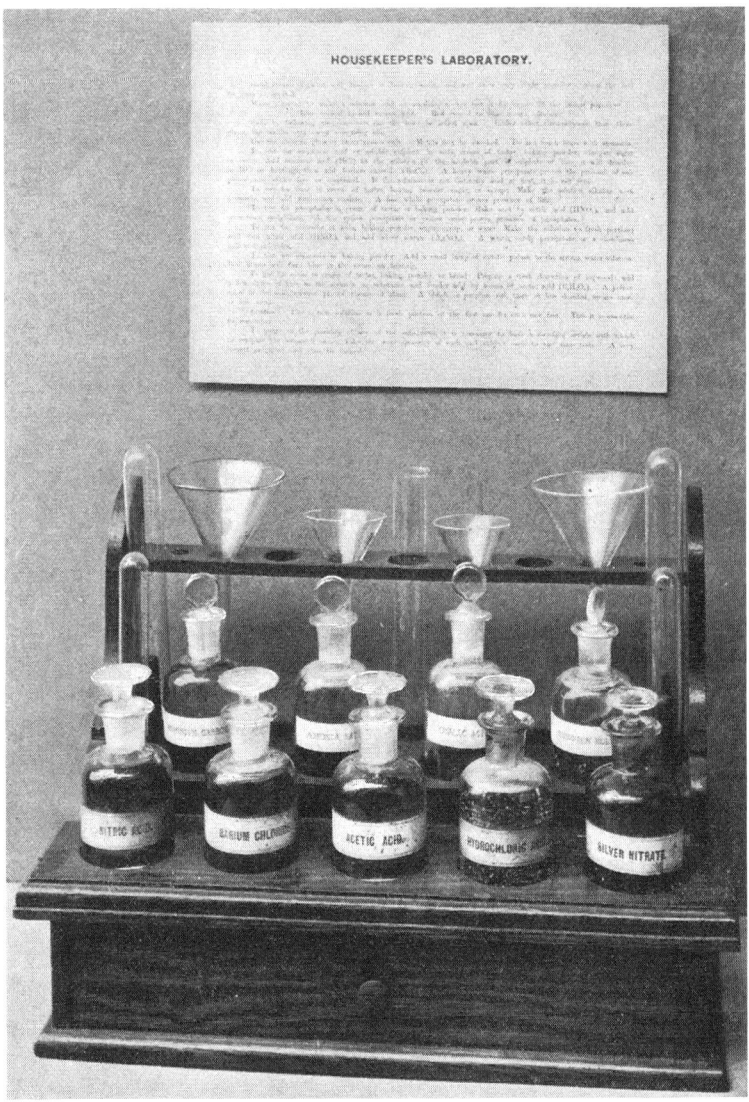

Fig. 3.1. "Housekeeper's Laboratory." Richards, *New England Kitchen Magazine*, Apr. 1895.

it—was perceived. A space of neither drudgery nor loving comfort, the home bedecked with laboratory equipment became a site where the housewife could become a domestic scientist.

Richards and her colleagues provided yet another way for direct application and ethos transformation by prescribing new scientific habits that women could practice within the home. Their twelve-volume *Library of Home Economics* functioned as both a correspondence course for women interested in "the practical application of the most recent advances in the arts and sciences to home and health" (as announced in the series' subtitle) and as a standard textbook in domestic science courses. Indicated above, these volumes instructed women to manage their homes in ways much different from traditional methods by asking them to adopt the practices of a domestic scientist. Margaret Dodd's *Chemistry of the Household* offers a salient, extended example.

Dodd begins her book by addressing and undoing those persistent concerns of domestic drudgery that were so prevalent at the time. She writes, "work that really interests does not prove as fatiguing as mere drudgery. An intelligent interest in the reason 'why' of daily happenings will surely make your daily duties go more easily and may lead you to discover simpler and more effective methods" (vi). Guiding readers in this pursuit, Dodd's chapters walk them through the supposedly mundane tasks of the day: washing dishes, preparing meals, and cleaning the home. Whereas each activity might be presumed a chore, Dodd sets out new domestic habits that would make this work interesting by explaining the scientific principles that undergird the task, supplying readers with an experiment to conduct in concert with this task, and then testing students on their emerging expertise.

For instance, Dodd instructs readers that the "morning bath will introduce us agreeably to the wonderful chemical substance, water, and with this substance we will begin our study of a day's chemistry" (1). Students are then prompted to learn about water as a solvent. Dodd writes,

> Water is nearly a universal solvent. It dissolves more substances and these in larger quantities than any other liquid. At a given temperature, water will dissolve only a certain proportion of the various salts and other soluble substances. When the water will take up no more, the solution is said to be *saturated*. Increasing the temperature generally increases the dissolving power of water for solids and liquids. The reverse is usually true for gases. When a saturated solution of

> a solid is cooled, crystals frequently form, many having beautiful shapes. (5)

So that readers can then see evidence of this process, Dodd invites them to conduct the following observation:

> In an earthen-ware or enameled dish dissolve as much alum as possible in a little boiling water. Pour the solution into a shallow dish or saucer, and set it away for a day or more where it will be undisturbed. Beautiful six-sided crystals will form in the dish. If strings are hung in the solution, the crystals will form upon them. Rock candy crystals are made from sugar cane in this way. (5–6)

Readers go on to learn about the scientific principles that govern other daily tasks such as the chemical reactions that govern bread-making (40), the properties of chlorine as a bleaching agent (82), and the types of gases that allow for illumination (98). Once students completed both their learning and experiments, they could test themselves with prompts such as "How do the hydro-carbons differ from the carbohydrates?" (55) and "Describe the manufacture of coal gas" (124).

This home instruction and testing transformed women's work, and a comparison with domestic advice manuals of old is illustrative of this change. Whereas domestic advice manuals such as Lydia Maria Child's *Frugal Housewife* instructed with simple directions such as "clean brass a kettle . . . with salt and vinegar" (11), the genre that Dodd's text belonged to explained the detailed chemical processes that catalyzed this cleaning so that readers not only understood what to do but also why and how the process worked as it did. The domestic science textbook also refused to let readers simply receive knowledge; instead its job was to engage readers actively in the learning process. Calling for experimentation, observation, testing, and reflection, domestic scientists identified ways for students to revise their negative perceptions of housework and adopt intellectually stimulating domestic habits. Therefore, just as Aristotle understood that ethos emerged from habituated practice, so too did domestic scientists. As Aristotle explained, "we become just by performing just acts, temperate by performing temperate ones, brave by doing brave ones" (bk. 2, ch. 1, sec. 4). In the same way, domestic scientists made it clear that students would become scientists by performing scientific acts. Conducting these experiments and seeing them as part of her new domestic habit, the woman was neither drudge nor angel of the house; she was, what one participant at the 1906 Lake Placid Conference called, a "highly trained home expert" ("Discussion" 13).

The Home on Display

While the spatial rhetorics discussed above were published mainly in specialized magazines, such as the *Journal of Home Economics* and the proceedings of the Lake Placid Conferences, and primarily spoke to an already-interested audience of educational leaders and women students, domestic scientists created other ways to reach publics that might not be alert to their project. Such public outreach was important since revision to the home and women's work in it was very much a public concern, and domestic scientists wanted both to educate and to garner support from the public for the specific changes they were advocating. As Mary Hinman Abel wrote of the leader of the domestic science movement, Richards had, as one her "chief interests," a desire to shape public opinion and to "seek out every available means to ... enlist and inspire helpers" ("Mrs. Richards" 347).

One of the more prominent means of outreach that Richards and her colleagues employed was demonstrating to the public what it meant to apply science to the home. These demonstrations focused on showing, not (so much) on telling, in order to let the public observe how science could change the home and, in turn, create new possibilities for women's professional ethos. As the previous sections made clear, when domestic scientists argued for the relevance of applying scientific thinking to work in the home, they were contending with (somewhat competing) visions of the home as a space both of monotonous drudgery and of loving comfort. But the home was also known as a *private* space, a perception that could have prevented domestic scientists from promoting their work. Public exhibits, however, enabled domestic scientists to make this seemingly private space a public one by inviting others to observe the newly renovated home and putting their scientific work on display. Popular and diverse on both large and small scales, exhibits became a signature move in the domestic science spatio-rhetorical repertoire as a way to reach greater audiences during this period, with Richards in particular believing in the "teaching power of exhibits" to arouse interest "in the problems of daily living" ("Exhibits" 397).

In this section, I explore how domestic scientists used display as a spatio-rhetorical tactic that opened the home to the public and educated people about its scientific renovations and about women's new professionalized ethos. As Lawrence Prelli writes, the term *display* can be traced back to the "Greek word *deiktikos*, which meant 'exhibit,' 'show forth,' 'make known'" (2). Displays are rhetorical because they are purposefully crafted to "direct [the] attention" of audiences, enabling them to see and even experience a scene in a particular way (12). I contend here that domestic scientists' spatial rhetorics of display enabled them to present their new spaces and their new ethos to audiences, prompting them to rethink their understandings of the home and women's work. Julie Nelson Christoph underscores the point that ethos is always a negotiation between rhetor and audience: "*ethos* is contingent on the cooperation and receptiveness of the audience" (663). Indeed, the previous section explored how domestic scientists used spatial rhetorics to address and revise audiences' preconceived notions of the home and housewife. But an audience's perception of a rhetor's ethos does not only pertain to past knowledge about that figure and her place in the world. Ethos can also be composed "on site" through the rhetorical displays and performances the rhetor enacts before the audience. Below, I focus on two instances where domestic scientists put themselves and their homes on display: the New England Kitchen, which was established in Boston in 1890 and aimed to provide low-cost nutritious food to the working-class citizens of the city, and the Rumford Kitchen exhibit at the 1893 Chicago World's Fair. I attend to the ways these kitchens functioned as "strategic performance[s]" that enabled domestic scientists to display before the watching public their new *habitus* and habits (Applegarth, "Genre" 45).

The New England Kitchen

On January 24, 1890, domestic scientist Mary Hinman Abel, in collaboration with Ellen Richards and with the financial backing of Mrs. Quincy A. Shaw and Edward Atkinson, opened the New England Kitchen on 142 Pleasant Street in Boston and began to serve meals to the working-class and largely immigrant inhabitants of the city.[9] Abel and Richards were quick to point out, however, that their work was not simply charitable. The project of the New England Kitchen was twofold. First, Abel, Richards, and their sister scientists who worked in the Kitchen aimed to identify, through rigorous experimentation, nutritious but low-cost food items for their potential clients. Second, they sought to teach their clientele about hygienic culinary practices and nutritious eating. While the latter aim certainly reveals what may be read as domestic scientists' sense of classed and cultured superiority, a concern I discuss in more detail below, the overarching goal was the Kitchen's pedagogical function. As Abel explains, "the *real work* of the *Kitchen*" is "to *teach* the *people to live more wisely*, both as to quality and cost; to accustom them to the taste of good food, so that they shall, after a time, wish to learn how to prepare it in their own homes" ("Study" 142).

While the primary audience for the New England Kitchen was the working-class immigrant population of Boston, Richards and Abel also advertised and welcomed others to visit the Kitchen and learn about their work. For instance, Richards presented on the Kitchen's achievements at a meeting of the Association of Collegiate Alumnae in 1890 ("Relation"), and she published articles on this endeavor in such serials as the *Forum*. Twentieth-century scholars Harvey Levenstein and Hamilton Cravens confirm that visitors beyond the intended customer-student often came to the Kitchen to observe its work, with Levenstein citing that physicians visited and recommended its nutritious food to patients (376) and Cravens noting that it "attracted much support from business and social elites" in the Boston area (128). Popular investment in Abel and Richards's work is also evinced by the fact that the New England Kitchen became a model for others around the country. Jane Addams sent one of her colleagues "to study the operation of the kitchen and confer with Mrs. Richards, and then set up a similar establishment at Hull-House" (Shapiro 147), and a pair of domestic scientists who worked at the Kitchen moved to Philadelphia to establish a version there (Levenstein 387). In fact, the New England Kitchen was so well known that one popular magazine dedicated to domestic science "borrowed [the New England Kitchen's] name as a mark of affection" (Shapiro 140). Thus, while the New England Kitchen spoke directly to the working-class immigrant population of Boston, a diverse audience kept a watchful eye on this endeavor and witnessed Richards and Abel's scientific experimentation and their teachings.

The key modes through which these domestic scientists enacted their pedagogies were display and demonstration. As Abel explains, the Kitchen's domestic scientists provided all visitors with an "object lesson" ("Study" 144), for the idea was that they would learn "*to live more wisely*" (142) by witnessing scientists at work. Put simply, the intention was "silent preaching by example" (137). To facilitate this silent preaching, the entire kitchen was exposed and open to view (fig. 3.2). Richards describes the composition of the space in this way: "the cooking is done on scientific principles and in sight of the customers" ("Relation" 5); there are "no covered or curtained spaces, ... every cooking process [is] open to the public" ("Scientific Cooking" 359–60). By putting domestic scientists on display, Abel writes, "[c]leanliness and thoroughness, as well as economy, [are] inculcated ... by means of the eye" instead "of the ear" ("Study" 141). Abel goes on to explain that "[i]ndirect teaching is often more potent than rules and maxims" (141).

A critical by-product of this pedagogical display was, of course, that domestic scientists were also showcasing to the public their transformed scientific kitchen and the expertise they wielded within it. Visitors observed, in Richards's words, domestic scientists "conduct[ing] scientific studies in food" ("Scientific Cooking" 355). On the stage of the exposed kitchen, these women "determine[d] the successful conditions of preparing, by scientific methods, from cheaper food materials, nutritious and palatable dishes" at an affordable cost (Richards, "Preface" 132). Richards records, for instance, that the Kitchen's domestic scientists conducted at least twenty experiments on beef broth and worked with cutting-edge culinary technologies such as the Aladdin Oven ("Scientific Cooking" 357). "Success," Richards asserted, "was won only through lessons of repeated failures, or, as scientific workers say, through negative results" (357).

The fact that these women were taking on this kind of work reveals how they were adopting the practices of the *real* scientist, but because the kitchen was on display for anyone to view, domestic scientists were also publicly

Fig. 3.2. "New England Kitchen," Pleasant Street, Boston. Abel, "Report," 1899, plate following p. 134.

performing their new ethos before their audience and demonstrating how they were applying knowledge garnered from the emergent fields of nutrition and dietetics to the everyday household duties of meal preparation. Indeed, Richards suggested how the Kitchen's scientists were enacting the kinds of application so highly valued in the new professionalized university. Writing in a pamphlet dedicated to the Kitchen, Richards invokes two famed German scientists known for their expertise in nutrition, Carl von Voit and Max von Pettenkofer, and asks, "How shall a scientific knowledge gathered by the labors of Voit, Pettenkofer and their pupils and co-workers be brought within the reach of the American citizen and housewife?" ("Scientific Cooking" 359). The implicit answer to the question was on display at the Kitchen: it was the domestic scientist at the New England Kitchen who translated nutrition science for her customers.

It is critical to note that as Richards, Abel, and their colleagues were demonstrating scientific ethos on the stage of the New England Kitchen, they were also crafting this ethos in contrast to their working-class immigrant clientele. Domestic scientists positioned themselves as the experts and their customers as the uneducated who needed to learn how to "live more wisely." Abel makes this distinction when she equates the Kitchen's pedagogical work with that of university laboratories. "[L]aboratories," she explains, "have a firm place in the educational system. More and more does the practical worker turn to the laboratory expert for the principles that must underlie his work" ("Study" 147). To Abel, the New England Kitchen was a laboratory that provided this same opportunity to its customers: when these "practical workers" come to the New England Kitchen, they too "turn to the laboratory expert."

Part of the distinction that Richards and Abel made between themselves and their clientele hinged on the domestic scientists' implicit relationship to an elite classed and cultured status. Certainly, to have New England in the Kitchen's name signals that Richards and Abel believed their clientele should adopt the kind of middle-class Anglo-American culture that was identified with New England. Cravens addresses this point when he writes of how Richards and Abel's menu reflected their classed and cultured stance, explaining that the duo offered "aggressively Yankee cuisine" that "attempt[ed] to make over [Boston] immigrants and poor into 'real Americans'" (128).

Perhaps not surprisingly, the ethos that Richards and Abel composed at the New England Kitchen and the expectations they had for their clientele were met with great resistance. Many potential customers balked at both the instructions and the food, and this negative reaction elicited great frustration from domestic scientists. Abel reports, for instance, that French and Irish "factory hands" were "the most incorrigible of all the communities" ("Study" 139), and she instructed other domestic scientists who were contemplating establishing a similar kitchen in their own cities to focus on "a neighborhood of Germans or English, Catholics or Protestants, not of Italians or Jews" (140). Thus, one failure of the New England Kitchen was the relationship that the domestic scientists built with their target customers, the ethos they created in relation to this audience, and the expectations they had for them. Even though the Kitchen stayed in operation until 1907, this audience never wholly bought into the New England Kitchen project, and, kudos to them, they refused to surrender their foodways for the ones the domestic scientists were prescribing.[10]

Even this particular failure of the New England Kitchen, however, speaks to how display and demonstration offered domestic scientists an opportunity to showcase their newly crafted ethos. Through this spatio-rhetorical tactic, domestic scientists prompted audiences to witness them in their new home environment and to see them as elite experts. In their reports, Richards and Abel point to a number of successes and failures of this pedagogical exhibit. But one point is clear, the New England Kitchen experiment was successful enough that domestic scientists continued to deploy this iteration of spatial rhetoric. Indeed, Richards's biographer Caroline Hunt argues that part of the New England Kitchen's success was its legacy: an important "outgrowth" of this experiment was "the Rumford Kitchen at the World's Fair at Chicago, an epoch-making educational experiment" (*Life* 220–21).

The Rumford Kitchen

In 1893 Richards, in collaboration this time with domestic scientist Maria Daniell, created the Rumford Kitchen for the Chicago World's Fair, the Columbian Exposition. Marking the four-hundredth anniversary of Columbus's arrival in North America, the Columbian Exposition was amazing in size: 27 million visitors attended the 65,000 exhibits in 200 buildings that covered over 600 acres in Chicago's South Side (Rothstein). While larger in scope than expositions that preceded it in cities such as London, Paris, and Philadelphia, the project of the Chicago fair was in line with its predecessors: to showcase cultural, technological, and industrial progress. Richards and Daniell saw their exhibit as an example of a specific kind of *domestic* progress because it introduced the public to the scientific kitchen by demonstrating how science could innovate cooking. As the guide to the exhibit explains, the Rumford

Kitchen "stands for the *application of science to the preparation of food*" (F. Walker 12).

Based on and similar to the work of the New England Kitchen, the Rumford Kitchen also used the spatio-rhetorical tactic of putting the kitchen and the domestic scientist's work in it on display. The Rumford Kitchen differed from its predecessor, though, in that the showcase was much grander in scale and spoke to a larger and quite different audience. While the New England Kitchen focused on inexpensive yet nutritious food for Boston working-class immigrants, the Rumford Kitchen addressed the middle-class, cosmopolitan visitors to the fair, and its project was epideictic rather than pedagogical. Prelli explains that a key component of display is often its epideictic character, as displays function by celebrating a person, an object, or even a set of values (15). Richards and Daniell certainly crafted a celebratory display of domestic science and invited their audience to see great value in the study of nutrition and the benefits a scientific method could bring to the culinary arts. As they did, though, they were also quite careful about the particular ways their celebrations intended to change public understandings of the home and woman's work in it.

The central epideictic and indeed persuasive project of Richards and Daniell's domestic display was to move visitors to associate the kitchen with science. Part of this spatio-rhetorical endeavor, however, was to *dis*associate themselves from the idea that domestic science was purely a woman's issue or was connected to arguments for women's rights. This point was especially important because there was space at the fair dedicated expressly to women's accomplishments in the aptly named Women's Building. This space both housed exhibits relating to women's advancements and offered a platform for a weeklong convention, the World's Congress of Representative Women—a congress at which five hundred women spoke, with activists such as Antoinette Blackwell, Julia Ward Howe, Lucy Stone, and Susan B. Anthony among that number.[11] Early in the exhibit planning, the Lady Managers of the World's Fair asked Richards to make her domestic science exhibit part of the Women's Building.[12] However, Richards declined this invitation and took a space outside the grounds of the Anthropology Building (Hunt, *Life* 286–88). It is likely Richards's decision hinged on an understanding that by situating her exhibit within the Women's Building, she would have associated domestic science primarily with women's issues. As discussed above, and indicated by decisions she made throughout her career, Richards was not interested in casting her work in this way. Hunt, Richards's biographer, confirms this point, writing that Richards saw her work as part of a "'home' movement," not a "women's movement" (*Life* 285). A spatial connection between the Rumford Kitchen and the Women's Building would have signaled the latter. Indeed, Richards's decision seems to have achieved its purpose, as an article in the *New England Kitchen* journal commends the location of the Rumford Kitchen, calling it a "modest little building close to the Anthropological, a fitting place since the development of the human race is largely dependent on food" ("Rumford Kitchen" 11). The Rumford Kitchen aimed for (and achieved) association with science and nutrition, not with women's concerns or even women's rights.

To strengthen this link, Richards and Daniell carefully composed the Rumford Kitchen so that greater attention was paid to the scientific home *without* explicitly articulating how this revision would revolutionize women's traditional role and work. Prelli argues that a display's rhetoricity often relies on the principle of selection. Echoing Kenneth Burke's theory of terministic screens, Prelli asserts, "whatever is revealed through display simultaneously conceals alternative possibilities; and therein is display's rhetorical dimension" (2). Richards and Daniell's display at the Rumford Kitchen demonstrates their intent to reveal and conceal elements of the kitchen so that the ethos they crafted for themselves and their colleagues was not a feminine or feminist one but a *scientific* one. The exhibit rarely invoked the figure of the woman, wife, or mother. Rather, its epideictic displays prompted audiences to participate in an enthymematic, logical deduction: if the space and activity of the kitchen changed, so too would the woman's domestic ethos.[13]

As a way of "constrain[ing] the range of possible meanings" for their scientific kitchen and their ethos, Richards and Daniell invited audiences to participate in two epideictic celebrations (Prelli 1). The first one commemorated the domestic innovations of eighteenth-century male scientist and inventor Count Rumford (Sir Benjamin Thompson), for whom the exhibit was named. A Massachusetts native who worked as a scientist throughout Europe, Rumford gained expertise in the field of nutrition and created such culinary devices as the double boiler. To learn about Rumford's accomplishments, visitors observed how he renovated the kitchen space by viewing a life-size diorama of his culinary laboratory replete with his inventions. By selecting Rumford as an exemplar, Richards and Daniell chose to highlight a man's contributions to domestic science rather than a woman's, and one could and likely should read this choice as yet another move to distance the exhibit from those asserting women's rights.

But this celebration of Rumford might also be read another way. While the focus was on a male figure, the exhibit drew attention primarily to how Rumford altered the traditional approach to the kitchen. Echoing the domestic science discourses that combatted domestic drudgery, the guide to the exhibit explains that Rumford engaged the kitchen as a site of inquiry, using the familiar mantra of "knowing how" as an inspiration for his experiments (Richards, "Count Rumford" 24). By orienting audiences to this scientific perspective on the kitchen, Richards and Daniell prepared them to recognize women's new domestic activity as salutary and to celebrate it as such. Furthermore, the invocation of Rumford and the changes he brought to the domestic scene could also be understood as an alternative route to arguing for women's scientific ethos. After expounding on Rumford's accomplishments of the past, the exhibit guide draws a conclusion for the present: "if a man held in so much honor and respect by the whole civilized world . . . found his greatest joy in planning kitchen utensils, surely it is not beneath the dignity of any modern investigator to follow in his footsteps" (F. Walker 13). Here Rumford is invoked to argue for the legitimacy of domestic science. By linking the kitchen to someone held in such high esteem as Rumford, Richards and Daniell infused the space with gravitas and persuaded visitors to see those (women) within it as pursuing rigorous scientific experimentation.

The second epideictic imperative also asked visitors to find scientific value in the home, and it did so by celebrating domestic science innovations since Rumford's time. To return to the above quotation, Richards and Daniell did not explicitly choose to celebrate those who "followed" in Rumford's "footsteps," even though there were many women doing so. These domestic scientists decided instead to emphasize the alteration of the home and to downplay women's newfound scientific expertise. While women's presence was tacit throughout the display, Richards and Daniell's second epideictic priority was to pronounce how traditional domestic tasks had become compelling scientific endeavors. The ethos construction was implied since it was up to the public to conclude that women would be the ones to take up this new work.

This enthymematic argument for both woman's presence in the home and her changed domestic ethos cultivated within it was elaborated on throughout the interior of the Rumford Kitchen exhibit. But, before visitors could learn about these innovations, they encountered the exhibit's exterior display, which had to resonate in a particularly significant way. As figure 3.3 illustrates, Richards and Daniell chose for their exhibit's exterior to replicate the look of a modest American home. To experience the scientific kitchen, then, visitors did not enter an unfamiliar laboratory-like space; rather they entered what looked like a traditional domestic scene. A spatial rhetoric of display, this exterior selection asked visitors to realize that even with all the changes one would note within the walls of the exhibit, the home was still the home and, by deduction, the woman still its prime inhabitant.

While the exterior of the exhibit likely struck cords of familiarity, the spatial rhetorics of its interior extolled changed domestic activities and encouraged visitors to value this new kind of work. As figure 3.4 indicates, the exhibit showcased culinary inventions since Rumford's time; it displayed charts and diagrams revealing new understandings of the human body and its chemical composition, and it set out a similar model of a laboratory created especially for the home that Richards championed. To amplify the idea that scientific expertise was now required for domestic work, Richards and Daniell supplied readers with the "Rumford Leaflets," a series of publications dedicated to domestic experimentation that visitors could take home with them.[14] These leaflets were not light reading. They engaged topics such as ventilation, digestion, and nutrition, and they leveraged specialized terminology and scientific formulae. Thus, with each celebratory display in the exhibit and with each leaflet in the series, the message was clear: the kitchen had changed. Along with this message, Richards and Daniell asked visitors to draw the unarticulated conclusion that the woman would be the one to master these new devices and wield this new scientific knowledge.

Fig. 3.3. "The Rumford Kitchen, Columbian Exposition, 1893." Richards, *Plain Words about Food: The Rumford Leaflets*, p. 10.

Finally, the pinnacle of the Rumford Kitchen was the demonstration of scientific cooking. Over the course of its two-month tenure, the Rumford Kitchen served over ten thousand scientifically tested meals to visitors. The exhibit guide clarifies that the Kitchen was by no means "a money-making exhibit"; rather its prime function was as "a scientific and educational [enterprise]" (F. Walker 11). Prelli describes how demonstrations often function rhetorically to offer proof for the claims asserted, and the Rumford Kitchen was no exception (15). Much like the New England Kitchen, the Rumford Kitchen put its food preparation in full view of visitors who observed the "simple yet efficient methods of preparing foods so as to retain the utmost nutrition and flavor" ("Rumford Kitchen" 11). Complementing these demonstrations, the Rumford Kitchen also supplied visitors with menus that included such information as the meal's nutritional value and serving size—details that were novel to exhibit visitors at the turn of the century. Of course, visitors concluded their experience by enjoying their meals, but they did so *within* the exhibit, viewing its displays as well as reading the surrounding charts and diagrams, menus and leaflets.

Fig. 3.4. "Interior Rumford Kitchen, Columbian Exposition, 1893." Richards, *Plain Words about Food: The Rumford Leaflets*, p. 16.

In this immersive, multimodal endeavor, Richards and Daniell continued to craft before their visitors the ethos of the domestic scientist. They asked visitors to celebrate domestic innovation by seeing, smelling, and tasting for themselves how science could improve the age-old domestic task of cooking. Like almost every other component of their display, Richards and Daniell chose to deploy spatial rhetorics that focused on the changed domestic task rather than the task's performer. But similar to the enthymematic arguments offered throughout the exhibit, when visitors joined in the epideictic moment of the kitchen's demonstrations, they were encouraged to affirm not just the new kind of cooking but also the new kind of cook.

The Rumford Kitchen was met with great success. Certainly, the exhibit served food to large numbers of people, and as visitors observed Richards and Daniell's selections and celebrations, they also seemed to like what they saw (and ate). An 1894 review of the exhibit in the *New England Kitchen* journal commends their work, stating that visitors were deeply interested in the domestic science innovations largely for the ways the exhibit presented its new knowledge in "concrete form" ("Rumford Kitchen" 12). The lunchroom was especially persuasive, with one report of a diner "express[ing] satisfaction that for the first time in his life he had been scientifically fed" (Hunt, *Life* 225). Thus, Richards and Daniell had achieved what they set out to do. Visitors did not associate their exhibit with feminine work or feminist activism; rather the public was willing to learn how the space and work of the kitchen had changed or should change with the application of science. Reflecting on the success of the exhibit, Hunt writes in 1918, "it all sank into the public mind, and all the more deeply because the public mind was quite empty of such information and ready to absorb" (225).

Exhibit Epidemic

The successes of both the New England Kitchen and the Rumford Kitchen prompted domestic scientists to produce more exhibits of this kind as a way to reach even more audiences. An exhibit "epidemic" thus ensued, with domestic scientists staging similar displays in various arenas ("World's Food Fair" 4). One significant example is the Mary Lowell Stone Home Economics exhibit, which was created for the annual meeting of the Association of Collegiate Alumnae in 1902. Elaborating on the work of its predecessors, this exhibit not only presented visitors with a model kitchen, culinary inventions, dietary charts, and nutritional information, but it also included visual displays of other types of domestic experiments such as tests on textiles that exposed the "effect of washing," ("Mary Lowell Stone" 59). The exhibit garnered such a positive response that association leaders, Richards among them, decided to take the exhibit on the road and showcase it in Baltimore, Trenton, New York, and Chicago. In 1904 this aptly named "peripatetic exhibit" followed the example of the Rumford Kitchen and became an installation at the World's Fair in St. Louis, the Louisiana Purchase Exposition (Abel, "Peripatetic Exhibit").

Beyond the highly visible exhibits, however, domestic scientists also displayed their work on a smaller, local scale. On college campuses such as the University of Illinois, domestic science and home economics departments opened their laboratories to the public for demonstrations that showcased model kitchens, bedrooms, and dining rooms fitted with new domestic innovations ("News" 92). Outside collegiate settings, women's clubs put on similar kinds of exhibits, with organizers in Roxbury, Massachusetts, "borrowing as much as possible" from the Rumford Kitchen to offer demonstrations in "connection with their winter's study of household affairs" ("Rumford Kitchen" 12). And finally, extracurricular women's institutes, supported in some cases by state governments, also used display and demonstration as a way to educate the public in general and women in particular about advances in domestic science. One report from the *Journal of Home Economics* highlights the women's institute sponsored by the Department of Agriculture of North Carolina, which continued the peripatetic tradition of the Lowell exhibit. This group "fitted up" a railway car "as a model kitchen" by replacing seats with an "oil stove, oven, ice box, kitchen cabinet, fireless cooker, sink, and necessary utensils" ("Women's Institutes" 163). Stopping at different locations three to ten times throughout the day, educators performed domestic science demonstrations for the North Carolina public.

Such diverse forms of display indicate domestic scientists' deep investment in this practice. Explaining the project of domestic science through crafted displays of spatial renovation and demonstrations of new domestic practice, rather than purely verbal expression, offered an effective way for Richards and her colleagues to convince audiences of their new field's goals and their expertise. The displays' "strategic performances" allowed domestic scientists to craft their ethos carefully yet implicitly before the eyes of exhibit visitors by selecting associations for themselves and defining themselves as scientists doing relevant, applicable, and rigorous work (Applegarth, "Genre" 45).

Domestic Activities beyond the Home

The final stage of domestic scientists' spatial rhetorics explored in this chapter is their shift in attention from work within the physical space of the private family dwelling to active participation and employment in public arenas such as government offices, philanthropic institutions, settlement houses, schools, hospitals, dormitories, and asylums. This move from the home to the public sphere might seem contrary to the agenda domestic scientists had been pursuing. Indeed, as this chapter has shown, these women expended a great deal of effort arguing that their scientific expertise should be applied to the complex problems of the family residence. But as the example of the New England Kitchen indicates, domestic scientists did not believe that women should only inhabit and wield expertise within their own dwellings. Domestic scientists also argued that there were sites beyond the home where they could work. The trick—and the spatio-rhetorical challenge—was to make clear that these sites were also within the bounds of the domestic scientist's ethos.

Ethos is an appeal to an audience in which the rhetor "argu[es] from authority" and asserts not only that she should be believed and trusted because of who she is and where she comes from but also that her expertise has authorized her to have jurisdiction over certain kinds of knowledge and even spaces (Halloran 60). Domestic scientists claimed authority in spaces beyond the home by using spatial rhetorics to recast these sites as domestic and therefore within their authoritative purview. Arguing that these spaces were similar to the home and held similar challenges, domestic scientists extended their spatial jurisdiction and thereby created greater possibilities for their professional occupation and advancement.

Ultimately, by advancing this set of spatial rhetorics, domestic scientists helped to propel what came to be known as the *municipal housekeeping* movement, a term that itself resonates with spatial significance. As Tiffany Lewis defines it, municipal housekeeping was understood as "women's application of domestic skills to tasks outside the home," with women taking up work that ranged from "clean[ing] the physical city" to "ridding politics of corruption" (469). Critical to this chapter's conversation, however, is how domestic scientists engaged with, yet differentiated themselves from, other proponents of this cause. While some advocates argued that women should embrace this kind of public work because it enabled them to leverage their "innate" investments in cleanliness and care, domestic scientists contended that it was their *scientific expertise* that made them especially suited for this intellectually rigorous and yet still domestic work. Thus the domestic scientists' intervention in the municipal housekeeping movement was to argue that women should enter these newly defined domestic-public spaces not as caring mothers but as trained professionals.

Claiming Space beyond the Home
Domestic scientists and municipal housekeeping advocates both claimed authority over spaces beyond the home by identifying them as domestic. Jane Addams makes this point clear in her speech "The Modern City and the Municipal Franchise for Women." Here, she argues for women's participation in city government by stating that while the American public may understand the city as "a great business corporation," which undoubtedly would fall under the jurisdiction of men, the public should instead see the running of the city as "enlarged housekeeping" and therefore suited to women's direction (3). The most pressing problems of the city, Addams continues, are neither military nor industrial (3) but "internal" (2). Among these problems are "unsanitary housing, poisonous sewage, contaminated water, infant mortality, the spread of contagion, adulterated food, impure milk, [and] smoke-laden air" (2). The city has thus "failed" because women, "the traditional housekeepers, have not been consulted" on ameliorating these material conditions and "men have been carelessly indifferent" to them (4). For Addams, the city's greatest problems are not within men's purview and skill set. While these problems are indeed public, they are also "internal" and decidedly domestic; as such, they are affairs to which women should attend.

Beyond defining the city as a home, advocates of this movement also created spatial parallels between home work and city work, equating the necessary activities in the home with the necessary activities of the city. As Mildred Chadsey writes in her *Journal of Home Economics* article, "Housekeeping is the art of making the home clean, healthy, comfortable and attractive. Municipal housekeeping is the science of making the city clean, healthy, comfortable and attractive" (53). Because of the similar work that both home and city require, Chadsey argues, women's expertise can easily transfer from one site to the other. She explains, "The first and most important function of any housekeeper is to keep the home clean" (54). Like the home, the city must also be kept clean: "The disposal of waste, such as garbage, rubbish, sewage, the cleaning of its street, the prevention of smoke and other noxious substances in the air, are all important measures in keeping the city clean" (54). Given the similar activities in these two spatial realms, Chadsey helps her readers deduce that "women, who for all ages have been the homemakers and housekeepers," are well prepared to move from the "individual" work of a single home to the "communal task" of the city (59). Such spatial equations and deductive arguments enabled advocates like Chadsey to convince audiences that women were not overstepping their bounds when they occupied themselves with these tasks; indeed, women were doing the same kind of work they had been taught to do, only this time in a slightly different setting.

Employing Scientific Expertise

The spatial rhetorics that extended the bounds of women's jurisdiction were articulated by stakeholders throughout the municipal housekeeping movement. Key to this discussion, though, were the varied and at times competing supporting arguments that bolstered these spatio-rhetorical claims. Some proponents stressed that women should be involved in "communal tasks" because of their innate womanly abilities, with one *Harper's Bazaar* contributor writing that since women have "always looked after little things," they are able to "attend with ease and thoroughness to those parts of municipal housekeeping which often escape the notice of men" ("Women and the Township" 22).[15] Such discourse, however, was not part of domestic scientists' rhetorical repertoire.

Domestic scientists argued that it was their hard-earned knowledge that qualified them to apply science to the home and to homelike spaces beyond it. Indeed, domestic science curricula guided students to make such larger-scale domestic applications by offering classes in mass water supply and sanitation, dairy management, and ventilation for factories and tenement houses, as well as nutrition and food service for hospitals, schools, public kitchens, settlement houses, and asylums. Anna Cooley, domestic scientist at Columbia University, extends this list, setting out that students take courses that enable them to gain expertise in the "work of organizations" such as the "Municipal League, Consumers League, Board of Health, [and] Trade Unions" as well as "sweatshop problems" (196). Such courses clearly prompted students to consider how their intellectually rigorous studies of the home translated into contexts beyond it.

As domestic science educators shaped their curriculum in this way, they often focused students' attention on working with less-privileged populations. Echoing the work of Richards and Abel in the New England Kitchen, domestic scientists identified this strand of their work as philanthropic at its core, but it was a particular kind of philanthropy: one that not only extended the domestic scientists' spatial authority but also challenged assumptions that this work was simple charity. Buell, for example, explains, "every question of public betterment . . . we now include as necessary factors in making the successful home" (93). Domestic scientists must therefore "not ask[,] is this particular effort going to benefit your home or my home? If it benefits any home, it is a part of our responsibility" (93). Thinking through this responsibility, domestic scientists were especially clear in their intention to prepare students for philanthropic work in spaces such as settlement houses or public kitchens. In her 1900 Lake Placid Conference presentation, Henrietta Goodrich explains, "[t]he old methods of charity . . . are universally condemned" (35); let rigorous study and investigation replace "the vagaries of sentimentalism" (35). Abel concurred. Reflecting on and defining the work of the New England Kitchen, she writes that it is the "scientific philanthropist" who works to improve life in the public sphere by studying particular situations and using "critical examination and proof from evidence [to] direct all wise effort" ("Study" 147). Erased, then, were unsophisticated and indeed feminine ideas about charity that municipal housekeepers might have adhered to. The domestic scientist as scientific philanthropist was emboldened by her expertise as she applied her knowledge to homelike spaces outside her particular residence.

In their entirety, the spatial rhetorics deployed by domestic scientists to rethink the site and significance of the family dwelling and to stretch understandings of domestic space reveal their investment in developing a rich and diverse range of professional options for women.[16] Scholar-scientists such as Richards occupied academic positions at colleges and universities across the country, of course, but domestic science students also went on to take positions as housing and sanitation commissioners, chairs of labor bureaus, children's bureaus, and women's bureaus; and heads of wage boards (M. Ryan, *Womanhood* 233). They became dieticians, nutritionists, founders and managers of settlement houses, union organizers, lobbyists, legal aides, and social workers (234). The spatial rhetorics that domestic scientists composed enabled them to take on these posts by deeming them sites that required women's newly cultivated scientific authority. Thus, domestic scientists were home experts, but because of their spatial transformations, their expertise could play out in numerous venues and spaces within and beyond the home.

Conclusion

The story told here about domestic scientists is likely unfamiliar to contemporary readers. Indeed, history has remembered the broader category of home economics in simple and mostly derogative ways. For many, this field seemed to offer women no more than a form of "glorified housekeeping" (Stage, "Home Economics" 3). As Sarah Stage writes,

> Home economics has not fared well at the hands of historians. Until recently women's historians largely dismissed home economics as little more than a conspiracy to keep women in the kitchen. For the generation of women who grew up in the 1950s and 1960s, the words "home economics" still conjure up memories of junior high school classes in cooking and sewing—hours spent making aprons and white sauce, twin symbols of prescribed middle-class domesticity. (1)

Certainly, it was this understanding of the field and profession that raised the ire and even revulsion of second-wave feminists such as Robin Morgan, who in her 1972 speech at the American Home Economics Association convention declared, "As a radical feminist, I am here addressing the enemy" (qtd. in Stage, "Home Economics" 1).

This chapter presents a more complex picture of who domestic scientists were and what their relationship was to the home. Given the findings offered, we might still see domestic scientists as having incited a "conspiracy to keep women in the kitchen," but through their spatial rhetorics, these women remade the kitchen into an intellectually rigorous space that not only necessitated scientific expertise and but could also transcend the bounds of the traditional family residence. Domestic scientists carefully orchestrated spatial rhetorics in ways that enabled them to claim educational opportunity and cultivate a scientific ethos so that they could gain professional stature inside and outside the home. Furthermore, if Aristotle is correct and ethos is the "most potent means of persuasion" (qtd. in C. Smith 2), then this chapter says much about how domestic scientists leveraged spatial rhetorics to make use of this potent persuasive force. To take a phrase from Hyde, domestic scientists demonstrated what it means to "dwell rhetorically" and to craft a new ethos by inhabiting (and renovating) a space with intention (xxii). Yet this chapter also makes clear that "completely controlling one's *ethos* is not possible" (Christoph 666); domestic scientists had to craft their spatial rhetorics in response to significant constraints. By addressing old and performing new iterations of home work, domestic scientists tried to change dominant perceptions of the home as a means of gaining respect for their work and for themselves.

And yet even in acknowledging domestic scientists' rhetorical prowess, there is no denying that many of these women disassociated themselves from the burgeoning women's rights movement of the period. Recall Richards's desire for domestic science to be a home movement, not a women's movement. Thus, Richards and her colleagues should likely be categorized as "conservative" women, whose commitments, using Charlotte Hogg's words, "fall outside our [contemporary] feminist frameworks" and who might have worked to "uphol[d] dominant and patriarchal cultural norms" (393). Certainly, while today's feminist scholars might prefer to have found domestic scientists railing against arguments that women remain in the home, this chapter revealed them doing just the opposite. Domestic scientists may not have been feminists, but they were active rhetorical agents who creatively engineered spaces to invent a new ethos for themselves and claim new educational as well as professional opportunities. I suspect that as feminist scholars continue to explore rhetorical questions concerning women and work, they may find even more evidence of tense relationships with feminism. For many working women, to associate with feminist causes might have come at too high a cost—financially, professionally, educationally, ideologically, or personally. A priority for feminist scholars then should be to explore what these costs were for women workers and to consider the varied—and even conservative—arguments they deployed to gain access to education, experience intellectual rigor, invigorate their professional standing, and support themselves and their families.

The ethos that domestic scientists crafted through their spatial rhetorics offers a commentary on their relationship to the women's rights movement that was gaining momentum during this period. But domestic scientists' construction of ethos reveals more than their political affiliations: it also has much to say about their classed, cultured, and even geographic locations. In instances such as the New England Kitchen and through their scientific philanthropy, domestic scientists drew lines between an "us" and "them"—those who had the expertise and knowledge, and those who needed to change their ways. Even though their efforts may have been made with the best intentions, the example of the New England Kitchen especially shows that the ethos domestic scientists created and the work they did could be read as a "not so subtle and unconscious form of cultural imperialism" (Cravens 128). In many ways, domestic scientists of the Kitchen were displaying and promoting middle-class, Anglo culinary and domestic culture for their customers. Once we recognize this happening with the New England Kitchen, we can and should consider how domestic scientists' overarching project may be read as one that composed a new vision of what the white middle-class (and now scientific) home was expected to be.

Even as we explore this notion of cultural imperialism, however, it is important also to consider the educational opportunities the field of domestic science opened up for middle- and working-class women, especially for those outside New England. The 1862 Morrill Act offered great opportunities for domestic scientists by establishing public colleges within every state with the condition that these institutions focus on practical arts such as agriculture, mechanics, and, indeed, home economics. The field of domestic science and home economics, therefore, often served the non-elite working- and middle-class woman student and provided *this* student with new professional opportunities and class mobility. Additionally and importantly, the first institutions to offer such courses were at places such as Iowa State, Kansas State, and the Illinois Industrial University (later the University of Illinois), so we might see too how this field created new options for rural women living, learning, teaching, and working in the Midwest.

What this chapter does not emphasize, however, is the raced component of home economics and domestic science. As such, the chapter implicitly suggests that this field only spoke to and was led by white women. Black women were involved in this field too, but their relationship to it holds a complexity that deserves dedicated scholarly attention. In 1890 the second Morrill Act funded separate land-grant institutions of higher learning for African Americans. With this funding, home economics courses became a strong presence at schools such as Kentucky State, Alcorn State, and Tennessee State University. In addition, courses in the domestic arts are also found in course catalogs at private institutions like Atlanta University and Spelman College (Shaw 77). Not surprisingly, this move to teach African American women domestic skills had serious political dimensions. Black women had been working within white homes from the onset of slavery in the United States, so educators had to think carefully about how they would couch the purpose of a home economics education for their students. As Rebecca Sharpless reports, upon the establishment of Utica Normal and Industrial Institute in Mississippi, parents were quite hesitant about this pedagogical option, stating they "[didn't] want their children taught to work for white folks" (qtd. in Sharpless 28). Stephanie Shaw's research extends this point, as she finds that many educational officials were sure to point out that "this emphasis on domesticity" did not "mean they were training domestic servants, for they were not" (78).

Thus, black educators had to clarify what a home economics education would do for its black women students and the relationship it would build (or not build) between their own and white communities. For instance, one leader at Hartshorn University explained that this arena of study was present in the curriculum so that the woman student would learn skills for work "at the head of her own family, and for the teacher or missionary at home or abroad" (qtd. in Shaw 78). Situated in this way, an education in home economics was an opportunity for students to gain a "taste" for "domestic elegance" and learn to be a "well bred cultivated woman" (qtd. in Shaw 78). Of course this particular kind of education and indeed ethos creation had political effects: educators believed that making women students into "homemakers" might not only strengthen black families but also "improve external perceptions of the black community" (78). It is important to note, though, that while some of the more elite black schools may have offered courses in the "domestic arts," the overarching project of places like Morehouse and Spelman was to provide an education to their students "comparable to the white New England women's schools" (79). Much like at Bryn Mawr, then, the emphasis at these institutions was on offering students classical study and creating "real intellectual women" instead of focusing on vocational instruction (79).

Another perspective on domestic science education was one that many African Americans resisted: teaching students domestic skills that would serve white families and publics. Vocational schools such as Tuskegee and Hampton offered black women students this option, as did the example of the problematically named Black Mammy Memorial Institute. This institute was featured with praise in an article by Riley M. Fletcher Berry in the October 1911 issue of *Good Housekeeping*. Berry explains that the institute was under the direction of Samuel F. Harris, founder of the Athens Industrial School. While Berry sees the institute filling a "crying need" for training students to be "cooks, maids, seamstresses, and laundresses," he also notes that the school is "directly opposed to the majority of the educators of the negro race" (562). There is obvious room for critique of educational programs such as the Black Mammy Memorial Institute. There is also, however, the possibility that matriculation at Tuskegee and Hampton (or even the Black Mammy Memorial Institute) might have certified black women in ways that later enabled them to take advantage of better career options and financial benefits.[17] Suffice it to say, closer examination of black women's experiences with domestic science education, home economics, and domestic service is necessary. But this brief exploration should underscore the overarching concern of this chapter: the complex and deeply intertwined relationship between ethos and space. It would seem that key concerns for black educators contemplating a domestic science education for their women students were *where* she would apply this knowledge and *who* she would become upon its application.

There is one final and especially compelling contribution this chapter makes to scholarly understandings of the relationship between ethos and space. As feminist scholars such as Donna Haraway and Adrienne Rich make clear, knowledge is locatable. It comes from a body situated in place and time, and thus both our knowledge and our ethos are rooted in the spaces we occupy. Lisa Shaver elaborates on this point by setting out that "presence is usually a prerequisite for reputation. Indeed, a person may leave a particular place in order to escape a bad reputation" ("No Cross" 66). Given this assertion, we might see, then, that the occupation of space both qualifies and indicts us, shaping our ethos in significant ways. But this chapter also complicates this idea. Domestic scientists' spatial renovations and ethos composition reveal that rhetors do not just build knowledge and identity from their designated locations. Rhetors can also *remake* their locations as a means to claim new kinds of knowledge and authority. Evacuating a space to gain a new reputation is not the only option available to rhetors. They can also renovate the space they already occupy to cultivate a new ethos. The spaces that rhetors occupy and generate knowledge from are not stable or static. A changed composition of a space and changed actions within it enable new knowledge and sometimes a new ethos. A rhetor's haunts are rhetorical and changeable. As such, so too is her ethos.

4. The Motherless Home
WORKING MOTHERS, EMOTIVE SPATIAL RHETORICS, AND THE WORLD WAR II CHILDCARE CENTER

> The hand that holds the pneumatic riveter cannot rock the cradle—at the same time.
> —G. G. Wetherill, "Health Problems in Child Care Centers," 1943

The epigraph to this chapter captures a moment of spatial anxiety over women's work during the World War II (WWII) years. During WWII more than six million mothers occupied jobs outside the home, and concerns quickly arose regarding how (or if) these women could care for their children. As G. G. Wetherill suggests, they could not be at home and at work at the same time; they could not simultaneously rock the cradle and hold the pneumatic riveter (634). The image accompanying Wetherill's 1943 *Hygeia* article furthers this spatial and embodied anxiety (fig. 4.1). With her child on her back and her riveter in hand, the working mother is trying to perform the impossible, and this image held true for millions of women across the country. While some of these women had worked outside the home before, war-related exigencies transplanted many mothers and their families away from their normal support networks, and women were now left to fend for themselves when it came to childcare. Thus the spatial anxiety expressed in the opening epigraph and image was not uncommon.

As Jane Carroll writes in her 1943 *Parents' Magazine* article, "Raising a Baby on Shifts," "Almost every newspaper and magazine we read these days has stories on the controversial subject of mothers working" (20). Writers decried the mother's absence from the home, with one in particular coining a new spatial reality for the period: the "motherless home" (*Proceedings* [1942]

Fig. 4.1. Rosie the Riveter with child in backpack. Reprinted from G. G. Wetherill, "Health Problems in Child Care Centers," *Hygeia* 21 (Sept. 1943), pp. 634–35 (image on p. 635), with permission from Elsevier.

68). Pointing to the consequences of this dire situation, newspapers reported rises in juvenile delinquency, truancy, child abandonment, and abuse; the term *latchkey kid* became common nomenclature. Stories of children being left on their own or locked in parked cars while their mothers worked in the factory were rampant. Agnes Meyer's aptly titled essay "War Orphans, U.S.A." captures the spirit of the moment: "All over the country it is the children who are suffering most from our pell-mell war effort, and the fact that mama has become a welder" (98).

This chapter explores how interlocutors set out to address the spatial problem of the "motherless home" by offering the solution of the wartime childcare center. During the war, federal and state governments, along with independent industries and communities, spent well over $75 million building thousands of childcare centers in war-impacted areas across the country (A. Cohen 30). The war nursery, as it was called, became a critical component of wartime operations because it not only addressed concerns for the fate of the American mother, child, and home but also increased working mothers' efficiency and productivity. As the following pages reveal, however, even though working mothers were in desperate need of sufficient childcare, it took great rhetorical effort to convince them and the rest of the country that the war nursery was the solution to the childcare problem. This chapter investigates the spatial rhetorics that helped establish these centers and distribute the mother's responsibilities beyond the home so that she could work and her children could be cared for.

This chapter also examines what happened to these centers once the Allies claimed victory in 1945. By that time, thousands of working mothers had begun to take full advantage of these centers, and there was significant debate over the fate of the childcare center. Advocates argued that mothers still needed to work and, realizing the critical support the centers could provide for their families, called for the centers to remain open. In contrast, government, industry, and other public officials asserted that it was time for the mother to resume her place in to the home in order to create room in the workforce for returning veterans. These powerful stakeholders challenged and defeated advocates' arguments, causing the majority of war nurseries to close just months after the war's end. Another objective for this chapter, then, is to analyze the spatial rhetorics that reversed support for working mothers after the war and prompted the removal of the childcare centers from the American landscape.

To make this two-part exploration, I focus attention on how spatial rhetorics shaped the *emotional* atmosphere surrounding the childcare center during and after WWII. I argue that during the war, when the country needed women to work, spatial rhetorics alleviated concern for the motherless home by equating the childcare center with the home and prompting the public and especially working mothers to cultivate for the center familiar domestic feelings of safety, nurturance, care, comfort, love, and even patriotism. The childcare center was a place like home, and as such, mothers and indeed the country could entrust children to it. After the war, however, and when the moment for supporting working mothers had seemingly passed, spatial rhetorics erased this investment in the childcare center as a homelike space and instead remade emotional ties to the postwar "victory home"—the white, suburban, middle-class home that promised the returning soldier not only comfort and peace but also the resumption of conventional gendered dynamics. In sum, spatial rhetorics mitigated concerns for mothers' exodus from the home during the war yet exacerbated those same concerns after the war by negating the emotional investments in the childcare center previously created.

To take up this spatio-rhetorical examination, I concentrate on the *emotive* spatio-rhetorics that defined both the home and the childcare center in

WWII. Throughout U.S. history, the white middle-class home has often—but not always—been defined as a locus of safety, nurturance, care, comfort, love, and patriotism. A primary way the home gained these qualities was because it was deemed *the* site to raise children, and it has been the mother's duty to create and sustain the emotional atmosphere of the home so that her children could thrive. This emotional atmosphere exemplifies what Yi-Fu Tuan calls "topophilia," a coinage that designates "the human being's affective ties with the material environment" (*Topophilia* 93)—ties that "differ greatly in intensity, subtlety, and mode of expression" (93). The home has, of course, been seen as a space where affective ties have great intensity; it is a site *for* topophilia. But the central concern of this chapter is built on the premise that home is understood to be a site of "felt value," and not merely because of individual and idiosyncratic affective bonds (*Space* 4). Rather, the idea is that people are continuously *taught* to love the home; we learn the emotional power it is *supposed* to wield. Deep emotional investment in the home is therefore a rhetorical construction composed not only through personal embodied experience but also through suasive forms that circulate in public and that prompt this emotional response. Spatial rhetorics, I contend, are one of these suasive forms.

This chapter's prime analytical concern is to consider how wartime spatial rhetorics transferred this emotional investment from the home to the childcare center during the war and then rescinded this transfer at war's end. To make this investigation, I leverage scholarship that engages the rhetorical nature of emotion. Building on the work of Brian Massumi, Jenny Rice explains that emotions have a "'narrativized' content that is shaped through specific cultural, social, and political contexts" (201).[1] For example, we may experience something that causes our hearts to race, but that personal, embodied, affective response becomes an emotion when we name it fear and then articulate the causes and concern surrounding that response and named emotion. Brent Malin elaborates on the rhetorical and collective dimension of emotion, explaining that an emotion is both "public and embodied"; it is "an important vector of shared meaningfulness that constructs, and is constructed by, communicative practices" (217). Robert Hariman and John Lucaites similarly elucidate the public and rhetorical dimensions of emotions, pointing out that emotions are "group properties, triggered by events or performances, established through communication, involving complex social forms, and producing social cohesion and persuasion" (16). I thus explore the multiple and multimodal ways that spatial rhetorics shape emotional articulation and investment. In particular, I investigate how spatial rhetorics named, described, enacted, and outfitted spaces (like the childcare center and the home) in ways that produced emotional attachment and understandings, creating or breaking emotive ties. Furthermore, given that emotion is a rhetorical production, I consider how emotional connections to a space are both purposefully composed and strategically revised, and I contend that these spatial rhetorics not only create emotional bonds but also prompt public action, shape public policy, spur material construction, and catalyze demolition.

To be sure, rhetoricians have been suspicious of rhetoric's capacity to generate and mobilize emotions. As Hariman and Lucaites observe, emotions have often been seen as "rhetoric's major liability" because rhetors can seemingly use pathetic appeals to manipulate audiences without leveraging valid forms of argumentation (6). But even with (or because of) this possibility, we cannot ignore how emotion functions as rhetorical fodder and suasive force. This point is especially true in the case of the childcare center and home during and after WWII: the emotions that spatial rhetorics generated greatly affected support for working mothers and their children. As we inspect the power of these rhetorics, we see how and why the tides changed regarding the public's comfort with releasing mothers from and (re)binding them to the home. Examining the ways spatial rhetorics helped to manage emotional investment reveals how the idea of the home as an emotional center where the mother *must* be present was muted during war and then pronounced again at armistice.

To think through the part emotive spatial rhetorics played in the establishing and dismantling of the WWII childcare center, this chapter first offers background on working motherhood and the home prior to WWII. Then, I discuss how the emotive spatial rhetorics characterized the wartime childcare center and endowed it with qualities traditionally associated with home—a process that made it possible for the working mother to entrust her children to this space so that she could work and mother, just not at the same time. The sections that follow explore the debate over the childcare center in the postwar era. I consider how advocates attempted to reassert emotive spatial rhetorics for the childcare center, arguing for its continued necessity, and how critics erased the parallels between the home and the childcare center, generating negative emotional responses to the latter. I also explore the ways these negative assessments of the childcare center worked in concert with spatial rhetorics that called for the mother's postwar return to the home and the (re)consolidation of domestic love and duty within the specified space of the family residence. I conclude by thinking about the relationships between emotions and spaces as well as the implications of this spatio-rhetorical examination of home for today's working mothers.

Before setting out on this investigation of emotive spatial rhetorics, I want to foreground questions of class, race, and culture. It is important to keep in mind the demographics of working mothers during this period and the dominant narrative told about working women and especially working mothers. As historian Maureen Honey explains, government propaganda campaigns depicted Rosie the Riveter as a young, white, middle-class woman who temporarily "entered the labor force out of patriotic motives" (*Creating Rosie* 19). The actual Rosies, however, were often "working class wives, widows, divorcees, and students who needed money to achieve a reasonable standard of living" (19). Many of these women had previous work experience but had lost their jobs or left the workforce during the Great Depression. Complicating the picture even further, Rosie was certainly not always a white woman; as Emilie Stoltzfus writes, "women of color" were the "invisible wage earners" of WWII (7). Focusing in particular on black women workers, Honey cites that "40% of all black women already were in the labor force when the war broke out as opposed to only 25% of white women" (Introduction 12). Since many women of color—black women and others—were already working before the war, their workforce numbers did not increase as much as white women's. For numbers of these women, however, their occupational status did change during the war years as they left domestic and agricultural work to take white-collar, industrial, manufacturing, and health-related jobs.[2]

Even though women of color and working-class white women were a large part of the female labor force, the story of Rosie the Riveter persisted, and the controversy over the working mother often turned on the assumption that she was a white middle-class woman leaving the home to enter the workplace on a temporary basis. Her investment in the war effort was patriotic, not economic. This depiction became especially problematic when deciding the fate of the childcare center at war's end. Since dominant discourse composed the wartime working mother as someone who *wanted* to work but *didn't need* to work, and since she was seen as a woman whose husband was returning from war and who had a home to return to, shutting down the war nursery did not seem too controversial. In reality, though, many of these working-class mothers did not fit this description. For them, the childcare center had become a secondary home and a critical component of their family's survival. Thus, this chapter keeps in the forefront how assumptions of white middle-class home life and traditionally gendered familial roles guided decisions regarding the childcare center and ignored the concerns of women who did not fall into this category. Before assessing the role spatial rhetorics played in the fate of the childcare center, however, it is necessary to establish women's role generally and the mother's role particularly in the pre-WWII workforce.

Working Mothers and the Home

As the twentieth century progressed, women entered the workforce in great numbers, so much so that after First World War, they made up 21 percent of all gainfully employed persons ("Our History"). In response to this influx, the Women's Bureau was founded within the Department of Labor in 1920, with its primary goal "to secure information which was not already available but which was needed to throw light on special problems which seemed urgently in need of consideration" (Women's Bureau, "Second Annual Report" 4). The interests of the Women's Bureau reflected the investments of the period, as it reported on the status and mode of women's employment, hours of work, working conditions, and minimum wages and salaries. Tracking women's employment statistics a decade after its founding, the Women's Bureau relayed that in 1932, even with the economic strains of the Great Depression, women continued to work outside the home, finding that "the total number of employed women increased between 1920 and 1930 from 8,549,511 to 10,752,116, an increase of 2 1/5 million, or 25.8 per cent" ("Fourteenth Report" 2).

While women from a range of backgrounds were moving into various occupations, the question of the working mother drew special attention. As Lynn Weiner explains, "the married woman who worked for wages had long been considered an aberration, a 'social accident' of scant public significance" (98). Such judgments were made because these working mothers were "usually poor or black," so their "status elicited little controversy" (98). After 1920, however, white middle-class mothers increasingly entered the workforce, and the "disjuncture between domestic ideology and the employment patterns of women resulted in the discovery and labeling of a new social problem" (98). The working mother had become "a symbol of female role transgression and social change" (98). To be sure, most concern centered on the white middle-class mother, but once this interest was piqued, the question of working mothers writ large garnered significant public attention. The Women's Bureau, especially, identified the strained working conditions and inadequate pay for mothers who *must* work to support their families. Its 1921 report stated that "[a]lmost every investigation which touches women in industry supplies additional evidence that women are working more often than not to eke out the insufficient wage of a husband or father, or supply the wage which had formerly been earned by a husband or father who has died or become incapacitated" ("Third Annual Report" 13). This report underscores the extremity of many working mothers' situations, citing that "her wage is below the minimum cost of living for an individual, while in many cases her responsibility is as heavy as a man's" (13).

Even though organizations like the Women's Bureau studied the conditions for working mothers, public interest often focused on returning these women to the home rather than helping them gain more equitable, livable wages. The exigencies of the First World War strengthened this investment, as tests qualifying young men for war indicated that potential soldiers had encountered "problems in early childhood [that] had caused physical or mental deficiencies that disqualified so many men for military service" (Kerr 160). Concerns were thus raised that mothers had not fulfilled their duties by creating nurturing homes for these would-be soldiers and that deeper investments must be made to home life. Not surprisingly, the Great Depression and its aftermath exacerbated this conversation. As the 1941 Women's Bureau publication announced, the "public still has to be convinced that married women have the right to work, that they may face an unescapable need to supplement and often supply the entire income, and that they can work without harm being done to the home and to the working standards of men and women wage earners" ("Women Workers" 1). Efforts were thus made to return working- and middle-class mothers to the home. The institution of mother's pensions was one response, as these pensions offered a subsidy to poor mothers for the service they were rendering to the state through motherhood and child-rearing. But the more global and pervasive rhetorical effort—even in the face of mothers' economic strain—was to reemphasize the importance of the home and the critical role the mother played in it.

For instance, the 1909 White House Conference on Children and Youth stated that the home was the "highest and finest product of civilization" (qtd. in Kerr 159). Writer Agnes Edwards Rothery concurred, writing in her 1912 *Home Progress* essay "The Successful Mother" that "[t]he greatest contribution that any woman can make to civilization is to help found a successful home. The family unit is the unit of the State and the home is the center of all social, economic, and educational good" (31). Rothery continues, "The successful family is the one that is strongly centralized, and by centralization we mean that happy state of harmony for which the mother is primarily responsible" (31).

The mother is, of course, the "magnetic centre" (34). Speaking in the midst of the Great Depression, President Herbert Hoover developed this point about the pivotal role the mother played in her child's life when he made the following remarks at the 1930 White House Conference on Child Health and Protection:

> After we have determined every scientific fact, after we have erected every public safeguard, after we have constructed every edifice for education or training or hospitalization or play, yet all these things are but a tithe of the physical, moral, and spiritual gifts which motherhood gives and home confers. None of these things carry that affection, that devotion of soul, which is the great endowment from mothers.

Joining with many other interlocutors, Hoover makes clear that even as women were increasingly entering the workforce, there were questions regarding how, why, and if mothers should be among this number. The rhetorical pull of the home was fierce, but this pull would change direction with the onset of WWII.

As many historians have recorded, WWII triggered a considerable jump in women's participation in the labor force (Honey, *Creating Rosie*; Milkman; Yellin). Because men were leaving the workplace to fight on enemy lines and given the increased need for production in war plants, government and industries recruited women to take up this work in great numbers. Jordynn Jack explains that "[b]etween 1940 and 1945, the percentage of women in the labor force grew from twenty-eight to thirty-four percent, which meant that the 1940s witnessed the largest proportional rise in female labor force participation in the twentieth century" ("Acts" 285). Even though a diverse set of women contributed to this war effort, the dominant message was that it was the white middle-class woman who was entering the workforce for the first time and for patriotic reasons, and the question quickly emerged as to whether she should take her place on the assembly line if she was also a mother.

This question and its responses elicited controversy. For example, the 1942 U.S. Manpower Commission offered an ambiguous statement regarding the recruitment of mothers. This statement condoned mothers working on factory lines, declaring that "[b]arriers against the employment of women with children should not be set up by employers" ("Employment" 1184). Yet, even as it made this claim, the commission reasserted the importance of the home and the mother: "The first responsibility of women with young children, in war as in peace, is to give suitable care in their own homes to their children" (1184). As Margaret Gerard explains in a 1945 article, though, the Manpower

Commission's recommendation was flawed, for while it publicized and encouraged industries to "choose for employment unmarried women first and then married women with older children," there were no "implements for enforcement," and, as such, the "plan [broke] down in all industrial areas" (493). Further complicating the point was the fact that young mothers were often ideal candidates for wartime work. As Gerard observes, this woman often "possesses mature physical strength but has not yet begun to feel the wear of years," and she often has "incentive to increase the family income beyond a marginal level . . . [to] enrich her children's as well as her own life" (493).

The Manpower Commission was not the only rhetorical force to send mixed signals to working mothers. Katharine Lenroot, the chief of the Children's Bureau, similarly admitted, "America's women must supplement men in the manpower of the nation. Theirs is the double task of winning victory and raising children" (18). But Lenroot was also quick to state that "while [women] have increasing responsibility for the war effort, it must not be overlooked that their primary duty is to their homes" (18). The general tenor of the moment, therefore, was one of conflict and concern. But even though there were calls for women to remain in the home and not work, many mothers simply had to work for financial reasons or were compelled to work out of their deep sense of patriotism. In fact, circulating throughout this period was the idea that "women who stayed home to care for children [were] slackers" (Kerr 162–63). Whatever their motivation, mothers joined the war effort: these women made up 9 percent of the workforce in 1920, but their involvement jumped to 17 percent in 1945 (Weiner 89). Mothers were working even in the face of the national and hotly debated question of whether or not they should do so.

Spatio-Rhetorical Anxiety and the "Motherless Home"

As the mother entered the WWII workforce, the spatio-rhetorical discourse circulating at the time was charged with intense emotional force over what would happen to her children and her home in her absence. The rhetorical situation surrounding her move into the war plant generated affective strains that interlocutors articulated as emotions of anxiety, stress, and concern. As Laura Micciche writes, emotion is a "rhetorical resource" (1). Emotions are "part of what makes ideas adhere, generating investments and attachments that get recognized as positions and/or perspectives" (6). This section explores the emotions generated through the descriptions, observations, and evaluations of the "motherless home" and the children who were (not) cared for within it. It also investigates how these emotive spatial rhetorics became resources that coalesced to enable the public to identify a national problem that could not be ignored.

Preliminary to a discussion of the motherless home, it is important to remember that throughout the First World War and the Great Depression, the ideological investment in and topophilia for the home were asserted over and over again. This construction of the home as the ideal site for the child's care, the mother's love, and the family's refuge continued and gained even more strength after the attack on Pearl Harbor and the onset of U.S. involvement in WWII. For example, a commission of the Children's Bureau reasserted the deep emotional connections to the home in its 1942 publication *A Children's Charter in Wartime*: "To children in wartime the home is vital as a center of security, hope, and love. To our fighting men the safety and protection of their families is the center of what they fight for. To men on the production front, the welfare of their families and homes is basic to morale" (2). As the charter explains, the home was a wartime flash point and emotional trigger. Soldiers were fighting for their homes, and because American families were facing war, destruction, and death, it was especially critical for children to feel the safety and security that the home (and implicitly the mother) should provide. Ideally and ideologically, then, spatial rhetorics such as these (re)inscribed the home as an essential place of safety, nurturance, care, comfort, love, and patriotism.

But even as the home was endowed with this deep emotional attachment, the actual experience of home challenged this depiction. The material reality, the embodied inhabitation, and the lived experiences of home at this time and the years leading up to it made it clear that the home was not as it should be. Owing to this mismatch, even greater anxiety ensued—anxiety that then contributed to the concern regarding the working mother and the motherless home. In fact, *A Children's Charter in Wartime* itself indicates that the real situation within the American home often does not reflect its articulated ideal. The charter states that due to work-related migration, the father's military service, and the mother's move into the workforce, there are now "problems in the home that affect every member of the family" (2). The home was seen as the ideal space for children, one that necessitated the mother's presence, but because of wartime needs and constraints, the home was in danger.

The charter's dual articulation of both hope and concern for the home was certainly indicative of the WWII moment. But to understand this moment, we cannot forget that American families had just lived through the effects of the

Great Depression, a period when families lost their homes due to bankruptcy and mortgage debt and when houses in many areas had simply ceased being built, with home construction in the United States "dwindl[ing] almost to zero" (Schroeder 4).[3] Further complicating this picture was the fact that families able to keep their homes had often been unable to keep them up. Houses across the country went "unpainted and unrepaired, their living value steadily declining" (4). Thus, due to the Great Depression, homes were consistently experienced as sites of financial strain. Even though President Franklin D. Roosevelt's New Deal operations had sought to address these home issues and the larger financial crisis, once the United States entered WWII, a different and equally troubling situation emerged regarding the physical state of the home.

After the United States declared war in December 1941, production needs grew, and war plants were built in key locations across the country. Families migrated by the millions to new cities that now hosted these plants, and when they did, quality living quarters were hard to find (Brown). The boomtown of Richmond, California, offers a representative example. Home to fifty-five different war industries, Richmond's population quadrupled from twenty-four thousand residents to one hundred thousand ("History & Culture"). Upon arriving in cities such as Richmond, however, families often found themselves in precarious, nontraditional living situations. Edmund Bacon reports in his 1943 article "Wartime Housing" that "[m]akeshift shacks were built, cellars were dug and occupied on the hope that the house would some day be finished, garages were occupied as homes . . . [, and] trailer camps multiplied, often under grossly exploitive and insanitary conditions" (128–29). Helen Weigel Brown elaborates on this situation in "Uncle Sam Houses His Children" (1944), writing that when families came to these new boomtowns, they immediately occupied all "available houses, apartments and hotels" (39). Once these spaces were filled, Brown reports, families "moved into store rooms, back rooms, garages, abandoned buildings, tents, trailers, every conceivable place that could shelter them. Many a newly arrived family was found walking the streets at night, with no place to go. Many another family with little children was found sleeping in the open in city parks" (39). To address this dire situation, "Uncle Sam" attempted to help families find more stable home environments. The government started a Share Your Home campaign that "urg[ed] families to 'move over' and make room for war workers," and it also built homes at rapid speed, constructing in 1944 over three hundred sixty thousand units for families and converting over six thousand spaces per month for daily living (Brown 79). All of this housing, though, was deemed temporary. Within two years after the war's end, these homes were to be torn down. But even with such federal efforts, the housing situation, especially at the start of the war, was dismal. Bacon makes this assessment: "The war has brought about wide-spread suffering among the civilian population resulting from intolerable housing conditions. Families are crowded together in inadequate spaces, privacy is violated, and the normal development of family life is hampered" (137).[4]

Given this reality, the embodied everyday experience of the home was not living up to its ideal definition as a site for security, comfort, and love. The already precarious physical state of the home made it almost impossible for the mother to create the ideal home, even more so for the fact that many of these migrating families moved to war-impacted areas so that the mother could work. Since she was now spending a great deal of her time at the war plant, her presence in the home would be limited. Public anxieties thus rose regarding what was happening to her children given her absence, especially so because childcare options for mothers and their families at the outset of the war were scarce. Many of these women had left traditional family and community networks and, consequently, had limited support to rely on. Due to these circumstances, women were often forced to patch together inconsistent help or to leave their children unattended. As quickly as mothers made their way into the workforce, then, reports circulated in outlets across the country that evaluated the situation for their children. These reports directed attention to the motherless home, and the spatio-rhetorical assessments they made expressed extreme anxiety about how the home, the working mother, and indeed the nation were failing America's children. Prompting alarm and action, these emotive spatial rhetorics made it clear that something must be done.

The introduction to this chapter offered an indication of the alarm and even panic over the mother's limited choices for childcare at this moment, but scores of other interlocutors helped to emphasize the gravity of this situation for American children and the American home. For example, at the 1941 Conference on Day Care of Children of Working Mothers with Special Reference to Defense Areas, Dr. Langdon of the Works Progress Administration made the following report:

> We have many instances cited, such as 800 women going to work in a factory one morning and 40 children being found locked in parked automobiles. That is very common and those are the children of the parents who are more concerned about their care. The children of the parents who don't care for them are running the streets. It is the

ones who really care who lock them in parked automobiles so that they will be sure to know where they are. That is really true and that is not at all uncommon, because there just is no place for them to go in many of these communities. (*Proceedings* [1942] 40)

While Langdon offers a disturbing description of the general childcare situation with the mother's absence, Lenroot's article in a 1942 issue of *New York Times* narrates one child's experience in the motherless home:

> Here is a two-room flat in a crowded section near a great aircraft plant. A knock on the door brings a tousled 4-year-old girl with a box of matches in her hand. She is alone and hungry, and has been trying to light the gas stove, as mother does, to cook meals. The teen-age girl who usually comes to "mind" her failed to show up this morning, it seems, and mother was afraid of losing her job if she stayed at home. (18)

Langdon and Lenroot describe mothers resorting to locking their children in cars, letting them roam the streets on their own, or even leaving them at home with matches in hand.

Still others aided in sounding the public alarm. For instance, Emma Lundberg makes clear in her Department of Labor bureau publication that mothers' employment in the war plant had caused a clear "disruption of home life" that should be seen as the "most serious hazard of wartime" (21). Katherine Glover agrees, writing that "when those who keep the home pots boiling, the hearths dusted, the children fed and cared for, leave the home shift for the factory shift, households and families are shaken from center to circumference" (14). Zeroing in on the wartime neologism *latchkey children*, Henry Zucker uses his 1944 article for the *Annals of the American Academy of Political and Social Science* to explain that the "house key tied around the [child's] neck is the symbol of cold meals, of a child neglected and shorn of the security of a mother's love and affection" (43). And what is more, one 1942 *Saturday Evening Post* article titled "Eight-Hour Orphans" describes the current status of the home and the child's care within it as a "tragedy" (20) and continues to generate public alarm with a warning: "No informed American needs a psychologist to tell him that children separated from home ties and without competent care during their most impressionable age are the troublemakers, the neurotics, the spiritual and emotional cripples of a generation hence" (106). These spatio-rhetorical assessments of the working mother's limited and even dangerous childcare options sparked a national conversation distinguished by its emotional tenor of grave concern.

Drawing from Jenell Johnson's work, one could read this moment as one in which a "visceral public" was formed, for here we see how people "cohere[d]" as a public "by means of intense feeling" (2) and how these "collective visceral feelings" of anxiety and fear "serve[d] as inarguable, self-evident rationales for policy" (5). The wartime childcare situation was a problem that needed to be addressed; the emotive tenor of the moment "join[ed] people together and move[d] them to action" (14). In short order, a range of institutions confronted this issue by creating childcare centers for these working mothers. Supporting this move, advocates leveraged spatial rhetorics that would assuage public anxiety by pointing to the childcare center as the key solution to the widespread concern surrounding the motherless home.

Composing the Wartime Childcare Center

Government, industry, corporations, and independent agencies addressed the public alarm over the motherless home by building childcare centers in war-impacted areas across the country. It has to be noted, however, that while these major stakeholders sought to ease concern for the working mother and to ensure the welfare of her children, there was another reason that drove their decision. Reports from war plants had revealed that without adequate childcare, working mothers could not do their jobs efficiently or effectively. As the booklet *Child Service Centers* sets out, there was great concern regarding "absenteeism, lateness, [and] early check-outs due to women with children" (2). Responding to these concerns, the federal government passed the Defense Housing and Community Facilities and Services Act of 1940 (otherwise known as the Lanham Act), which authorized the spending of more than $50 million on childcare centers and consequently established 3,102 centers across the country (Kerr 163). Forty-seven states built childcare centers in areas directly affected by the war effort, taking advantage of federal financial support while also contributing more than $26 million of their own funds (163). On a local level, community groups such as the Child Care Development and Protection Committee in Watertown, New York, created centers that addressed their community's specific needs, and industries such as the Kaiser Corporation in Portland, Oregon; Vancouver, Washington; and Richmond, California set up war nurseries either on-site or in their communities.

The creation and management of these centers were not untouched by racial prejudice, however. Jim Crow ideology sanctioned that schools and public facilities should, by law, be separate and presumably (but not in practice) equal. Thus, as Emilie Stoltzfus notes, "given the fact that some 95 percent of the wartime child care programs nationwide were administered through school systems, many . . . were legally (or *de facto*) segregated" (100). There were exceptions to this rule. Some centers, like the Kaiser Centers and the Ossing Center discussed below, existed outside the purview of state-sponsored segregation and thus allowed for and even celebrated the fact that children of diverse backgrounds played together in these settings. Even with these apparent progressive stances on race relations, however, reports reveal that at many of these non-state-sponsored sites, African Americans still experienced implicit forms of prejudice. For example, one Kaiser report explains that black mothers hesitated to enroll their children because they felt "less welcome" than their white counterparts ("Historic American Buildings Survey" 29). In response to both explicit and implicit discrimination, childcare centers were established specifically for African American children. As childcare advocate Thomasina Johnson reported at the Congressional Hearings on Wartime Care and Protection of Children of Employed Mothers, by 1943 "259 units for 12,335 Negro children ha[d] been established by communities throughout the States where separate facilities are required by law" (qtd. in "Wartime Care" 74–75). But even though some centers were designated for black families, the rhetorical and material focus stayed on white mothers and their children. The country was most concerned with how it could win the war without also putting the traditional (read: white) American family and home in danger.[5]

When it came to building these childcare centers, their physical construction and placement must have wielded significant spatio-rhetorical power. These centers were created to support working mothers and their families, to ease their childcare stresses, and to enable these women to be more efficient at work. In terms of their material formations, the WWII childcare center emerged on the landscape in a variety of ways. As Katherine Glover writes in "Women at Work in Wartime," "There is no set or single pattern for child care centers. They vary as the life and pattern of American communities vary" (17). Childcare centers were established in apartment buildings, schools, churches, community centers, and even on-site at factories and war plants. The spatio-rhetorical impact was significant: driving to work, running errands, walking through the neighborhood, mothers saw these centers as new fixtures on the landscape, and their existence alone announced their availability and support. As Carole Blair explains, "Architecture, like natural language use, expresses degrees of significance not just through its symbolic substance but by its very existence" (34). The material reality of the wartime childcare centers garnered attention: their "existence mark[ed] them with at least a potential for public attention that would not have been available in their absence" (36). Just by being there, simply by appearing in the visual field in material form, the childcare center initiated a first and critical spatio-rhetorical move that would have helped both to shift the emotional tenor of conversation about working mothers and to pacify the anxieties expressed during this period.

The physical existence and location of the Kaiser Child Service Centers in Vancouver (Washington) and Portland (Oregon) were especially significant. These two centers were massive in scale. With fifteen service rooms, each site was able to care for 375 children per work shift, which amounted to 1,125 children a day. Important in terms of spatio-rhetorical concerns, these centers were located at the entrances to two war plants. Such placement created another moment for relief, signaling to women the convenience these centers offered. As the writer of a 1944 *Architectural Record* article explains, the Kaiser Child Service Centers are located "on the straightest possible line of travel to save time, gasoline, and expense to the working families" ("Designed" 84). Passing these massive buildings before entering work, women would no doubt have been persuaded to see that there was now an option for them and their children—and a convenient one at that.

The mere creation of these sites helped to shift the emotional atmosphere from anxiety to relief. Center advocates also knew, however, that different modes of persuasion—different kinds of spatial rhetorics—were necessary to convince working mothers to take advantage of these sites. For even though the unattended home could turn out to be quite dangerous for children, many mothers initially chose it over the childcare center. These women's reservations were due not just to ideological understandings of the home but also to negative perceptions associated with childcare centers of the past, for the war nurseries of the WWII period were not the first federally sponsored childcare centers. During the Great Depression, the government subsidized nursery schools for financially destitute families, and these sites were often seen as desperate options for those with impoverished, broken, or dysfunctional families. For many WWII-era mothers, placing a child in such a facility signaled poverty, negligence, and government dependency.

Adding to this understanding, the childcare center was also often depicted as a site for strict regimentation and detached, callous treatment. In her

1942 article "Help Mothers Win the War," Ethel Beer articulates mothers' concerns regarding the childcare center, writing that in the past it was often seen as a "custodial institution," a "rudimentary affair" that only provided "shelter for children while their mothers worked" (193). Even though working mothers during WWII were experiencing extreme pressure to find adequate childcare help, such negative perceptions of childcare centers suggested that these sites could not do the emotional work that the home provided. Lacking that critical affective atmosphere, the center could not act or feel like the home should. Mothers therefore hesitated to entrust their children to these spaces, as they preferred the ideological, if not actually present, space of the home. Dorothy Baruch's series of articles in the *Journal of Consulting Psychology* substantiate this claim. In one installment, Baruch writes that in the first months of the war nursery's inception, many mothers preferred the "'halo' of the home" to the "'havoc' of the school" (45).

To convince working mothers and the public at large of the childcare center's value, supporters embarked on a two-part spatio-rhetorical campaign. The first worked to endow these spaces with the emotional tenets of home by casting the childcare center as a place where children would feel safe, cared for, comforted, nurtured, and loved; here, too, they would even learn patriotism and democratic principles, just as they would have in the home. The second spatio-rhetorical initiative was to move beyond the equation between childcare center and home (childcare center qua home) and to argue instead that the center *surpassed* the home in terms of its suitability for children and the exemplary support it provided to working mothers. Within this second argumentative strand, the childcare center was not just a home; it was a *superhome that could do a better job than the traditional home.

Coupled together, these two spatio-rhetorical moves assuaged anxieties regarding the motherless home by offering a new, emotionally laden understanding—or presence—for the childcare center. As Chaim Perelman and Lucia Olbrechts-Tyteca set out, presence entails "the displaying of certain elements on which the speaker wishes to center attention in order that they may occupy the foreground of the hearer's consciousness"; presence is the rhetorical work that "aspires to give the mind a certain orientation, to make certain schemes of interpretation prevail, to insert the elements of agreement into a framework that will give them significance" (142). During WWII, childcare center advocates composed a new emotional presence for the childcare center that would "crowd out other considerations from the viewer's mind" (C. A. Hill, "Psychology" 29). This new childcare center was not the cold institutional space of old; instead it was a homelike space that could meet and even surpass the expected and deeply revered emotional aspects of domestic life. Such comparisons between the center and the home did much for the working mother: with an equally good (or even better) space available for child-rearing outside the home, she could delegate her motherly duties and enter the workspace without concern.

Childcare Center as Home
Promotional materials publicizing the goodness of the wartime childcare center pervaded the national scene. In terms of governmental efforts, the Office of War Information strongly advised magazine writers at posts throughout the country to include positive depictions of childcare centers in their stories (Honey, *Creating Rosie* 81). For example, the 1944 *Magazine War Guide* explained, "Mothers need to be convinced of the advantages of the community services for their children. . . . Magazines have done much, may care to do more, in interpreting what steady reliable care for children of war workers means" (qtd. in Honey 81). In addition to this national effort, local agencies publicized centers through signs on streetcars and busses, posters in employment offices, movie trailers, and maps that alerted the public not only to the existence of these centers but also to the reliable service they provided ("Extended School Services"). Individual war plants advertised and dedicated articles to their childcare centers in company newspapers, such as Kaiser's *Bo's'n's Whistle*, and the Kaiser Centers also created promotional booklets that celebrated their work (*Child Service Centers*). Moreover, such outlets as the *New York Times, Parents' Magazine, Collier's, Journal of Home Economics, Women's Home Companion*, and the wartime periodical *Education for Victory* exerted great effort to proclaim the good work of these centers.

As the headline of one *New York Times* article indicates, the goal for advocates was to show how centers were "solving big problem[s] for mothers" ("Nurseries"). Advocates pursued this goal by mobilizing a specific kind of spatio-rhetorical project: the childcare center, they argued, could take on the emotional work of home. Like the home, it could be a place of safety, nurturance, care, comfort, love, and even patriotism. However, as director of the Kaiser Centers, James Hymes, noted, the American public and especially mothers were not immediately convinced: "[mothers] will not place their youngsters any place until they have seen the institution in operation" (qtd in. "Nurseries" 17). Thus, the first and most pervasive spatio-rhetorical challenge for proponents was to enable mothers and the public at large to peek in the childcare center and observe its good work.

PEEK IN

Proponents provided audiences with this opportunity to peek in the childcare center by publishing articles that showcased children in centers engaged in their daily activities. This showcasing relied on two intertwined and emotionally compelling spatio-rhetorical tactics: photographs and detailed description. As Janis L. Edwards explains, photographs have the rhetorical power of "simulat[ing] reality"; so by presenting photographs of childcare center activity to interested audiences, advocates offered them the "visual equivalent of 'being there'" at the center (181). To complement these visual efforts, the photographs were accompanied by vivid textual description, or *enargeia*. As Gerard Sharpling explains, *enargeia* is the "graphic portrayal of living experience . . . [that] take[s] the audience into the presence of an object by attempting to place things before the eyes" (173). Through *enargeia*, spatial rhetorics described the childcare center with vivacity and detail, and in so doing, they exercised the "power to evoke a wide range of sense impressions, and hence emotions, from the reader" (174). Asking readers to witness the childcare center through these visual and descriptive spatial rhetorics prompted the erasure of old and the creation of new emotional ties to the childcare center. Ultimately, these combined efforts made it possible for the childcare center to act and feel like home.

Figure 4.2 displays the kind of photographs commonly included in articles that promoted childcare centers. Here, seven young children are happily playing with dough; the accompanying caption explains that a two-year-old child chants, "roll, roll, roll," while a four-year-old claims to be "making biscuits." Viewing such photographs and reading their explanatory captions, audiences were able to see for themselves happy children playing, eating, learning, and napping. Such seemingly simple visuals did much to counter memories of past childcare options. Here, observers would note that *these* centers are not sterile places where children are simply sheltered. They appear instead to offer children a comfortable, safe, and enriching space in which to grow.

Supporting the overwhelming number of visuals that showcased the goings-on at the childcare center was *enargeia* that offered detailed descriptions of the child's day. Ruth Carson's *Collier's* article "Minding the Children" provides one example:

> Children play in the big, sunny room that was the living room, and outdoors in the back garden. They have a quiet time in the former library with crayons, picture books and storytelling, have naps on

"Roll, roll, roll," chants the two-year-old. "I am making biscuits," announces a four-year-old at Center Nursery School, Seattle, Washington

Fig. 4.2. Childcare center children at table. Louise Kiskaddon et al., "Creative Activity in Nursery School," *School Arts* 43 (1943), p. 291; used with permission from Davis Publications.

canvas cots in the big upper room, have their midmorning fruit juice or milk, eat noon dinner off gay pottery in the dining room. A nurse is on the lookout for colds and such, and there's an isolation room upstairs for sick children. (46)

Similar to Carson's description of children in the big, sunny, quiet, and healthy childcare environment is Kaiser's event schedule for a child's day at the center, published in its promotional booklet (fig. 4.3). The booklet explains to readers the child's activities hour by hour. As it does so, it highlights not only the thought and care put into each activity but also the positive effects each one has for the child. Snacks, for instance, "keep energy high," while "comfortable cots" allow the child to "relax and rest," thus "provid[ing] a good balance to vigorous play" (12). In sum, the schedule asserts that as children move through each activity, they experience a "full, happy day" (12).

Cumulatively these visuals and descriptions enabled readers to sense a positive atmosphere decidedly different from childcare centers of the past and even from the contemporaneous home. As Ruth Steelman reports in her study of a center in Greensboro, North Carolina, the center is a place that offers children "an attractive environment" where teachers "encourage individual growth rather than mass training" (13). Such visions of the childcare center

The Motherless Home   **141**

11:15 A. M.
REST
Comfortable cots where the child can relax and rest provide a good balance to vigorous play and insures a happy, well child.

2:30 P. M.
OUTDOORS
More play. Another chance to practice getting along well with people—and to have fun doing it.

11:30 A. M.
LUNCH
A story first, and then this as a typical lunch: Liver loaf, creamed onions, buttered potatoes, crisp raw carrots, milk, and for dessert, a creamy rice and fig pudding.

3:00 P. M.
SNACK
A high spot in the afternoon and one that the children look forward to is "snack" time— milk, a sandwich and a slice of apple to help keep energy high.

12:15 P. M.
SLEEP
Every child has a nap. Being in a group makes it easy for children to learn good habits in sleeping and dressing.

4:00 P. M.
HOME
With memories of a full, happy day; with things to talk about; with tomorrow's fun to look forward to.

Fig. 4.3. A child's day in the center. *Child Service Centers*, descriptive booklet, Kaiser Company, Inc., 1945, p. 12; Oregon State Library holdings. Courtesy Kaiser Permanente Heritage Resources.

would have been reassuring to say the least, as the implicit point throughout these particular spatio-rhetorical efforts was that the home did not have to be the only environment that could cultivate and care for the child. The center could do this work as well.

SAFETY AND SECURITY

Another key spatio-rhetorical strategy was for advocates to emphasize the safety and security that children enjoyed in the center. Photographs in newspaper articles and promotional materials again showed children in safe environments under careful supervision and away from physical danger. Figure 4.4 from the Kaiser booklet displays children at play on sliding boards and jungle gyms, with others running happily in a well-kept yard replete with shaded areas. The accompanying caption guides readers' attention in this way: "Parents like the fact that the outdoor playground, away from all traffic, is completely enclosed by the building itself" (*Child Service Centers* 17). Countering prevalent visions of children in the unattended home with matches in hand or running freely in the streets, these images of children at the childcare center assured viewers that safety and security would no longer be a concern for working mothers or the American public. Even more importantly, the center went beyond basic safety. The installation of jungle gyms and play yards cast the childcare center as a site of enjoyment where children would exercise and have fun—a space, in short, where children could thrive.

The issue of safety, however, took on an additional resonance at the center. Advocates described its environment as one that enabled children to feel *emotionally* safe and stable. As Elta Pfister writes, the childcare center is "designed to give the child a place where he feels he belongs during the hours when his parents are at work" (203). This sense of belonging and safety was identified as crucial for stakeholders, and advocates were sure to point out that the emotional support supplied by the childcare center catalyzed positive change in the children under its watch. Pfister makes this claim, writing that when children first entered the childcare center, "[e]asel paintings made at school by children whose mothers were working or away from the home usually indicate a disturbed, unhappy situation in their lives" (203). After spending time in the center, however, there was a marked difference in these children. Pfister celebrates the effects of the center in this way: "[A]fter a few weeks of happy

Parents like the fact that the outdoor playground, away from all traffic, is completely enclosed by the building itself. There is an inner grass court surrounded by covered cement porches. Groups are divided into age levels by low fences. There are wagons, sand boxes, wheelbarrows, swings, climbing apparatus, large outdoor building blocks and tricycles. The wading pool in the center of the playground is a favorite in summertime.

Fig. 4.4. Outdoor playground at the Kaiser Centers. Child Service Centers, descriptive booklet, Kaiser Company, Inc., 1945, p. 17; Oregon State Library holdings. Courtesy Kaiser Permanente Heritage Resources.

belonging to the group in a Child Care Center with regular work, play, rest, and eating periods, the same children indicate by the painting medium, and through other projective techniques, that they are becoming much less tense, participate more freely in group activities, and life is smoothing out for them" (203). The childcare center's emotional supports of safety and security were clear. Throughout the tumultuous war period and while mothers worked in the war plant, the childcare center did the work of home by providing a safe haven for the nation's children: because of the center, "life [was] smoothing out."

LOVE

As advocates reconstructed the childcare center into a site that would protect and safeguard children physically and emotionally, they also highlighted important spatial activities within the childcare center that replicated the affective care children would ideally receive in the home and from the mother. A major concern for childcare center advocates was the promise of making children feel loved. Mary Elizabeth Evans uses her *Journal of Home Economics* article to detail how center teachers take on the nurturing practices of the mother: "[W]e found that *children who are away from home all day need affection and occasional 'cuddling' from their teachers*. While we did not initiate any cuddling, we did not discourage a child when he showed a desire to be held or fondled, by suggesting that he join the group or get down from our lap" (259). Hymes, director of the Kaiser Centers, similarly describes the spatial activities of the teachers working the night shift at the childcare center: "Teachers on swing shift must be prepared to give more outward affection and warmth than day-shift nursery school teachers. They must be people who can 'cuddle' children" (227). Not surprisingly, photographs corroborated these descriptions of the loving care that children received in the center. Figure 4.5, for example, displays the teacher tucking a child in for his nap. The title of the article featuring the photograph is "While Their Parents Build Planes," and the visual completes the sentence: while the parents build planes, the teacher in the childcare center loves and cares for their children.

PATRIOTISM

As promotional materials underscored the love, safety, and security that children in the childcare centers experienced, they also set out how children were learning love of country and democratic principles. Just as the home was seen as the site to instill American values and ways of life, childcare centers were endowed with this purpose as well. Another photograph featured in "While

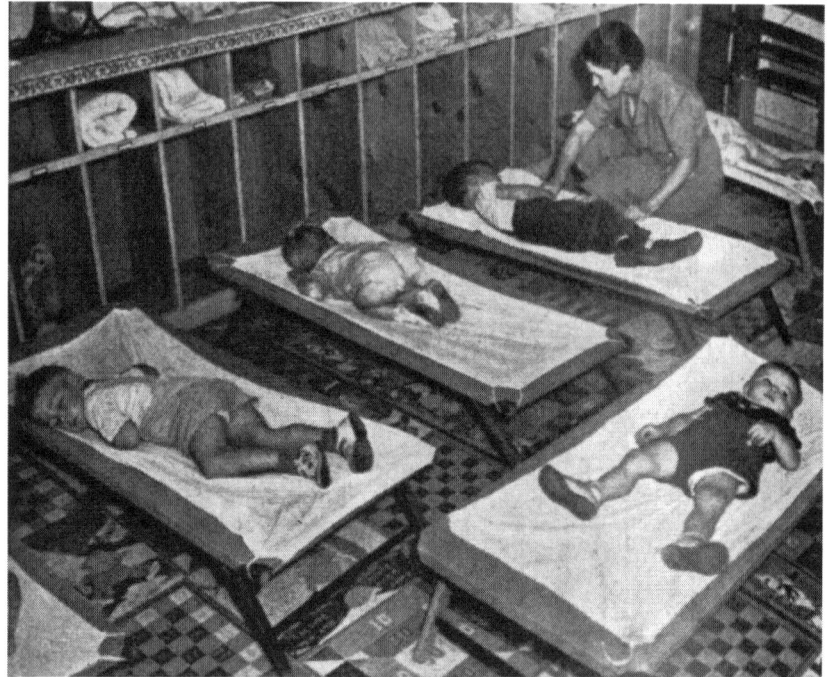

Fig. 4.5. Tucking in at naptime. "While Their Parents Build Planes," *Women's Home Companion* 70 (Mar. 1943), p. 10.

Their Parents Build Planes" is of children playing under a raised American flag (fig. 4.6). The caption below the visual explains, "Every morning the flag is raised over the playhouse which the children built from a Lockheed engine crate and which takes turns being a fort, a Red Cross hospital or a pony express station" (8). The caption goes on to state that children have also created a "Victory garden" on-site at the center. Likewise, in her *Women's Home Companion* article, Dorothy Budd describes how children at the Ossing childcare facility learn democratic ways of life. She writes, "The midmorning snack is one of the high spots at the Ossing recreation center's nursery school. Here you see democracy in action. Children of every race and creed learn to get along well together" (58). While this kind of integrated childcare center was not the ruling principle at sites across the country, Budd takes this moment to describe how one childcare center instilled this particular form of ideal democratic practice.

These two examples emphasize the ways the center allowed for children to learn democracy and patriotism, but other advocacy materials took this idea and moved it in a slightly different direction by consistently attributing to the center a different kind of patriotic role. That is, due to the fact that

Fig. 4.6. Pony Express at the childcare center. "While Their Parents Build Planes," *Women's Home Companion* 70 (Mar. 1943), p. 8.

centers were enabling women to work, these sites were depicted as a vital part of the war effort. The pamphlet *When Mother's Away* articulates this point: "A day nursery which is soundly planned and soundly operated will, without question, help to win this war. It will maintain and preserve the morale of the women who have to work in war industries. It will protect and safeguard their children. It will preserve their family life" (National Assn. of Day Nurseries 35). Beer's aptly titled article "Help Mothers Win the War" makes an even grander patriotic claim; she writes, "In this crisis it is evident that the day nursery can help mothers win the war. It is as sure a weapon as the gun on the battlefield. And it should be used to the greatest extent. Therefore let us adopt the slogan:—'FORWARD MARCH THE DAY NURSERY'" (195). From this perspective, the childcare center, like the home, was a site of patriotism. It supported both family and country in the cause.

Through all of these spatio-rhetorical efforts to peek into the childcare center, audiences witnessed how the center was taking on the emotional work of the home: it was a site for safety, nurturance, care, comfort, love, and even patriotism. Photographs especially enabled audiences to see center activities with their own eyes, and the examples suggest these moments were not staged. Rather, in the terms of Cara Finnegan, the candid nature of these photographs functioned as "visual synecdoche" in which the pictured children were not positioned as unusual but instead as representative of all children in childcare centers across the country (205). Finally, we might notice in both the photographs and the descriptions a lack of overt argument. Advocates did not mobilize a rhetorical offensive. Instead, by observing photographs and reading descriptions, audiences were prompted to revise negative perceptions of childcare centers and consider how the center had realized cherished domestic practices.

Childcare Center as Superhome

While many advocates equated the childcare center with the home, others went a step further. They claimed that the center was so good at caring for children that it *surpassed* what the home and mother could do. These proponents leveraged spatial rhetorics that suggested how the center could exceed the home's and the mother's capacity. Such spatio-rhetorical moves defined the center not as a home but rather as a superhome, and they aimed to garner from audiences even deeper respect for the center, strengthening both mothers' and the public's emotional ties to this site.

A primary way advocates took up this work was by explaining how the center fostered a better environment for child-rearing than the home could. Articles consistently praised the ways that children at centers learned the values and practices often taught in the home, such as manners, consequences to their actions, self-reliance, and personal responsibility. Center proponents pushed this point further, however, to celebrate the fact that the group situation enabled children to learn more effectively than they would at home. For instance, the article "Cooperation on the Home Front" displays a photograph of children playing together, with the caption above explaining, "Young children learn to get along in a group in a way that it would be hard to duplicate at home" (fig. 4.7). This point is also made in the detailed daily schedule for children published in the Kaiser Centers' booklet: "Being in a group makes it easy for children to learn good habits in sleeping and dressing" (fig. 4.3). Among these good habits, the center's group environment cultivates sharing, as the booklet explains: "Things that must be used together are good medicine to prevent 'spoiled' children" (*Child Service Centers* 11). These spatial rhetorics described the group situation of the childcare center as one that made learning important behaviors and habits easier for children; best of all, of course, by virtue of the center's environment, children would not grow up to be spoiled.

In addition to highlighting the positive effects of the center's group atmosphere, promotional materials also praised the center's unique built environment, underscoring how these sites were outfitted for the sole purpose of childcare. In "Cooperation on the Home Front," Finck lists the following critical components of a childcare center that would be difficult to replicate in even the best middle-class home: "rope swings, slide, ladders and climbing apparatus, sandboxes, hollow blocks" as well as "[c]lay, paints and crayons, scissors, blocks, hammering equipment, toy cars, airplanes, trains, animals for creative play; doll-corner equipment, books, child-sized benches, tables, easels" (25). Similarly, Eunice Barnard lauds the spatial composition and construction of various childcare centers across the country, writing of how lucky the children are to "live all day in a Lilliputian paradise" (107). Barnard elaborates on the uniqueness of these spaces: "Round about is a realm of adventure and delight: blocks just right for small arms to lift; swings, slides, ladders, wagons, sand, clay, dolls and brooms and pots and pans. Here, too, menus are planned for baby digestion instead of grandpa's or Aunt Kate's" (107). Unlike the home, which had to cater to various constituents like grandpa or

Fig. 4.7. Group play. Originally published in Barbara Hubley Finck, "Cooperation on the Home Front," *Parents' Magazine*, Aug. 1945, p. 25; all rights reserved.

Aunt Kate, the center's only concern was for the child. Because of the special attention the childcare center gave to children and how well suited it was for them, advocates prompted working mothers and other audiences to deepen their appreciation for this space.

As another mode of arguing for the superior work of childcare centers, proponents also composed spatial rhetorics that highlighted the people who worked within these spaces, explaining that these workers were often experts in their fields and that the services they provided surpassed what any ordinary home (and, implicitly, any ordinary mother) could do. Credentials of center leaders were a focus, and these figures were mostly women who, perhaps not surprisingly given the findings in the previous chapter, were often trained professionals with degrees in home economics, child psychology, child welfare, and nutrition. Praise for their professional status was often coupled with descriptions of their expert caretaking and nurturing skills. Barnard, for instance, claims that the teacher in the childcare center is "a goddess trained to know what makes children tick or at least what different ways they should tick at ages two, two-and-a-half, three and so on" (107). This woman is a "molder of character, a creator of physical and emotional poise" who "has at her command a vast store of scientific data on child reactions and child behavior unknown twenty years ago" (107). Given descriptions such as these, the everyday mother's qualifications and abilities would likely have paled in comparison.

While expert childcare providers certainly ensured that children were safe and well cared for, many centers also enacted other spatial activities that offered additional modes of support for working mothers and reinforced the perception of the childcare center as a superhome. For instance, advocates realized that after leaving work, mothers were often overwhelmed by having to care for children and tend to the full range of domestic duties. As Glover writes, "At present the woman in a war plant usually rotates from the assembly line to the clothesline to the kitchen stove" (23). To help mothers manage their duties at home, a number of centers across the country took on the work of laundry, mending, shoe repair, errands, grocery shopping, and even the preparation of a hot evening meal for mothers to take home (Swartz). By assuming these domestic responsibilities, the childcare center, suggested proponents, accomplished and surpassed the home's work. Furthermore, the relief these services afforded would have been immeasurable for mothers. By dispersing domestic labor beyond the confines of the family residence, the center eased the mother's daily burdens so that she could work and mother (but maybe not grocery shop).

By virtue of these combined spatial rhetorics that suggested the childcare center could accomplish and even exceed the work of the home, working mothers and the public at large gained confidence in it. Indeed, spatial rhetorics created a new presence for the childcare center and crowded out the negative emotional atmosphere previously attributed to this space. By 1944 more than six hundred thousand children were enrolled in centers across the country, and the image of this space and people's emotional engagement with it had changed. As Baruch reports in 1945, "Distrust has been replaced with confidence. The first apprehension in leaving small children 'to be regimented' has been replaced by a sense of security and firm knowledge that children were not being lined up and treated like robots, but that each was receiving care and guidance which took into account his own individuality and needs" (45). As the popularity of and reliance on these centers grew, mothers and advocates confirmed how the emotional support and affective characteristics of the home had transferred to the center. Working mother Rena Burns attests to the crucial function of the childcare center in her family's life:

> I have three small sons; twin boys 3 years old. Billy is 6. *The nursery to them has been home for some time.* They have the proper food, rest and play that a growing child must have. They have had the love and patient care of mothers at the nursery, that made them realize that their own mother had to work while dad was in the Army or wherever he might have to be. Most of all to we mothers who had to work to keep our home fires burning until our husbands and fathers were home[,] [t]he nursery was a place that we know that our minds could be free from worrying if they were playing in the street, or if they were fed, or all the other things that the nursery has done for them. (A3869; emphasis added)

Here the topophilia expected to be felt for the home is attributed instead to the childcare center, as Burns articulates her deep love for the center and the support it provides her family.

While Burns goes so far as to see the center as a replacement for the home, where "mothers" at the center take care of her children, figures like Steelman more moderately identified the childcare center as a secondary, yet vital, domestic space. Though the center should not "strive to supplant the family unit," Steelman asserts, it should be a "supplement to the home" (13). Likewise, in its evaluation of the Kaiser Centers, *Architectural Record* finds that these places "serve the children in the capacity of a substitute temporary home quite as in the capacity of a school" ("Designed" 88). Finally, the close, necessary relationship between home and center was fused even more strongly in the Office of Civilian Defense's *Services for Children of Working Mothers in War Time*. This 1943 publication states, "When parental supervision and attention are diminished because the mother takes an essential war job it is reasonable to turn to the school to compensate in some measure for what the child lacks at home" (8). Spatial rhetorics such as these reveal how the childcare center had become a space that offered the emotional supports of home and had even come to compensate for what the home could not provide during this time of stress and concern.

The Postwar Childcare Center

At the war's end in 1945, the exigency that had brought about the war nursery suddenly lifted. The childcare center as a site offering the emotional sustenance of home and the relief of distributed domestic work soon became a source of anxiety for some in peacetime. Soldiers came back from war expecting to find jobs waiting for them and the resumption of traditional gendered dynamics at home and at work. But women's domestic return did not always go as planned. To be sure, while dominant discourse depicted a scenario in which the white middle-class woman eagerly returned to the white middle-class home, this expected domestic restoration was met with a good deal of resistance, as women from various raced, cultured, and classed backgrounds balked at the idea. A survey conducted by the Women's Bureau revealed that after the war, 75 percent of women polled had stated that they intended to continue working outside the home (Close 131). In another survey, one hundred women were asked about their postwar work plans and reasons for them: fifty-seven said they needed to "support themselves and in many cases others"; twenty-one stated they needed to remain in the workforce "for some special economic reasons," such as to "buy a house, pay off debts, [or] educate children"; and twenty-two replied that they liked working or being independent" (Women's Bureau, *Handbook* 33).

Such intentions prompted public alarm. Eric Johnston expressed this concern in his essay "Aprons or Overalls," in which he explains that "to meet the crisis" of war, "we have set aside many of our traditions, not the least of which is that 'women's place is in the home'" (15). Women, he writes, "will not willingly leave the factory and shop to return to the kitchen" (15). Margaret Mead similarly focused on the question of women's relationship to work and the home in the postwar world in her essay "The Women in the War." She declares that the American public has a problem on its hands: "Across the pages of the mind march lines of women, in slacks holding large fat pay envelopes which they brandish more effectively than the traditional rolling pin" (279). Assessing this situation, Mead deduces that many American citizens are asking and indeed worrying, "'Will women return to the home?' . . . Perhaps women have all left the home, perhaps there won't be any homes!" (278). As indicated by this comment, new tensions arose in postwar public discourse regarding what the woman's and especially the mother's relationship to the home might be.

The fate of the childcare center was directly tied to this conversation. The initial postwar plan was to close centers immediately. From the perspective of funders, the exigency for childcare centers had passed. After armistice, women were no longer needed at the war plant, so childcare centers should close. Such thinking motivated government officials to move to terminate childcare funding shortly after the Japanese surrender, announcing that there would be no more federal support of childcare beyond October 1945. This announcement was not a welcome one for many working mothers. As the numbers above suggest, mothers were among those women who needed or wanted to work, and because of the situation in which they found themselves, they argued the childcare center must remain open. To fight the closing of these centers, mothers and childcare advocates created activist groups such as the New York Child Care Parents Association and the Philadelphia Association of Day Nurseries, waging their protests in a number of forms. As Emilie Stoltzfus writes, childcare activists "held mass meetings, picketed city halls, successfully requested public hearings, conducted letter writing campaigns, developed pro–day care radio spots, and lobbied decision makers" (39).

This section explores how activists petitioned for the continued support of childcare centers by reasserting the wartime spatial rhetorics that defined the childcare center as a homelike space for the new postwar context. These advocates wanted the emotional investment in and respect for the childcare center to continue, and they argued that the American public should recognize how the center, as a secondary or even primary home, continued to address pressing and present circumstances. The spatial rhetorics analyzed in this section in many ways respond to the question Sara Ahmed poses in *The Cultural Politics of Emotion* when she asks, "What sticks?" (11). By this she means, how do emotions get attached and remain tied to ideas, objects, norms, and practices? And she considers the part that emotions play in how "subjects become invested in particular structures" (12). In posing and responding to Ahmed's question, this section explores how advocates attempted to use spatial rhetorics to make the wartime affective associations for the childcare center "stick" in their postwar world. These activists did so by buttressing the spatio-rhetorical emotional investments established during the war and therefore arguing for these temporary sites to become permanent.

A primary move for many of these activists was to counter the claim that the exigency for the childcare center had passed. The government and other funding entities saw the centers as wartime initiatives, but for many families the circumstances of war persisted. For example, in her article "After Lanham Funds—What?," Kathryn Close admits that the childcare program "was planned solely as an emergency device to meet wartime needs" (131). Close argues, however, that the country should realize that while this emergency measure may have seemed temporary, it could be read as similar "emergency" programs have been in the past: they "have usually unearthed an area of long time need and have contributed experience valuable for future efforts to meet that need" (131). Close then applies this thinking to working mothers and the wartime childcare center by asking, "Is the whole experience justified only as one method of helping to win the war? Or has it revealed anything about children and mothers that have long time implications for communities?" (131). Answering this latter question in the affirmative, Close articulates the need for the center to become a permanent fixture on the societal landscape, writing that "children in some 2,000 nurseries throughout the country are not only receiving good physical care while their mothers are away working, but in their playtime hours are subject to the direction of trained teachers with varying degrees of skill in the techniques of child development" (133). Close attempts to regenerate the wartime emotions for the center and make them "stick" by reminding her audience of the expert care that children have received and should continue to receive.

Baruch deepens this argument when she too rethinks the question of exigency to argue for the relevance and continuance of the childcare center. Baruch reminds her readers of the patriotic service the childcare center paid to the country when they had taken "their place on the war front" (56). As the center did its wartime work, however, onlookers realized the benefits of the childcare center: the mother does not have to be the sole caretaker of the nation's children. Through the instantiation of the childcare center, Baruch argues, the American public has come to the "conviction that its children belong to the community, and that the total community has responsibility for them" (48). Childcare centers thus have "shown themselves worthy of continuing to serve children and parents in the postwar world, not as facilities set apart and outside of what is commonly done for children and parents, but as a well-integrated and cohesive part of what all the schools of the nation must eventually undertake" (56). Even though the center was at first deemed temporary, Baruch calls on readers to acknowledge how the center addresses a new, critical, and ongoing exigency: it enables the community to aid the family and share in the responsibility of child-rearing.

A different yet substantial emotive spatio-rhetorical claim within activists' protest rhetoric was to focus more directly on the homelike qualities of the childcare center that were identified and displayed during the war, while also assessing the distressed status of the home for many families in the postwar world. Activists argued that the war permanently damaged the home and that the childcare center should be recognized as a site necessary for raising the nation's children. One California mother articulates this point in a letter to her governor:

> Face it Governor, Face it America. The American home is broken. War casualty and emotional maladjustments and economic conditions, forces many a mother to get out and make a living for her family. You *can't* desert the *future* America! . . . The Child Care Centers are aware of their great task. Its teachers are trained to mold their impressionable young charges into sociably desirable and trustworthy citizens. . . . Governor, the "child care centers" are our salvation!! (Dyer 1–2)

Recasting wartime rhetorics that encoded the childcare center as a homelike space, this mother argues that the center had replaced this revered site. The postwar home is "broken," and the childcare center is now the only site that can cultivate in children American ideals and values.

The move to have audiences question the ideal postwar home, respond to the reality of the domestic situation, and recognize the value and necessity of the childcare center was reiterated in Margaret Culkin Banning's *Rotarian* article "Will They Go Back Home?" Here, Banning makes it clear that "sentimental statements that a woman ought to have a home or that a mother belongs with her children" will get the American public nowhere (29). Instead, the situation must be attended to "honestly and realistically" (28). Banning argues that homes "are not so safe universally, nor so attractive as sentiment cracks them up to be" (29), and for many mothers, "eight hours on the job . . . look[s] better than the bleaker prospect without it" (29). Turning to the question of the childcare center, Banning suggests that this space is an critical option for mothers in dire situations, for they find that the center can do what the home fails at: "children are getting on better when they are cared for in competent nurseries than when they are brought up in homes with inadequate equipment for child care" (29). Banning's spatial rhetorics reiterate the assessment that the postwar home is "broken," and she couples this evaluation with an attempt to strengthen the wartime bond to the childcare center as an exemplary site for child-rearing.

Banning's words echo the wartime claim that childcare centers were *better* than home, and this idea of the center as a superhome resonated in many advocates' postwar spatial rhetorics. In his 1945 statement before Congress, California childcare advocate "Mr. Healy" reminds his audience that childcare centers were staffed by highly trained experts—nutritionists, childcare specialists, and medical professionals—who carried out innovative programs for the children at their sites. Healy goes on to report his own observations of centers in his state, explaining that children were "given opportunity to play with other children in surroundings few homes can afford. Competent women specially trained in the care of children guided them in their activities. Excellent meals prepared by dieticians were served to these children" (Healy 8657). Activist Rhoda Kellogg takes this argument in a slightly different direction in her 1945 *Education for Victory* article. She writes,

> Even if the vast majority of these young mothers of today were competent and able to assume the whole responsibility of child care, they would be the first to realize that homes cannot provide the child the companionship, the physical equipment, the nutritional service, and the educational opportunities that are available in a well-run nursery school. (10)

Through such claims, Healy and Kellogg elaborate on the wartime assertions that the childcare center could do the work of the home and do it better. Even the mother is outdone in these scenarios. The childcare center does exactly what the home can no longer achieve: it successfully (and expertly) nurtures and educates the next generation of American citizens.

Through all of these attempts, advocates called for the childcare center to become a permanent fixture on the landscape by attempting to make the wartime emotions generated for this space "stick" in the postwar world. Building on the work of Judith Butler, Ahmed argues that emotional stickiness—the sense that a felt relationship to an object, idea, or person is permanent—actually happens through repetition; it is through "the repetition of norms," Ahmed writes, "that worlds materiali[z]e" (12). The repetition of emotional appeal occurred in postwar America. Yet, this effort to make the public's regard for the childcare center stick was not achieved. The next section explores how different spatial rhetorics countered these attempts to adhere positive affective bonds to the childcare center. Critics did so by crafting spatial rhetorics that (re)established negative associations with this space and ensuring that these associations would be the ones to stick. Moreover, they enhanced this rhetorical effect by creating or renewing emotional attachments to the traditional home, or what became known in postwar America as the "victory home."

Dismantling the Childcare Center and the Resurgence of Home

While childcare center activists supported working mothers by leveraging spatial rhetorics that attempted to remake wartime emotional investments, critics sought to weaken this bond not only because the wartime exigency had passed but also because it stood in the way of a larger national concern that gained power and volume during this period. Mead's question—"Will women return to the home?"—reflects the anxiety over women's place in the postwar world. Responses to this question contributed to a vibrant and dominant conversation that Malvina Lindsay defines in her 1946 *Washington Post* article as the "back-to-the-home movement" (6). This movement argued for "enlarging the influence of the home in American life," and its claims were based on the premise that working mothers were white middle-class women who eagerly wanted to (or at least should) return to and rebuild the white middle-class home.

The Kaiser Centers' May 1945 issue of the *Bo's'n's Whistle* offers an example of this discourse in its article "'The Kitchen'—Women's Big Post-War Goal," accompanied by a two-sided cartoon (fig. 4.8). On the left side of the cartoon, a mother, dressed as a worker, runs back to the home; on the right, the same mother, dressed as a homemaker, sings happily in her kitchen doing the dishes with her children at her feet. The article puts these words into her mouth:

> [W]hen the war is finally won the thing we want to do is to take off these unfeminine garments and button ourselves into something starched and pretty. . . . In all parts of the country we'll be hunting up vine covered cottages where we can hang frilly curtains, put geraniums in the windows and spend some time with our kids. . . .

Fig. 4.8. "'The Kitchen'—Women's Big Post-War Goal." *Bo's'n's Whistle* 11 (May 1945), p. 7.

Sure we believe in women's rights and equal pay for equal work and, furthermore, during the war it has been swell proving to you that we could take it, day in and day out, rain or shine, doing any kind of job that needed doing. But after we have done our duty in giving our best energy to help with the war, and when that job is finished, well—just hand over the knitting needles. And string up that hammock under the old apple tree. (7)

Representative of the back-to-the-home movement, discourses like this asserted that the woman's deepest desire was to return home. The family residence was the only space for America's children, and the biological mother was the only person who could perform the country's vital home work.

Not surprisingly, a priority within this movement was to question the relevance of the wartime childcare center, for its presence stood in direct opposition to the movement's goals. The childcare center was a material reality and an emotional resource that allowed mothers to leave the home and let others raise their children. Critics therefore set out to dismantle the childcare center by employing spatial rhetorics that worked to break emotional ties to, and dissolve positive feelings for, the wartime childcare center, all the while (re)generating a topophilia for the traditional home and the mother's place within it. As Ahmed writes, emotions do not just "stick"; they also "move" and "slide" (14). This section reveals how critics' spatial rhetorics enabled the wartime investments in the childcare center to "slide." For just as emotional "[a]dhesion involves not only sticking to a surface, but giving one's support and allegiance," the converse of this point is also true: emotional dissolution and detachment operates through retracting support and denying allegiance (100).

Before examining the spatial rhetorics that directed women from the war plant to the home and aimed to discontinue the childcare center's work, it is important to note how race, class, and culture inflected this conversation. Inspection of dominant spatial rhetorics reveals that the main concern was to reconstitute the white middle-class American home and to rebuild the traditional white middle-class family. The mother this discourse focused on—and, indeed, composed—was the one who *could* leave the war plant; she did not need to work. Her efforts during the war were constituted as primarily patriotic, not economic, and now that the war was over, it was expected that her patriotism be expressed in the form of rebuilding the home and supporting the family within this space. Even though thousands of mothers from variously raced, classed, and cultured backgrounds needed to work for economic reasons, dominant discourse centered attention on the idea that childcare centers were unnecessary because they served the middle-class woman who could easily return to the home. In terms of race, too, as we will see, the prime concern was to create a *white* middle-class home in the postwar environment. To compose this home, segregation was a critical principle that shaped the vision of the middle-class home and the newly formed suburban neighborhood. The spatio-rhetorical debate regarding the childcare center was thus conditioned by much larger priorities for what the postwar home should be and the mothers who should run it.

The first and most overt spatio-rhetorical move was for critics to undo positive connotations characterizing the war nursery as a homelike space. Just as childcare center advocates in wartime had made a new presence for the center to "crowd out" previous negative perceptions, postwar critics harkened their audience's attention back to those prewar depictions of centers as unhealthy, regimented sites that impede a child's development. Dr. Benjamin Spock offers one example in his 1946 *Common Sense Book of Baby and Child Care*. Here, Spock places the subject of "working mothers" in a chapter titled

"Special Problems" and contemplates the effects a mother's decision to work has on her children:

> Some mothers *have* to work to make a living. Usually their children turn out all right, because a reasonably good arrangement is made for their care. But others grow up neglected and maladjusted. . . . You can think of it this way: useful, well-adjusted citizens are the most valuable possession a country has, and good mother care during early childhood is the surest way to produce them. (484)

For readers of Spock's book, the decision seems like an easy one: either mothers place their children in childcare centers and risk them growing into "maladjusted" adults, or they stay home and raise children to become "useful, well-adjusted citizens."

Seconding Spock's claims, editorial writer Edward Crawley resurrects prewar depictions of the center by arguing that it is a "dangerous fallacy" to think that a childcare center can be an "acceptable substitute for a home environment" (8). He bases his critique on the premise that childcare centers are spaces that foster "maladjusted personalities" in children (8). According to Crawley, childcare centers are "fertile ground for delinquencies"; they are sites where children's "earliest and hence most lasting impressions of behavior [a]re gained through the pattern of regimentation directed by the state" (8). Negating wartime understandings of the childcare center as supplement to the home or even a superhome, critics like Crawley rekindled public fears by reminding audiences that this space could likely be an institution that makes children into delinquents.

In addition to regenerating prewar emotional relationships to the childcare center, critics also redefined these sites as places that enabled a different kind of delinquency. Rather than seeing childcare centers as supportive resources for hardworking mothers, critics defined them as places that allowed middle- and upper-class women to shirk their maternal duties and take up less important, even frivolous activities. Cleveland Board of Education president Norma Wulff makes this point: "Those centers were set up originally by the government to help women take war jobs while their husbands were in service. They were not set up as a convenience for women who want to make a little extra money" (qtd. in Stoltzfus 73). Walter MacDonald, a journalist for *World Telegram*, offers a similar assessment in his article "Rich Parents are Chiseling City on Child Care." As the title of the article suggests, women using childcare are "fur-coated mothers" affluent enough to drop off their children in taxi cabs or "1947 automobiles" (P1). From this perspective, the childcare center is a convenience for uncaring middle- and upper-class mothers who do not *need* to work and who neglect the duties of home. These emotive spatial rhetorics revised the respect and love for the childcare center generated during the war and encouraged the public instead to see the center as a site of ill repute, one that enabled mothers to be careless.

MacDonald's journalistic efforts represent yet another particularly stinging condemnation of the childcare center. In articles such as "Child Care Chief's Furor Born in Paris Red Front" and "Reds Howled for Child Care Funds," MacDonald played into postwar America's deepest fears. As the sections above detailed, wartime childcare centers were often depicted specifically as doing the work of the *American* home, cultivating democratic values and even providing a critical space to develop patriotism. MacDonald challenges these spatio-rhetorical definitions by presenting the childcare center as a communist institution. MacDonald calls for the closure of these sites by recasting the childcare center as the "pet of pro-Communist groups," even going so far as to describe the New York childcare activist campaign in particular as one "organized with all the trappings of a Red drive, including leaflets, petitions, protest demonstrations, mass meetings, and hat-passing" ("Reds" P4).

Emboldening MacDonald's attack, Agnes Lewis of the Blue Star Mothers of America also describes childcare centers as "communistic" (13). Lewis argues it is crucial for women to "stay in their own homes to care for their children," for if they do not, the United States will replicate the practice of the Soviet Union (13). Recasting claims such as Baruch's that praised the center for enabling communal responsibility for children, Lewis argues that the center takes children out of the hands of the individual mother, forces her to work, and puts them under the care of multiple caretakers. She continues, "America is built on the bedrock of family ties and we refuse to imitate the Soviet Union, where 6,000,000 children are in such centers while mothers are in forced labor camps" (13). In the infancy of the Cold War era, describing the government-sponsored childcare center as a communist institution instead of an American home was a strategic and powerful blow that was sure to produce new forms of anxiety and suspicion regarding the center and its work. Furthermore, if the childcare center was the place where a group of "red" teachers bred future communists, the counterpoint had to be true: the home functioned as the bastion of American democracy and way of life. Through logical deduction, it was apparent that childcare centers could not raise the next generation of Americans; only mothers could raise good citizens at home.

These overt challenges to childcare centers worked to erase positive feelings for this space as a homelike place and to prompt reevaluation of the center's relevance in postwar American life. Propelling these claims were other spatial rhetorics regarding motherhood and the home that aided in the dismantling process. Most directly, critiques of working mothers dominated the period, and with the condemnations came the celebration of mothers in the home. Joseph Schuyler illustrates this argument when he writes in *Catholic World*, "We place the mother of a home on a pedestal of devotion and honor; a woman in a factory is just another cog in the industrial machine" (30). Elaborating on this move to glorify and reassert the presence of the mother in the home were the claims of figures such as Agnes Meyer, Frederick Crawford, J. H. S. Bossard, and Esther McGinnis. Interestingly, these figures' arguments seem to echo the claims of the turn-of-the-twentieth-century domestic scientists examined in chapter 3 when they reclaimed the space of the postwar home as a site that necessitates the mother's expertise and focused attention. For example, in her *Atlantic Monthly* article "Women Aren't Men," Meyer asserts that the "role of the wife and mother has become infinitely more exacting and difficult," and this increased difficulty is due to the fact that society has "amassed so much factual knowledge of the importance of the home as the basis of society, of the importance of marital relationships, of child guidance and education in general" (33). Thus, the women should not "apologize for being a 'mere housewife,' as so many do," but rather "make society realize that upon the housewife now fall the combined tasks of economist, nutrition expert, sociologist, psychiatrist, and educator" (33). Connecting this argument to the particular exigencies of postwar life and the war's disruptions to the home, Meyer argues that once women assert that "no job is more exacting, more necessary, or more rewarding than that of housewife and mother," they will then "feel free to become once more the moral force of society through the stabilization of the home" (33).[6]

Crawford contributes to the refrain that women must reclaim motherhood and promote the home as a sacred space. In his contribution to the collection *American Women in the Postwar World*, he writes, "The home is the basic American unit. Homemakers are essential to the morale and well-being of male workers and also are the first line of prevention of juvenile delinquency. A woman who is away ten hours a day cannot do a full-time job of homemaking" (30). Furthering Crawford's argument is J. H. S. Bossard's assertion published in the *Journal of Home Economics*:

> [I]t is vitally important to bring to American womanhood a white glow of appreciation to the role of the homemaker in our rapidly changing society. Homemaking is more than housekeeping. It is more than the acquisition and utilization of skills and aids. It is, in its ultimate essence, the creation of a social situation in which a normal family life may develop. And it is this family life which molds the personalities of its members. It is the homemaker who stands revealed today as the maker of men and of women in an era desperately in need of the best that favorable circumstances can develop from human capacities. (387)

The point was implicit yet clear: there could be no replacement for the home and the mother within it. The exigency and extreme situation of wartime America were now over. It was time to return attention to the home.

While Bossard implicitly references the turmoil of war and the effects it had on the American home and family, McGinnis addresses this point head-on in her 1945 *Journal of Home Economics* article, where she writes, "War intensifies problems, brings separation of families and new places to live, tests the strengths of family ties and the soundness of upbringing. It reveals the weaknesses, the lack of discipline, the overprotection which lead to homesickness, nervous breakdowns, and inability to 'take it'" (193). For McGinnis, the childcare center is not the answer to these problems. Rather, it is only the home that can offer a solution, for as she explains, "The kind of home a person has come from has a powerful influence on character" (193). The home is the sole determiner for a socially accepted personality: "whether a person is outgoing and likable or shy and withdrawn, whether he is able to be demonstrative in his affections or is full of 'touch-me-not' inhibitions" depends on the home the mother has created (193).

This conversation regarding the power and significance of the home might have lost traction had there not been a new material reality on the landscape. But undergirding this attention to the mother, the home, and the glories of homemaking was the physical presence of the victory home. As noted, during the war, many families moved to war-impacted regions and lived in makeshift housing, thus creating a situation in which, by war's end, "there were 3,600,000 families lacking homes" (C. Clark 196). In response to this situation and to the fact that thirteen million service people were returning home (196), there was an absolute building boom after the war. With the National Housing Agency estimating the need for 12.6 million homes to be built (Blandford 378), companies such as Abraham Levitt and Sons took advantage of wartime innovation and mass production to build prefabricated, low-priced homes in postwar suburbs such as Long Island, New York; Park Forest, Illinois; Greenbelt, Maryland; and the aptly named Levittowns in both Pennsylvania and New York. The homes in these planned communities often took the form of the traditional Cape Cod style—a style "reminiscent of early-American saltboxes"—that aimed to make buyers "feel that they were claiming a piece of the American tradition" (Baxandall and Ewen 131). Yet, while the exterior architecture of these homes was traditional, the interior was modern: "each house featured radiant heating, General Electric stove and refrigerator, Bendix washing machine, venetian blinds, and an unfinished attic for future expansion" (131).

The returning veteran and his wife were primed to purchase one of these victory homes. As a 1946 *Monthly Labor Review* article recites, the idea of home ownership is "deeply ingrained in our history, and has been universally accepted and encouraged by business, government, and labor" ("Effect" 561). When the war came to a close, though, this investment gained force. Not only did President Roosevelt identify "the right of every family to a decent home" in his 1944 Second Bill of Rights (part of his State of the Union Address), but the GI Bill also provided returning servicemen with low-cost mortgages and low-interest loans, making the prospect of buying a home a new reality for many American families.

Postwar public discourse and advertisements regarding home ownership and home products were also inflected by Cold War fears of communism and McCarthyism. As Rosalyn Baxandall and Elizabeth Ewen record, the National Association of Manufacturers "sentimentally identified home ownership with patriotism and democracy, touting it as a bulwark against Communist invasion and government interference in private lives" (107). The message here was that a "nation of renters . . . was unstable and un-American" (107). To promote this message, the Federal Housing Administration "assisted private industry in advertising designed to create a suburban home ownership market" by "circulat[ing] literature and pamphlets, sponsor[ing] exhibitions, and cooperat[ing] with local realtors to promote subdivisions" (112). Clifford Clark extends this point, writing, "Popular home magazines, interior decorators, architects, appliance makers, and building-material manufacturers joined" in this "exuberant chorus of optimistic voices" that "fuel[ed] what became the largest surge of home construction since the 1920s" (194). Buying and outfitting a home was the ultimate American postwar dream.

The rhetorical impact of these victory homes must have been significant for all Americans but especially the working mother. Miles Orvell explains that the victory home "existed exclusively" for its "singularity and insularity" because contained within this space was all a family needed (185). Thus, while wartime spatial rhetorics surrounding the childcare center celebrated the dispersion of domestic duty, with the center performing many of the mother's responsibilities, postwar life announced consolidation. This "self-contained world," as Dolores Hayden explains, was "expected to consist of a male breadwinner, female housewife, and their children" (*Redesigning the American Dream* 23). Hayden elaborates on this postwar housing model, assessing that it offered an "architecture of gender, since [these] houses provide[d] settings for women and girls to be effective social status achievers, desirable sex objects, and skillful domestic servants, and for men and boys to be executive breadwinners, successful home handy men, and adept car mechanics" (17). The physical presence of these victory homes thus operated as a spatial rhetoric that called on women to take up specific forms of postwar motherhood and gendered practices.

The figure of the singular, self-contained home was reinforced by the fact that in these planned communities were thousands of homes almost identical in their architecture. Orvell explains that these neighborhoods were so uniform and "efficiently packed with house after house, that a stranger would be hard put to find his or her way into or out of it" (185). As working women were being called to the victory home, then, they were seeing thousands of others in identical circumstances; just like their neighbors, they too were expected to find their place in domestic life. And as many—but not all—made this return, they contributed to the postwar baby boom that started or extended their maternal responsibilities. C. Clark remarks "the phenomenal increase in the birthrate [that rose] from 2.2 births per woman in the 1930s to 3.51 by the end of the 1950s" (205–06). The general feeling of the moment was that owning a home and (re)creating a family life were the right and only choices. If a woman decided to (not needed to) leave the home to work and make use of a childcare center, she would disrupt this new vision of the American dream.

One final point regarding the victory home: the desire for and the act of owning one of these homes certainly signaled the achievement of middle-class existence, and in fact "the middle class grew proportionally larger" during this period, with the "median [annual] family income jump[ing] from $3800 in 1949 to $5700 [in 1959], an increase of about 50 percent" (C. Clark 206). This suburban existence was not just classed, however; it was also raced. As Thomas J. Sugrue explains in "Jim Crow's Last Stand: The Struggle to Integrate Levittown," while the planned community in Levittown, Pennsylvania, attracted a "heterogeneous mix of suburbanites," housing discrimination reigned supreme, making it so that "only 347 of 120,000 new homes were available to blacks" (176). Black families were thus not able to dream this American dream but instead were forced to live in "old, rundown housing, mainly in dense, central neighborhoods left behind by upwardly mobile whites" (176). Moreover, Levitt and Sons was not the only home manufacturer that worked in this way. The pervasiveness of this endeavor is reflected in the fact that the Federal Housing Authority also refused to "approve mortgage funds for integrated communities" (Hayden, *Redesigning the American Dream* 23).[7] The victory home therefore signaled victory for a particular kind of *white* middle-class family and focused attention on the return of the *white* middle-class mother to this space.

The comprehensive function of the emotive spatial rhetorics that both "unstuck" attachments to the childcare center and created bonds with the victory home catalyzed the most significant act in the dissolution of support for working mothers: the closure of the childcare center. Within a year after the war's end, most federally funded and industry-funded centers had closed their doors. The center's presence in large part became an absence. The act of spatial silencing is key here. The support itself was not only gone, but the material reduction and even erasure of the childcare center from the nation's landscape also muffled attention, conversation, and concern.

The withdrawal of this support certainly affected the working mother. However, just because dominant emotive spatial rhetorics helped shut down these centers and called mothers home, it did not mean these women simply stopped working. Historian Howard Dratch records that while the number of women in the workforce did "dip in 1945–47," it quickly "grew beyond war levels" (169). This growth indicates that, more than ever before, mothers needed care for their children outside the home. Without large-scale federal funding, individually owned and operated childcare centers began to emerge around the country. Compared to the war nursery, these new centers decreased in quality and increased in cost, placing a new and different economic and emotional stress on working mothers and their families (169).

Conclusion

This chapter centered on the role *emotive* spatial rhetorics played in the establishment and dismantling of the childcare center in the WWII era by exploring how these rhetorics created (and then strained) emotional ties to the center as a homelike place to which working mothers could entrust their children. At the beginning of the war, the idea of the "motherless home" incited anxiety. The establishment of the childcare center and the spatial rhetorics that surrounded it quelled these concerns and reassured mothers and the public that children were protected and loved in an environment made for them where they could thrive. Once the war was over, though, and when the *country's* need for women to work had passed, dominant spatial rhetorics generated new forms of fear regarding the childcare center and the working mother. During the war, the childcare center took the place of the motherless home, but afterward, there could be no replacement for the home or mother. Dominant spatial rhetorics in the postwar United States remade the white middle-class home and family, and these American institutions could not abide the spatial, financial, and emotional support for the working mother found in the form of the childcare center.

This chapter's analyses revealed how power animated the spatio-rhetorical discussions regarding the childcare center. Edward Soja writes, "We must be insistently aware of how space can be made to hide consequences from us, how relations of power and discipline are inscribed into the apparently innocent spatiality of social life" (*Postmodern Geographies* 6). At first glance, the dismantling of the war nursery may seem to make sense. The exigency had passed; women were no longer needed to contribute to the war effort, so the childcare center should close. However, the seemingly "innocent" closing of these centers does indeed "hide consequences from us." Many postwar mothers still needed and even wanted to work, but their reasons for doing so did not count as much as the national imperative to remake the white middle-class home and return the mother to it. Building from the work of Dolores Hayden, this chapter demonstrates how to inspect both the innocence and consequences of spatiality, exposing how "power struggles" often emerge through the "planning, design, construction, use, and demolition of typical buildings" (*Power* 30). By attending to the creation and demolition of the childcare center, we have observed what Soja would call a "spatial injustice," seeing how the fate of the working mother and her family was in many ways reliant on the raced, classed, and cultured vision that dominant society had for them (*Seeking Social Justice* 73).

As this chapter also detailed, a critical factor in the spatio-rhetorical debate was the generation of emotions to align people with or indispose them to an understanding of the childcare center as a homelike space. The chapter shows how spatial rhetorics appeal to audiences and prompt them to feel a certain way about a space, its activities, and its inhabitants. This emotional attachment, this topophilia, is critical in terms of persuasive effect: how the public felt about the childcare center as a loving, American home or as a regimented, communist institution mattered in terms of the support the public gave to it. Because issues of motherhood, children, and the home often trigger an intense emotional response, it makes sense that this debate generated a "visceral" public, one that "emerge[s] from discourse about boundaries" and "cohere[s] by means of intense feeling[,] . . . draw[ing] attention to how feelings and bodies shape public life" (J. Johnson 2–3). Certainly this debate focused on where the boundaries of the home should be drawn: Could maternal love and domestic duty be dispersed to sites beyond the home? Could other women care for and love working mothers' children? The intense emotions that attended these questions and their answers substantially affected the childcare center's existence. Malin writes that "[t]o understand emotion communicatively is to appreciate the negotiated, public aspects of emotive meaning" (217). This chapter shows how through spatial rhetorics, emotions were deployed, negotiated, and renegotiated as a means of offering support to and then retracting support from working mothers.

Another project of the chapter was to disturb and dimensionalize the dominant vision of the WWII working woman. To be sure, the most recognizable image of the woman worker that persists today is that of Rosie the Riveter in the form of J. Howard Miller's "We Can Do It!" poster (fig. 4.9). The National Archives, which holds the rights to this image, ranks it among its top ten most-requested items (Kimble and Olson 536), and the *Washington Post* has named it the "most overexposed item" in the Washington, D.C., souvenir market (qtd. in Kimble and Olson 536). As James J. Kimble and Lester Olson explain, this image has become "a modern American legend," and it suggests how, in WWII, women "bravely and patriotically" turned "manpower into woman power" (534). This chapter counters Miller's "Rosie" with the image of the *mother* Rosie displayed in figure 4.1: the woman who attempted both to "hol[d] the pneumatic riveter" and "rock the cradle—at the same time" (Wetherill 634). Indeed, during the war this image represented millions of mothers who came to the war plant with much different concerns than a single or married woman without young children would have.

This chapter placed in the foreground the figure of the mother and troubled the idea that patriotism was the prime exigency for these women. Issues of economics and class played a major role in why mothers decided to work. While the chapter focused on these concerns, there could be more emphasis on how

Fig. 4.9. "We Can Do It!" poster. J. Howard Miller, Westinghouse Electric Corporation, 1942.

race and culture animated women's work and motherhood during this time, and more research should certainly be conducted on this score. Whiteness "haunts" this chapter, as the figure of the white mother and white American home functioned as an unarticulated premise for many of the arguments regarding the necessity of the childcare center during and after the war (Kennedy et al. 19). Building on the work of Vicki Ruiz, Naomi Quiñonez's research helps to complicate and nuance the vision of the WWII woman worker. Quiñonez explores the fact that numbers of these Rosies were actually *Rositas* and considers that, for many Mexican American women, the war offered them new opportunities: "the percentage of Mexican American women in clerical and sales positions increased from 10.1 in 1930 to 23.9 in 1950," giving these women access to "white-collar positions [that] were heretofore unattainable by most Mexican American women" (250). Quiñonez thus concludes that through the process of taking on these new positions, many Mexican American women were able to "step out of their traditions and take on new customs and expand their experiences and ideas of the world" (250).

Maureen Honey, however, resists celebrating the WWII era for women of color, reminding her readers in *Bitter Fruit: African American Women in World War II* that "few areas of American life were integrated at that time, and employers could routinely avoid hiring workers they considered inferior" (Introduction 8). Women of color certainly experienced the "double bind" of racism and sexism during this period. For black women in particular, new opportunities may have opened up for them during the war, but these women often "found themselves at the bottom of the list when it came time to fill well-paying positions" (8). For black mothers, even though some childcare centers highlighted the fact that their integrated sites reflected "democracy in action" (Budd 58), centers were often segregated or caused black families to feel "less welcome" than white mothers and their children ("Historic American Buildings Survey" 29). Even more troubling is the fact that after the war, the focus once again centered on the white middle-class home and the white middle-class mother within it. As Honey explains, "not only were black women excluded from the mainstream rhetorical picture" that the back-to-the-home movement promoted, but they also "were not in an economic position to give up gainful employment for a full-time homemaker role" (Introduction 11). The racism that shaped the postwar housing boom also "made the nonworking suburban housewife ideal of the mid-forties a particularly alienating, largely unattainable goal for African Americans" (11). Thus, the story of Rosie as a working mother is told quite differently when the assumption of whiteness is revoked and we investigate how racism, classism, and sexism inflected *these* Rosies' experiences.

Finally, this chapter's findings speak loudly to exigencies of our twenty-first-century context, for discussions about working motherhood and childcare persist within our national discourse. To be sure, the numbers of working mothers have continued to rise: a 2013 survey from the Bureau of Labor Statistics revealed that 69.9 percent of mothers with children under the age of eighteen worked (Women's Bureau, "Mothers"). And as Catherine Rottenberg reports, the strains of being a mother and a worker become especially acute for women of color and working-class white women:

> [S]tatistics show that in 2009, 27.5 percent of African American women, 27.4 percent of Hispanic women, and 13.5 percent of white

women were living below the poverty line. Moreover, 35.1 percent of
households headed by single moms were food insecure at some point
in 2010, meaning that they didn't have enough food at all times for
an active, healthy life. Many working mothers are working double
shifts, night shifts, or two to three jobs just in order to provide for
their families. (159)

The increase in working motherhood, however, has not brought on affordable, high-quality childcare. Sheryl Sandberg, author of *Lean In: Women, Work, and the Will to Lead*, finds that "child care costs have risen twice as fast as the median income of families with children. The cost for two children (an infant and a four-year-old) to go to day care is greater than the annual median rent payment in every state in the country" (99). A 2015 White House report offers another vantage point on this issue, stating, "At a time when 60 percent of households with children do not have a stay-at-home parent[,] . . . center-based child care for an infant in three out of five states costs more than tuition and fees at four-year public universities" (Stevenson). In many ways, one could read this situation and conclude that the country is at (yet another) childcare crisis point.

Indeed, former president Barack Obama and leaders within his administration read the situation in this way, and as a heuristic to think through this crisis pointed to the WWII childcare center as an exemplar for replication. In his 2015 State of the Union Address and in a speech given at the University of Kansas that same year, Obama explained that "because it was a national priority" during WWII and because "having women in the workforce was critical," "this country provided universal childcare" ("President Obama"). Obama continued, "Research shows that it was good for the kids and good for the parents." But even though U.S. leaders knew the benefits, and even though, as Obama clarified, "almost every other advanced country on earth continued to do it, learned from us and did it," decision makers in the United States discontinued the practice soon after war's end. Obama refrained from explaining why the country dismantled the wartime childcare center, and instead he asked, "If we knew how to do this back in 1943 and 1944, and here we are in 2015, what's the holdup?"

This chapter offers some answers to what the holdup might be when it comes to providing working mothers and their families with affordable, high-quality childcare. As I have shown, when those in power needed and wanted women to work, they made spatial and indeed emotional changes: they built childcare centers; they offered take-out dinner and laundry services; they ensured children were well cared for and happy; and they composed discourses that assuaged anxieties around working motherhood and the dispersal of domestic duty. When those in power did not want or care if women worked or if they preferred to envision and enforce the idea that the best place for children and their mothers was in the home, those spatial and emotional supports for childcare were revoked. This chapter therefore suggests that part of the present-day hesitation may come from a resistance to admitting that the ideal home and ideal mother are not enough; the childcare center is a necessity. The concerns are financial, but they are also spatial and emotional, and until we address all of these concerns, the holdup is likely to continue.

5. Home Work
SPATIAL RHETORICS AND FEMINIST RHETORICAL SCHOLARSHIP

> The production of knowledge about the past, although critical, has not always been an end in itself but rather ... has provided the substantive terms for a critical operation that uses the past to disrupt the certainties of the present and so opens the way for imagining a different future.
> —Joan Wallach Scott, *The Fantasy of Feminist History*, 2011

History, especially feminist history, has heuristic, performative, and political power, for investigation into the past can function, in the words of Joan Wallach Scott, "to disrupt the certainties of the present" and "ope[n] the way for imagining a different future" (34). In this concluding chapter, I build from Scott's comment to consider the futures *Domestic Occupations* helps to make possible. Here, I move beyond the arguments of each individual chapter to the collective projects of the book. I meditate on the contributions this study makes as a whole, and I identify new paths scholars might take by virtue of the work accomplished within this text. The goal of this conclusion, then, is to envision how this spatio-rhetorical history of home and this investigation of women's work might shape new kinds of thinking and new kinds of scholarship. But before I take up these projects, let me offer a brief summary of the study.

A major purpose of *Domestic Occupations* was to offer a (not *the*) rhetorical history of the (white middle-class) American home from 1820 to 1950. My intention was to craft this particular feminist history by attending to the material, ideological, pictorial, emotive, discursive, and embodied site of the home and the ways this site's spatial rhetorics constrained and made possible women's work outside the domestic arena. As I did so, I also composed rhetorical histories of other spaces related to women and their sites of work, such as the school in chapter 2 and the childcare center in chapter 4, and my purpose throughout was to explore how the rhetorical presence of the home shaped women's new work opportunities as schoolteachers, domestic scientists, and World War II laborers on the home front. The objective thus has been to consider how understandings of the home and experiences within it inflected particular women's career opportunities, focusing on the complex rhetorical operations that at times tethered them to home and at others freed them to explore different career paths.

Throughout each chapter, I elaborated on the definition of spatial rhetorics I first identified in the introduction, and I considered how each case study offered specific insights into spatio-rhetorical practice. That is, I explored how women's work was affected by the gendering of space, the opportunities and constraints for ethos development, and the management of emotion. Certainly the focus on gender, ethos, and emotion in each respective chapter does not mean these concepts *only* pertain to the case study they are attached to. These concepts could also move across and beyond their particular chapters. For instance, chapter 2 explores the spatio-rhetorical process that regendered the school from masculine prison to feminine home and consequently enabled women to enter it and become teachers. But the chapter also suggests that as women moved into the newly renovated and regendered school, the collective professional identity—the ethos—of the teacher changed: when the school was composed as a site for corporal punishment, the schoolmaster was its executioner. But when the school was recomposed as a homelike space, the ethos of the teacher changed. The teacher needed to be one who would love and care for students, who could "keep school" like she would "keep house."

The same holds true for the ways emotions inflected spatial definitions and practices studied throughout this book. To be sure, the childcare center debate was distinguished by how interlocutors attempted to create and break emotional bonds to this space by defining it as a home or as a communist institution, but domestic scientists also contended with such emotional ties. Remember that Ellen Richards worked assiduously to divest the home of its traditional emotive character, writing, "Love is all right, but it is not today enough to keep a house" ("Wanted" 10). And the gendering process observed in chapter 2 can also be identified in chapter 3: one could easily argue that domestic scientists regendered the home from a feminine space of love and comfort to a masculine site of scientific experimentation. Thus, the rhetorical focus of each chapter elucidates how spatial rhetorics animate ideas about gendering, ethos, and emotion, but these concerns could also have been emphasized within other chapters as well.

Why Write (More) Rhetorical Histories of Space?

As I note above, this study can be read as a rhetorical history of the home (and the school and the childcare center). In bringing the study to a close, I am interested in thinking through these equations: Why write more histories like this one? What are the benefits of composing rhetorical histories of space and exploring further the significance of spatial rhetorics? In this section, I offer four responses, building on the arguments generated in each individual chapter and across the study as a whole.

First, investigations of spatial rhetorics underscore the ways that spaces—our ideas about them, our inhabitations within them, our outfitting of them—shape our experiences. As Kenneth Burke understood, scene matters. And chapter 2 of this study makes clear that when the school was defined as a public, dilapidated, and dangerous prison, the white middle-class woman could not occupy it. But when the school was renovated in material, structural, and ideological ways into a space that was clean and private, when it became a place for comfort instead of punishment, the school then resembled the white middle-class home, and, as such, it was a space the woman could enter. Certainly this study should prompt scholars to consider how other kinds of spatial creation, practice, renovation, and redefinition elicit and craft certain kinds of experiences.

Recent work in public memory studies further attunes us to these issues regarding the coupling of space and experience. For example, in "Spaces of Remembering and Forgetting: The Reverent Eye/I at the Plains Indian Museum," Greg Dickinson, Brian Ott, and Eric Aoki set out that their work is to "identify the implications of activating memory" in the space of this museum, thinking specifically about how "visitors experience (i.e., 'read') the symbolic and material dimensions of [this] spac[e]" (28). Carole Blair elaborates on this point as she assesses the ways memorial sites "do obvious work on the body. They direct the vision to particular features, and they direct—even control—the vector, speed, or possibilities of physical movement" (46). Blair does not argue, however, that memorial spaces are the only sites to do this work. Memorial sites are just one genre that exposes "rhetoric's materiality," and she suggests that we can consider how sites beyond the memorial also do the work of "construct[ing] communal space, prescrib[ing] pathways, and summon[ing] attention" (28).

Working alongside Blair, this project explores how spaces "ac[t] on the whole person of the audience" (49–50). Yet, divergently, *Domestic Occupations* offers an important perspective on spatial rhetoric by *not* focusing on extraordinary or prominent memorial spaces that we expect to manifest great care in terms of their construction and engineering inhabitants' experiences. This study examines instead the everyday: the home, school, and childcare center. By doing so, it responds to Dickinson's prompting to "take the banal seriously" ("Joe's Rhetoric" 23). Such attention is important, Dickinson claims, because mundane sites, by virtue of their regular inhabitations, "provide the material/rhetorical resources of which, in which[,] and through which we create our bodies and ourselves" (6). This emphasis on the everyday is also a feminist move. As Nan Johnson writes, feminists "have seen the problematic underside of 'tradition' and the 'exemplary' and headed steadily in the direction of the ordinary and everyday ways that rhetoric and writing are experienced" ("History" 15). *Domestic Occupations* prompts feminist rhetorical investigations of other spaces we encounter every day—meeting rooms, restaurants, playgrounds, shopping malls, doctor's offices, laundromats, and athletic fields—and invites analyses that say something significant about how we experience space and make paths through our world.

Second, by attending to spatial rhetorics, we can conceive of how they allow for or bar access to particular spaces. As chapter 3 elucidates, turn-of-the century aspiring women scientists could more easily gain entry to laboratories on college campuses if they made clear that their application of science would (re)turn them to the home. Such attention to spatial access (and constraint) speaks directly to important discussions today within disability studies. As the authors of "Multimodality in Motion" explain, "[t]raversing public and private spaces inevitably means finding a way to access those spaces. This simple fact is thrown into relief for those who experience barriers to access, and often [goes] unnoticed by those whose bodies, minds, abilities, and resources allow them to occupy the role of the default user" (Yergeau et al.).

From a disability studies perspective, one example of how spaces can be redesigned for greater access is at Gallaudet University. Here, architects have created "DeafSpace"—space engineered so that it is attuned to how deaf people communicate and how they "'read' the activities of their surroundings . . . through an acute sensitivity of visual and tactical cues such as the movement of shadows, vibrations, or even the reading of subtle shifts in the expression/position of others around them" ("DeafSpace"). A goal for DeafSpace is to build environments that enable "spatial awareness 'in 360 degrees' and facilitate orientation and wayfinding." Such spatio-rhetorical attention underscores not just the flexibility of space but also the imaginative possibilities for spatial creation so that access, inhabitation, and communication are possible in ways they may not have been before. As David Harvey writes in *Spaces of Hope*, "the infinite array of possible spatial orderings holds out the prospect of an infinite array of possible social worlds" (161). This study, then, helps to set the course for thinking through questions of spatial access and how rhetors can imagine possible social worlds through the deployment of spatial rhetorics.

Third, it is critical to repeat the point that spatial rhetorics offer insight into the workings of power and the politics of spatial occupation. Of course, power animates spatial relations and designations. As Foucault notes, when we write histories of space, we are composing "histor[ies] of powers . . . from the great strategies of geo-politics to the little tactics of the habitat" (149). Chapter 4 of this study elucidates Foucault's point, for when the government wanted mothers to work during the war, it provided childcare centers to which women could entrust their children, and it participated in a spatio-rhetorical campaign that defined these spaces as homes where children would be safe, loved, and happy. When the war was over and it was expected that women would to return to the home, a new dominant discourse emerged—this one defined by spatial silencing. Through closing centers, the government and industry leaders helped to shut down conversations about working mothers and the supports they needed to survive and thrive. Chapter 4, especially, prompts us to think about spatial silencing through the demolition of childcare centers, but it also calls on us to consider how power and politics infiltrate and inflect other spaces.

Indeed, it is not difficult to pinpoint sites of spatial contest. The list is long, including such spaces as Native American lands, lunch counters, Wall Street, Alcatraz, busses, and even bathrooms. In fact, as I compose this chapter, a virulent debate is being waged over how transgender people should (or should not) occupy bathrooms designated as men's or women's. As Emma Green writes in her 2016 *Atlantic* article, "America's Profound Gender Anxiety," bathrooms are "one of the last remaining gendered spaces in public life, where women and men are divided and body parts exposed. And transgender people consistently struggle with bathroom access—which can lead to higher rates of suicide—making this a key issue for advocates." The legislative battles over bathroom bills and the experiential understanding that bathrooms are sociopolitical spaces marked especially by gender reveal the poignancy of claims made by theorists such as Henri Lefebvre and Mary Ryan, who have argued that "the appropriation of the social spaces of everyday life is an essential precondition for the political empowerment of subordinated groups" (Ryan, *Women* 92). By conducting historiographic and present-day studies of spatial rhetorics, we see *how* this appropriation occurs (or does not occur) through overt maneuvers of occupation, renovation, and legal redress as well as subtle acts of spatial definition and description.

Fourth, this study reveals how spaces help to constitute specific kinds of gendered, raced, classed, and cultured ethos for their inhabitants. Even more, though, it pushes this point further to explore how spaces themselves not only impart identities to their inhabitants but also possess such identities themselves. A prime concern throughout the main chapters is to consider the ways the home was (re)constructed as a white middle-class space and to enunciate how whiteness was the prevailing assumption when interlocutors were composing and wrestling with specific understandings of home. In taking up such work, this study speaks alongside Tammie Kennedy, Joyce Irene Middleton, and Krista Ratcliffe's *Rhetorics of Whiteness: Postracial Hauntings in Popular Culture, Social Media, and Education.* Here, they write that whiteness often "haunts" discourse (19), and the authors offer this example to add depth to this point: "[i]f a sentence states that a man walks down the street, he is assumed to be white; thus, whiteness haunts the term *man* as a racial identity marker and, thus, functions as an unstated norm" (19–20). But as these scholars attest, and as this study works to prove, "whiteness can haunt more than just a term" (20). *Domestic Occupations* examines how whiteness haunts spaces. This study has attempted to state the unstated assumption of spatial whiteness, to consider what it meant to compose the white middle-class home over and again—differently yet repeatedly—and to interrogate how this assumption of whiteness has both ignored the experiences of others and shaped the gendered, raced, cultured, and classed experience of the women who have occupied and attempted to move from this space. More work can and should be done on this score, so that rhetoricians can gain a deeper sense of how rhetorics cause spaces to gain and lose gendered, raced, classed, and cultured identities of their own, and how these identities animate one another and act on those who attempt to enter and dwell within them.

Spatial Rhetorics and the Home

As one of its prime endeavors, *Domestic Occupations* reveals how, in three specific instances, the space of the white middle-class home was defined and redefined in ways that greatly affected possibilities for women's work. A key understanding culled from this study is that the ideological figure and material reality of the home *changes* across time and circumstance. This study makes clear that home has not always been what we might think it was. To be sure, the home was defined throughout the nineteenth and twentieth century as we would expect: it was as a site of idyllic care and comfort, separate from the bustle and business of public and civic life. But, as chapter 3 illustrates, domestic scientists rejected this understanding, arguing that the home could also be a site of serious scientific experimentation. Extending this point, *Domestic Occupations* also demonstrates that spatial rhetorics can *transfer* traditional understandings of home to sites other than the physical space of the family residence. Chapters 2 and 4 describe how other spaces became homes, and when they did, new opportunities opened up for women. But the home has been much more than a spatial parallel to the school that enabled women to become teachers; it has been more than a site for scientific experimentation; and it has been more than a space for domestic replication to which working mothers entrusted their children. So where else might we look to unpack the rhetorical importance of the home? How else might we inspect the spatio-rhetorical renovations to the home and the significance of these revisions?

Domestic Occupations invites scholars to think beyond the subjects of this book and to consider how *other* women may have experienced the home. As indicated in chapter 3, domestic service would be one prime place for exploration, but bell hooks's essay "Homeplace (a site of resistance)" offers another telling example. Responding to the idea that white women often attempt to escape the home and domestic duty, hooks identifies a different meaning of home for black women. She underscores the importance of home for these women and their families, writing that the "construction of a homeplace, however fragile and tenuous . . . had a radical political dimension" because here was a site where "one could freely confront the issue of humanization, where one could resist" (42). hooks continues, "Black women resisted by making homes where all black people could strive to be subjects, not objects, where we could be affirmed in our minds and hearts despite poverty, hardship, and deprivation, where we could restore to ourselves the dignity denied us on the outside in the public world" (42). hooks's definition of home is much different from those investigated in this study. For hooks, home is a space of resistance that can "heal the wounds inflicted by racist domination" (42).[1] Reading hooks's words confirms that understandings of the home are intersectional and that the woman's relationship to it changes given her raced, cultured, classed, and gendered position. Further investigations into the rhetoricity of the home and the spatial rhetorics that animate it would pursue concerns such as hooks's and could, pushing this point even further, take (at least) four additional forms.

First, we might consider other important moments when the home was under debate and reconstruction, such as the material feminist movement. As referenced in chapter 1, Dolores Hayden's *The Grand Domestic Revolution: A History of Feminist Designs for American Homes, Neighborhoods, and Cities* and Polly Wynn Allen's *Building Domestic Liberty: Charlotte Perkins Gilman's Architectural Feminism* take up this subject, investigating how figures like Charlotte Perkins Gilman, Melusina Fay Peirce, and Victoria Woodhull devised a form of feminist activism that defined domestic work as *real* work and imagined how the home could be renovated through "architectural innovation" to create a better work environment for women (P. Allen 23). As Hayden writes, these women enacted this project by "develop[ing] new forms of neighborhood organizations, including housewives cooperatives, as well as new building types, including the kitchenless house, the day care center, the public kitchen, and the community dining club. They also proposed ideal feminist cities" (*Grand Domestic Revolution* 3). Both Hayden's and Allen's exemplary studies, however, were published in the 1980s, and while feminist rhetoricians have explored the *educational* and *civic* value of sites such as settlement houses, we might return to this subject and expand it by thinking about the spatio-rhetorical importance of material feminists' arguments, exploring how their physical changes to the home offered new arguments about women's work and domesticity.[2]

Another site of study would be to consider the home from the perspective of domestic violence, with feminist rhetoricians asking questions such as these: How have traditional perceptions of the home and spatio-domestic realities prevented women from escaping violence, reporting the crimes against them, and advocating for themselves and their families? Conversely, how do spatial rhetorics that define and describe the home inhibit audiences from listening to these women's claims? Such a project would investigate how the traditional perception of the home as a site of care, comfort, and safety—a space for familial intimacy and privacy—stands in the way of reporting, intervention, and advocacy. In other words, this work would examine how dominant understandings of home perpetuate the idea that this site is a space of "absolute freedom and ontological security" instead of a "site of fear and isolation, a prison" (Mallett 71).[3] Additional attention might also be paid to the spatio-rhetorical role of the shelter and how this space is meant to offer the refuge, care, and protection the home is supposed to provide but does not. Given the fact that one in four women experience domestic violence at the hands of an intimate partner and that three women are killed every day by current or former male partners ("30 Shocking Domestic Violence Statistics"), Gloria Steinem's assessment rings true: "the home in our country is the single most dangerous place for women" (qtd. in Starr). Feminist rhetoricians thus might consider the role that spatial rhetorics play in allowing this space to be inhabited in this way and how they could work to intervene in this spatial discourse and violent practice. More globally, feminist scholars would unpack how "the hegemonic representation of home ... comes at great cost to those who dwell and belong differently" (McAlister, "Ten Propositions" 119).

Spatial rhetorics of home could further be explored by examining how these rhetorics operate to establish and disrupt traditional perceptions of family life and familial relations, especially when it comes to *masculine* gendered practices. To the latter point, Jennifer Courtney offers one compelling example in her study of twenty-first-century domestic advice books targeted at men that "complicate the tradition of domestic counsel by presenting cleaning tips with an unexpected masculine ethos" (67). Courtney explains that these texts invite men to take up new "domestic behaviors," all the while "alleviating anxiety" that they are sacrificing their masculinity by so doing (67).[4] Feminist scholars might then turn more attention to this emergent genre to examine how domestic activities are engendered masculine so that readers see that this work is what "real men" do (71).

Fourth and finally, domestic spatial rhetorics invite investigations that couple space with sex and sexuality, the work of Joan Faber McAlister being illustrative on this score. In "Figural Materialism: Renovating Marriage through the American Family Home," McAlister traces the emergence of the post–World War II master bedroom as an "intimate retreat" that was physically larger and distanced from the other bedrooms in the home (293). McAlister underscores the rhetorical significance of this change to the home's floor plan, arguing that it made the "sex life of the married couple highly visible" and suggested that couples now "had access to erotic pleasures once denounced as threats to monogamous marriage without abandoning the obligations that underlie [its] respectability" (294). While the focus in this particular essay is on heteronormative sexual practice, feminist scholars might continue to explore how architectural change and even trends in décor say much about the sexual lives of the people who inhabit these ever-shifting domestic spaces. The four examples identified here gesture toward the possibilities beyond those studied in *Domestic Occupations*, and they reveal how generative this conversation about *domestic* spatial rhetorics could be.

Women, Work, Space

While a main project for this study has been to consider the operations and significance of spatial rhetorics in general and spatial rhetorics of home more particularly, this objective was always paired with a dedicated investment in the ways these rhetorics shaped particular aspects of women's experience: their working lives and their ability to obtain new career opportunities. Thus, as noted in chapter 1, the term *occupation* plays a dual role in this study, as it means *both* the inhabitation of a space *and* a kind of work. The chapter also explains that the three instances of women's spatial negotiations studied here do not exhaust opportunities for research. The historical period from 1820 to 1950 was alive with rich conversations about women's work both outside and inside the home. Interlocutors debated issues of compensation, working conditions, and professional opportunities; they set out new career paths and professional training; they composed career advice books and "vocational autobiographies"; and they conducted research on who the working woman was and what the public's concerns for her work should be (Applegarth, "Personal Writing" 531). *Domestic Occupations* attends to the ways that women became teachers, domestic scientists, and wartime workers. It gains significance, though, by specifically investigating how the physical and ideological construction of the home shaped expectations about the women who should occupy it and whether or not they could work outside it.

The examinations within *Domestic Occupations* that explore the spatio-rhetorical dimensions of women's work in these three arenas advance a wider conversation about the rhetorical complexity of women's work experiences. As noted in chapter 1, this book speaks directly to Sarah Hallenbeck and Michelle Smith's assessment of feminist rhetorical scholarship. They write that feminist rhetoricians have attended primarily to women's civic engagements, the barriers they faced when entering public debate, and the strategies they leveraged to shape conversations of civic import. Hallenbeck and Smith argue, however, that such attention to women's rhetorical activities has created a "too-narrow focus on national citizenship and civic participation"—one that distracts us from considering how women argued for basic economic sustenance, financial independence, and professional advancement (205). They urge scholars to consider instead "work-related" rhetorics and to "unearth 'work' as a historically situated, rhetorically constructed, materially contingent project" (201). *Domestic Occupations* helps to realize what this new scholarly emphasis might look like, especially by meditating upon the *spatial* dimensions of women's work and exploring how women's ties to the home shaped their access to particular kinds of work spaces. In this section, I consider what a spatio-rhetorical emphasis adds to this emerging conversation around women's work.

Beyond the School, Laboratory, and War Plant
Domestic Occupations prompts scholars to look beyond the school, laboratory, and war plant to consider whether and how women's changing ties to the home affected other work-related contexts, thus inviting more research that explores how work spaces have been made (un)acceptable for women's entrance. It is important to remember that the quotation that propelled this study was one that created a spatial equation between the home and the school. At the opening of his school for girls in 1822, Joseph Emerson set out, "Next to the domestic circle, the schoolroom is unquestionably the most important sphere of female activity" (8). Women could be teachers—they could move from home to school—because the school was a space similar to the home. Interrogating this idea of spatial parallels, scholars might examine how spatial (dis)similarities have affected particular kinds of women's work. Virginia Penny's 1863 claim offers yet another example for investigation. In *The Employments of Women: A Cyclopaedia of Woman's Work*, she asserts, "Many men would banish women from the editor's table and author's table, from the store, the manufactory, the workshop, the telegraph office, the printing case, and every place, except the school room, sewing table, and kitchen" (vii). While Penny identifies the occupational spaces (un)available to women, the purpose of her book is to challenge these spatial barriers and to "counter the false opinion that exists in regard to the occupations suitable for women" so that "women have free access to all those in which they may engage" (vii). Penny writes that she would "love to see thrown open to women the door of every trade and profession in which they are capable of working" (vii). Penny's goal, then, is to argue for women's professional access, and feminist rhetoricians might explore how she and others argue for that access through texts like Penny's five-hundred-page encyclopedia. The broader concern here is to inspect more closely how rhetors have defined, equated, or distinguished work spaces in ways that informed possibilities for women's work and of course to consider how race, culture, class, sexuality, and ability status inflected these options.

Feminist rhetoricians can certainly pursue such investigations by looking back to history, but we also might turn attention to the spatial rhetorics that continue to animate and engender work environments today. Much like they were for Ellen Richards and her colleagues, twenty-first-century scientific workplaces are often still hostile to women and minorities. Such hostility was evidenced by a 2014 survey reporting that "70 percent of women scientists had faced sexual harassment while working in the field, and 26 percent had experienced sexual assault" (Beck). As another more specific example, in 2015, British Nobel laureate Tim Hunt argued for sex segregation in laboratories with the reason being that "girls" create "trouble" within these spaces. Hunt went on to explain the trouble that "girl" scientists cause: "you fall in love with them, they fall in love with you and when you criticize them, they cry" (qtd. in Soper). Thus, according to Hunt, allowing women into the lab charges the space with sexual and emotional meaning that prevents real scientific work from being accomplished. Hunt seems to want to reinstate the spatial segregation present at MIT in Richards's time, when, as Richards wrote, she was cordoned off from her peers "very much as a dangerous animal might have been" (qtd. in Stage, "Ellen Richards" 21).

While this call for spatial segregation is disheartening (to say the least) to encounter today, feminist rhetoricians might attend to how women scientists crafted a spatio-rhetorical response to Hunt's assertions. Using the hashtag #distractinglysexy, numbers of women scientists tweeted pictures of themselves in their workplaces poking fun at Hunt's claim that they were distractions to their male colleagues and impediments to the rigorous work accomplished therein. Scientist Sarah Durant, for example, tweeted a picture of herself at work in the field along with a comment: "nothing like a sample tube full of cheetah poop to make you #distractinglysexy"; Ines Varela Silva offered a visual of her taking notes on-site, adding this tweet: "doing fieldwork in Mexico while being #distractinglysexy in between 2 bouts of crying" (Herman); and Danielle Spitzer posted a photo of herself covered from head to toe in a lab suit, tweeting, "It's just really hard working in a coed lab because I'm too distracting to the male scientists #distractinglysexy" (Waxman). Feminist rhetoricians might reflect upon how these women scientists deployed Twitter to situate themselves in their scientific work spaces, purposefully displaying the *un*sexiness of their work. As discursive and visual spatial rhetorics, these tweets reveal moments when women scientists redefined their work spaces and asserted their workplace experience in the face of powerful claims that saw these spaces and experiences otherwise.

Feminization of Professions

The case studies of *Domestic Occupations* also add dimension to understandings of the feminization of professions by indicating how spatial rhetorics contribute to this gendering and evaluative process. Scholars who pursue such questions often attend not only to who takes up certain kinds of work but also to how gender animates the kinds of activities necessary for a job and the preparation needed to perform it. When an occupation gets defined as feminine; when it requires attributes of care, nurturance, comfort, and service; when it is seen as a natural extension of women's gendered identity; and when it is overpopulated by women, that work often becomes feminized, devalued, and underpaid.

In contrast to the feminization of professions, Sharon Bolton and Daniel Muzio explain that masculine professional status relies on how workers "do gender" in a specific way: they "comply with behavioural and interactional norms that celebrate and sustain a masculine vision of what it is to be a professional . . . thus marginalizing the 'feminine' and devaluing, ignoring and unsupporting the work that women do" (283). Nell Noddings agrees and explicates specific ways that "power and prestige" are cultivated in "masculine" professions: "less and less direct contact between professional and client; highly specialized languages; great monetary expenditures required in preparatory education; an increase in internal talk as contrasted to interaction with the larger community; and an overall exclusivity marked by racism, sexism, and classism" (402).[5] Certainly, the gendering of professions is inflected by such activities, but *Domestic Occupations* also highlights how spatial rhetorics affect this process. The spatio-rhetorical analyses of chapters 2 and 3 especially make clear that when mainly white middle-class women moved into new professions such as teaching or science, they had to contend with (and make use of) the material attributes and ideological understandings of home. Feminist rhetoricians might build from these analyses to investigate how the spatial rhetorics of home translate (or not) into feminized (and masculinized) professional spaces and thereby contribute to the gendering of professional practice. Or more broadly, we might inspect how the spatial rhetorics that circulate through an occupational site invite and expect feminized or masculinized work.

Such an approach could certainly apply to a 2014 report from the Department of Labor revealing that women continue to dominate service professions, disproportionately occupying jobs as secretaries, elementary and middle school teachers, registered nurses, and home health aides ("Most Common

Occupations"). A spatio-rhetorical perspective on these findings would consider how the "gendered geograph[ies]" of the office, school, and hospital (as well as occupational spaces where women do not dominate) help to engender these professions by equating them with (or distancing them from) the home and specific kinds of home work (M. Ryan, *Women* 82). Furthermore, we might consider how these spatial equations contribute to the evaluation of the work conducted therein. As Daphne Spain writes, the home has mainly been seen as the "spatial institution containing the least amount of socially valued knowledge" (235). Feminist scholars should investigate how a spatial relationship to the home might contribute to negative assessments of the work conducted within a space, citing that the spatial activities require minimal intellectual expertise or rigor and should therefore be compensated accordingly.

Women's Work and Feminism

Yet another point of complexity *Domestic Occupations* brings to the fore is the (dis)connections between women's work and feminism. More specifically, this study indicates the complicated ways that woman's spatial relationship to the home can factor into her work possibilities and her feminist politics. In chapter 3, for example, Richards's rhetorics revealed the domestic scientists' wariness of feminism, seeing as they did that any overt alliance with this political stance could damage the public's perception of their scientific work, their access to scientific education, and their ability to compose a professional ethos. Richards was clear in pointing out that domestic science championed the home, not women's rights (C. Hunt, *Life* 285). Chapter 3 also showed how activists for women's education such as M. Carey Thomas and later feminists like Robin Morgan railed against the domestic science project, identifying Richards and her colleagues as "enem[ies]" who operated in conflict with the feminist cause by directing women back to the home (qtd. in Stage, "Home Economics" 1). Thus, for some, articulations of feminism had the potential to impede (domestic) science careers while, for others, tightening ties to the home signaled regressive work opportunities and conservative politics.

Chapter 4 moved in a different direction as it acknowledged a distinction between mothers who needed to work and those who wanted to work. Even if some mothers may have wanted to retake their place in the home after World War II, many could not afford to and therefore depended on the childcare center for their livelihood. While the chapter may have centered more on the mother's *need* to work than on the woman's *right* to work, activists during this period did capitalize on the wartime economy and the work women were performing to question women's traditional ties to the home. Susan B. Anthony II, for example, pursues such a project in her 1943 book *Out of the Kitchen—Into the War: Women's Winning Role in the Nation's Drama*. Anthony zeroes in on what the exigencies of the war have made possible for women, citing that World War II is the "historical turning point which put millions of women in pants" (97). A central point for Anthony is to pit the home against the world of work by defining woman's home ties as a sign of fascism and her release from the home as an indicator of democracy. She writes,

> Democracy's task is to elevate woman so that the world is her home—not the home her world.... Democracy must encourage women to be servants of the world. The conditions of war are definitely pulling women out of the house into the world. The peace must not push them back into the house, unless they wish to go there.... Woman's place is in the factory, the office, in the professions, in the fields and at the council table—wherever human labor, human effort, is needed to produce and create. (244)

Anthony concludes her book with these words: "America must unlock millions of doors that have imprisoned millions of women. Women must be let out—liberated from the homes, so that they can take their place in the war of the world today—and in the work of the world tomorrow" (246). For Anthony, women's work opportunities, feminism, and democracy are intimately linked, and central to their shared concerns is spatio-rhetorical politics.

Domestic Occupations thus calls on scholars to explore the often-thorny relationship between feminism and work and to attend to how allegiances to the home shape this relationship. Scholars might investigate the fraught battles for the Equal Pay Act and Equal Rights Amendment as well as feminist activists' involvement in the labor movement and, conversely, labor union leaders' involvement in the feminist movement. They might research advocacy groups and unions such as 9to5, National Association of Working Women; the International Ladies' Garment Workers Union; the Women's Trade Union League; the National Consumers League; United Farm Workers; the Women's Bureau; the National Federation of Business and Professional Women's Clubs; and the United Cannery, Agricultural, Packing, and Allied Workers of America (to name just a few). And they might examine the rhetorical interventions of leaders within these organizations and others such as Lucy Parsons, Leonora O'Reilly, Mother Jones, Lucy Gonzales Parsons, Rosina Tucker, Luisa Moreno, Maida Springer-Kemp, Jessie de la Cruz, Elizabeth Gurley Flynn,

Dolores Huerta, and Emma Tenayuca. Studies that triangulate work, feminism, and spatial rhetorics would add depth and nuance to understandings of the difficult negotiations that women from varied raced, classed, and cultured backgrounds often have had to make as they argue for their right to sustain themselves and their families and to pursue work they need and desire.

Emotive Spatial Rhetorics and Working Motherhood
The final concern of this section is to reflect upon how *Domestic Occupations* emboldens feminist rhetorical inquiries that inspect the strains (and the joys) of working motherhood. One of the main reasons why women's spatial ties to the home have traditionally been so strong is because of the emotional labor they are expected to perform there. Women are to generate what Andrew Downing, quoted in chapter 2, called "home feeling" (79) and to foster what Tuan has defined as "topophilia," or love and affection for, in this case, domestic space. Women have been seen as the chief cultivators of these dominant and distinctive domestic attributes largely for one reason: their children. Children are the prime reasons for the mother making the home into a loving and caring space where these inhabitants can grow and thrive. Surely, as chapter 4 makes clear, public debates about the "motherless home" were emotionally charged because the mother was not present to give it the "home feeling" that children needed.

The tensions between the working mother and the emotional domestic environment she is expected to create for her children are more implicit in chapters 2 and 3. In chapter 2, women could move from the home to the school because new pedagogical practices deemed it fit for women to transfer their "inherent" abilities to love and care for children in the home to the newly renovated space of the school, where they would now love and care for their students as "mother-teachers." We might pause, though, to consider how, in chapter 3, domestic scientists even more covertly worked at the intersections of working motherhood, emotion, and the home.

In large part, domestic scientists chose to conduct their work in the home because, by doing so, they would not be seen as shirking their domestic duties. We can assume, then, that a reason these women sought to conduct their experiments at home was because their children were there. What I find so interesting in domestic scientists' writing, however, is the limited presence or, more accurately, the absence of their children. In books like Margaret Dodd's *Chemistry of the Household*, for example, children are subjects to be studied. In a water experiment, say, it is the work surrounding the care of children—such as drawing a bath—that gets examined, experimented on, and perfected. Largely absent from the domestic scientists' texts are indications of the actual, unpredictable presence of children or the emotional dimension of motherhood. Children of domestic scientists do not seem to fight with their siblings or wake up in the middle of the night; they also don't seem to snuggle, act silly, or practice their "I love you's." The absence of children and the emotions they trigger within the home is unsurprising: domestic scientists wanted to display themselves as rigorous scientists, not loving mothers. They needed the home to be seen as a site for science, and the child's presence in their spatial rhetorics would remind readers that the home could be a site for love, not scientific experimentation.

Given this explicit and implicit theme throughout all of this study's chapters, feminist scholars might dedicate more attention to the rhetorical dimensions of working motherhood and the *emotive* spatial rhetorics that animate these women's lives. That is, feminist scholars might explore how working mothers negotiate, manage, and recast the emotive spatial rhetorics that shape their occupational and mothering experiences. Twenty-first-century working mothers certainly experience the spatial anxiety of needing to be two places at once. Metaphorically, we are still asked to "hol[d] the pneumatic riveter" and "rock the cradle—at the same time" (Wetherill 634). As such, feminist scholars might consider how working mothers' narratives are often brimming with emotive spatial rhetorics in which they articulate how their expected presence at home and at work elicits often-conflicting feelings of anxiety, joy, fear, hope, anger, resentment, love, triumph, disappointment, and fatigue.

Key to these types of investigations, however, would be for feminist scholars to remember, as this study attempts to do, that the emotions spatial experiences generate are tied to material realities. That is, this study suggests that the emotional stress working mothers undergo is likely catalyzed by material absence and structural inequity. Emotive spatial rhetorics are often indicators of the need for material and structural supports such as automatic and fair parental leave policies; excellent, affordable, and accessible childcare; convenient and comfortable lactation rooms; and flexible scheduling and possibilities for working remotely. Seeing working mothers' emotive spatial rhetorics as evidence of individual, idiosyncratic felt experience turns attention away from the collective, material, systemic circumstances that mothers across differences face. We cannot pretend that the emotional stresses working mothers deal with are not a consequence of inadequate structural and material support. Lack of this support is what elicits emotive spatial rhetorics and what makes or breaks working mothers and their families.

Spatio-Rhetorical Research Methods

The final project for this conclusion is to reflect on the research methods that propelled this study. I engage in this reflection largely in response to Barbara L'Eplattenier's call for rhetoric and composition scholars, in particular, to "incorporate more explicit discussions of our primary research methods into our historical research" so that those in our field can "highligh[t] the uniqueness of archival study and creat[e] the depth and breadth of knowledge required to begin generalizing about the tools our discipline needs and uses" (68). In looking back at my research process—a process marked by calculation, planning, and thoughtfulness as well as failure and serendipity—I offer three significant insights that might help others pursue spatio-rhetorical research of their own. However, before identifying these insights, I begin by laying out my basic process and my major challenges.

Most obviously, my objective for *Domestic Occupations* was to understand and assess the spatial rhetorics that affected real, three-dimensional, historical spaces that I believed made an impact on working women's lives. My interest in these spaces, though, was at the level of the collective and general, not the individual and particular. That is, I was not aiming to recover specific spatial experiences; I was not, for instance, analyzing the spatial rhetorics of a *particular* home, school, laboratory, or childcare center. Instead, I was attempting to unearth a more general spatial experience. My goal was to understand how these spaces, in general, were constructed and understood. The spatial rhetorics I attempted to discern, then, were the dominant spatial rhetorics that defined and assessed what schools, homes, and childcare centers were and could be. In each chapter, I attempted to identify, as well, how interlocutors intervened in these dominant spatio-rhetorical narratives: the male schoolteachers who tried to recover and masculinize the feminized classroom; the domestic scientists who remade the home into the lab; the childcare center proponents who sought to maintain the idea that the center was a home after the war had passed. While I dedicated more time and attention to these interventionist spatial rhetorics in some chapters than in others, a priority of mine was to understand the resistant spatial rhetorics that tried to renovate popular and powerful ideas about a space's meaning and operation.

A number of methodological problems emerged as I set out to recover these collective yet historically situated spaces and to inspect the spatial rhetorics that defined and shaped them. To be sure, any historian worth her stripes would say that a first methodological step should be to visit that research space because, as Gesa Kirsch would argue, "being there in the physical location is invaluable" to assessing the rhetorical situation and significance of your artifacts (20). Of immediate concern for this study, though, was that there was not, as noted above, just one space to inspect. Instead I was interested in how spatial rhetorics created a general and dominant understanding of these sites. Another issue was that it was difficult to find homes, schools, home laboratories, and childcare centers that were still standing and maintained from the periods I was interested in. Because these were (in many ways) ordinary spaces, because their materiality (and real estate) was substantial, and because many of these sites (like the World War II childcare centers) were purposely demolished, they could not be visited and studied.[6] Finally, as the investigations of this study illustrate, spaces change over time. We cannot return to the nineteenth-century school, the turn-of-the-twentieth-century home laboratory, or the wartime childcare center. Even if they had been preserved, they would be different in this twenty-first-century context—not only in terms of their use but also in terms of their surroundings. The spatio-rhetorical scene would have changed dramatically.

Given these objectives and challenges, my methodological work was to identify artifacts that would offer clues to people's spatial experiences, perceptions, and assessments of these sites in the time periods under examination. What I found was that to learn about space and spatial rhetorics, I had to be creative with my artifact gathering and analysis. In stepping back now and reviewing my process as I conclude this study, I discern three key methods that enabled me to gain a deep understanding of what spatial rhetorics are, how they operate, and how to make sense of them.

First, to capture the ways people argued over, discussed, and experienced the spaces I chose for this project, I had to make use of a range of artifacts and documents. As I detailed in chapter 1, my method was multimodal and, I should add, multigenre. This study could not have taken shape had I relied on only one mode or one genre; focusing just on the newspaper article or the photograph would not have been enough. Instead I needed to identify the various ways these spaces were represented and engaged: through personal letters, school reports, and conference proceedings, as well as photographs, drawings, exhibits, architectural plans, and more. Additionally, a key part of this multimodal, multigenre research method was to attend to the emotional atmosphere rhetors attributed to a space. I was interested not only in how people saw a space but also in how they experienced it emotionally. Thus, I found myself zeroing in on the ways that rhetors expressed comfort, anxiety, peace, or alarm as they argued over, narrated experiences within, or even simply described a space.

As I culled these various materials, I also sought out whether and how these artifacts engaged with one another, attending to the ways a drawing of the eighteenth-century school was (or was not) in conversation with teacher reports on the school environment, and then how these reports were (or were not) speaking to the architectural plans for the new school. My process was not just to collect artifacts in different modes and genres but also to place these various artifacts in the same rhetorical situation, to see how they might interrelate. Setting up these artifactual conversations was critical since I aimed at understanding the status of the *general* rather than the *particular* home, school, and childcare center. Since my goal was to discern dominant discussions about these spaces, I found myself consulting hundreds of artifacts of various sorts, attempting to discern patterns of agreement across them. Equally important, too, was to learn how rhetors intervened in these conversations through diverse modalities and genres, for it was clear that domestic scientists in particular made use of a varied spatio-rhetorical arsenal when they set out to remake their homes: the conference proceeding, the *Journal of Home Economics* article, the home laboratory, and the Rumford Kitchen exhibit were all at their disposal. And finally, throughout my research and writing process, I had to remember that every artifact of any mode and genre was rhetorical. No photograph, drawing, display, report, or observation was offering disinterested insight into the "real" space. Instead, every artifact was seeing the space from a particular vantage point.

Second, my original intention was to analyze artifacts that offered evidence of spatial debate. Chapter 4 especially examines artifacts that signal rhetors arguing over whether or not the childcare center should stay open, what this space says about working motherhood, and how this space supports or disturbs the welfare of American families. In reviewing the totality of the artifacts I analyzed for the entire study, however, I observe that while a number of materials were overtly functioning within the argumentative mode, the majority were definitional and descriptive: this is what the home laboratory is; this is how a domestic scientist would outfit it; this is how she works within it. While spatial descriptions and definitions may seem less intriguing than overt arguments about space, I found they revealed much and even possibly more about how people experienced, understood, and assessed the spaces under study. As Edward Schiappa writes, descriptions and definitions are distinctly rhetorical and important: "Whenever we name or describe a phenomenon or class of objects or define a situation [or, I would add, a space], we entitle to [it] a specific status that invites appropriate attitudes and behaviors in response. In short, we are engaging in a persuasive act" (169). Spatial descriptions and definitions operate by interpreting and seeing a space in a particular way, and in so doing they "advance certain interests and not others" (170). Even though description and definition may not often trigger what Nathaniel A. Rivers and Ryan P. Weber call "rhetorical fireworks," I found these rhetorical tactics to be illustrative and informative, maybe even more so than overt argument, because they indicated what interlocutors understood a space to be (188).

Relatedly, I found that a primary way rhetors composed spatial definitions was through spatial equation or spatial metaphor: asserting that one space was *like* or actually *was* another kind of space (the school is a prison, the home is a lab, the childcare center is a home). As Nedra Reynolds explains, spatial metaphors "come from somewhere . . . and they then go on to influence our responses to other places; they are formed through the material worlds and the ways in which people experience place and space" (*Geographies* 13–14). The metaphors in *Domestic Occupations* that interlocutors created were immensely revelatory because they made it so that one space was perceived as another, and, as such, understandings, evaluations, and even arguments about both spaces emerged. I want to underscore, however, that these metaphors were not merely imaginative and creative; they were also material. When domestic scientists said the home was a laboratory, these women made it thus by equipping the home with their scientific equipment. Spatial equations should therefore push scholars to consider not just the creative power of this rhetorical strategy but also the material realities that correspond with them and the consequences of these changes.

Third and finally, a significant part of my analytical process was to discern the temporal register in which these spatial rhetorics were functioning. That is, I found it important to identify whether a rhetor was describing what a space *was* in the past, *is* in the present, or *should be* in the future. These temporal distinctions were important because while, once again, the rhetor may not have been engaged in overt argument, she was, through her assessment, identifying a past, present, or future spatial practice. Attuning oneself to these temporal distinctions offers insight into what stakeholders believed a space was, is, or should be and indicates moments of spatial (dis)satisfaction and change.

Surely, these three methods are not the only inroads to pursuing a spatio-rhetorical project. My intention, though, is for them to offer scholars a "way in" to initiating projects of their own and to act as reflective prompts for others already engaged in this work, as the field continues to invent ways to study spatial rhetorics. The ultimate goal for *Domestic Occupations* is to offer scholars a heuristic to think expansively and productively about women's work and spatial rhetoric. Echoing Scott in this chapter's epigraph, I hope this study acts as an invitation for others to conduct additional scholarly investigations and, most importantly, to imagine better spatial futures. There is still a great deal of (home)work to do.

Notes

Works Cited

Index

Notes

1. Contending with Home: Spatial Rhetorics and Women's Work

1. This magazine was affiliated with another publication also produced at the Lowell Mills, the *New England Offering* (later titled the *Lowell Offering*).
2. Shirley Wilson Logan examines the ways Anna Julia Cooper engages this discussion in "'What Are We Worth': Anna Julia Cooper Defines Black Women's Work at the Dawn of the Twentieth Century."

2. From Prison to Home: Spatial Rhetorics Regender the Nineteenth-Century School

1. The cultural expectation of corporal punishment is also found in Walt Whitman's and Washington Irving's literature.
2. This conversation about girls' schooling was vibrant and consistent. As Cott explains, "every submission to the American Philosophical Society's prize essay contest in 1795, on the topic of American system of education, proposed universal free schools open to both sexes" (103).
3. Cott writes that while women did not occupy the school in great numbers, a few women were teaching in schools as early as the 1760s. These women mainly taught during the summer session because the student body was made up primarily of girls since most boys were working at this time of year (30).
4. During this period, women were also teaching other people's children out of their own homes through the makeshift operation of the dame school. See Perlmann et al.; Perlmann and Margo.
5. As Barnard's work makes clear, with the exception of Michigan, the focus was mostly on northeastern and, specifically, New England states. Mann writes of inspecting schools in every Massachusetts county—about eight hundred schools—and receiving reports from one thousand additional school leaders regarding the state of their schoolhouses. In their publications Mann and Barnard often reproduced these leaders' reports in their entirety.

6. Alonzo Potter and George Emerson's *School and Schoolmaster* (1848) discusses both improvements to school teaching and to school architecture. In 1851 Barnard published *Practical Illustrations of the Principles of School Architecture*. In 1871, and as the first U.S. commissioner of education, Barnard submitted *School Architecture: Plans for Graded Schools* as a government report that reached beyond New England to Louisiana, Missouri, California, and Michigan.
7. Uriah M. Judah's contribution to the *Republic* magazine remarks the popularity of this image: "The numerous readers of this volume must be perfectly familiar with a scene that has been admirably pictured by the ingenious artist, of the 'Village School in an Uproar'" (227).
8. Certainly, gender scholars could continue to explore this attack on women teachers by also considering how male teachers were often feminized owing to their professional choice. As Jackie Blount writes, school teaching "had become so thoroughly female-identified by the early 1900s that men who taught young children sometimes were widely regarded as effeminate and submissive" (85).
9. For a more detailed examination of the Indian Industrial School at Carlisle, see Adams; Enoch; and Spack.
10. See VanHaitsma for discussions of how the teaching profession created opportunities for women to sustain same-sex relations and collaborate together as educators.

3. The Domestic Scientist's Home Experiment: Spatial Rhetorics and Professional Ethos

1. Such discourse about the changing nature of the home was extremely popular, with domestic scientist Caroline Hunt noting that that "the passing of home industries and of the rise of factory methods of production would before any audience be a twice told tale" ("Woman's Public Work" 12).
2. As I discuss in chapter one, Gilman was part of a radical group of activists we now define as material feminists whose goal was to "socialize domestic work" (Hayden, *Grand Domestic Revolution* 28) by demanding that all "household labor and child care become social labor" (5).
3. Activist Lucy Stone similarly observes that before the Industrial Revolution, women's "sphere was at home, and only at home." But once the "spinning wheel and loom" were "superseded by machinery, . . . something else had to take their places." And when looking for something to fill this newfound time and energy, women have "tr[ied] new occupations" and "reach[ed] out after far better things" (59).
4. Within home economics, there was deep interest in connecting the home to the business world and learning to run it like a business. Bertha Terrill

writes in *Household Management*, "As the economic importance of the home is more fully realized, the business side of home-making is emphasized. The home has a close and intimate relationship to the business world in general. The housewife in her customary purchases comes in touch with retail trade of almost every variety and adds her contribution" (37).

5. See the title pages of texts within this series (Dodd; Terrill).
6. Home economist Mary Roberts Smith of Stanford University articulates this hesitation in her 1902 "Report of Committee on Courses in Home Economics in Colleges and Universities," where she writes that leaders at women's colleges such as Smith, Vassar, and Wellesley are "afraid to introduce [home economics courses] because it might appear to lower their standards" (18).
7. The Smith-Lever Act of 1914 also helped to spread the influence of home economics, as its purpose was to create outreach possibilities between land-grant institutions and their surrounding agricultural communities through extension services. Propelled by this act, home economists and domestic scientists offered practical instruction to women who were not able to access collegiate courses.
8. Richards also published this article in *Chemistry of the Household* (Dodd) and *The Profession of Home-Making*. The visual was also featured in the Rumford Kitchen exhibit.
9. Abel and Richards based their kitchen on the "People's Kitchens" that were popular in Germany but made the New England Kitchen their own by adding the pedagogical and display element (see Levenstein).
10. The dissolution of the New England Kitchen was slow and complicated. Due to the fact that immigrant clientele never wholly invested in the endeavor, Abel and Richards came to focus their attention on using the Kitchen to create school lunch programs, but soon after this shift, the founders turned to other pursuits. In 1907 the Women's Educational and Industrial Union took over and recast operations (see Levenstein).
11. For more information regarding the rhetorical significance of women's speeches at the World's Congress of Representative Women, see Maddux.
12. For additional information regarding the Women's Building at the Chicago World's Fair, see Corn and coauthors; Gullett; S. Hunt; Weimann; and Wood.
13. An enthymeme is a rhetorical syllogism in which an argument is made through logical deduction. The distinctive feature of the enthymeme is that a step in the syllogism is unstated such that the audience must fill in that unstated step on its own. For instance, "I want a dog because I am lonely" is an enthymematic argument: the unstated logical step in this claim is that dogs provide companionship. To understand this enthymematic argument, the audience must identify and accept as true the premise of dogs as companions.

14. The Rumford Leaflets are collected in *Plain Words about Food*.
15. For a detailed discussion of this aspect of municipal housekeeping see Gottlieb; T. Lewis; and M. Ryan, *Womanhood*.
16. Another sign of domestic scientists' interest in extending their scientific expertise beyond the home was Richards's proposal to change the nomenclature of her field of study and excise the overt reference to the home. In place of home economics or domestic science, Richards suggested "euthenics" as an alternative name for the discipline. Elaborating on the definition of this term in a similarly titled monograph, Richards worked to define euthenics as the "science of controllable environment" (*Euthenics*). Ultimately this attempt at renaming was not successful.
17. For more information on the Black Mammy Memorial Institute, see Patton and coauthors.

4. The Motherless Home: Working Mothers, Emotive Spatial Rhetorics, and the World War II Childcare Center

1. While not the concern of this chapter, a great deal of attention has been paid to the distinction between affect and emotion. See Gregg; Hawhee; Massumi; and Rice.
2. For a discussion of African American women's involvement in WWII, see Hartman; Honey, Introduction; Mullenbach; and Yellin. For studies concerning Latina and Mexican American women's contributions to the war effort, see Portales; Quiñonez.
3. For a detailed description of how home ownership was affected during the Great Depression, see Wheelock.
4. Given that this period was also governed by Jim Crow ideology, it is no surprise that this housing was often segregated, with the worst options left to African Americans and other people of color.
5. On the matter of race, a report from the Maritime Child Development Center in Richmond, California, states,

> At Kaiser's northwest shipyards, the director of the Child Service Centers later stated that they believed they had failed to attract black mothers, largely because they had hired no black staff members, and had not done enough to help the African American population overcome their anxieties over leaving their children in the care of others. ("Historic American Buildings Survey" 29)

The report goes on to state that "[m]any other centers did discriminate racially, with virtually all nurseries in the South excluding African American children" (29).

6. As women were being pushed out of the war plant and into the home, new child-rearing theories called for mothers to dedicate their full attention to children; those women who did not offer such focused care were often seen as delinquent or even abusive (E. Rose 194–95).
7. Sugrue's chapter goes on to explore the civil rights campaign to integrate Levittown, Pennsylvania, and the resistance to this integration. See also Harris; Kushner.

5. Home Work: Spatial Rhetorics and Feminist Rhetorical Scholarship

1. In "Homeplace (a site of resistance)," bell hooks also writes of the "tension between service outside one's home, family, and kin network, service provided to white folks which took time and energy, and the effort of black women to conserve enough of themselves to provide service (care and nurturance) within their own families and communities" (42). This tension, hooks continues, is "one of the many factors that has historically distinguished the lot of black women in patriarchal white society," and it is the work of black communities to "honor this history of service" and to "critique the sexist definition of service as women's 'natural' role" (42). hooks further develops her personal attachments to home in *Belonging: A Culture of Place*.
2. See Dayton-Wood or Garbus for work that focuses on settlement houses as sites of education.
3. See also P. Cohen.
4. See also M. White; Moisio and Beruchashvili.
5. In making this claim, Noddings references G. Sykes's 1987 paper "Teaching and Professionalism: A Cautionary Perspective" presented at Michigan State University.
6. The Rosie the Riveter World War II Home Front National Park in Richmond, California, does preserve the Maritime Powers Child Development Center on the park grounds. Visitors to the park can view the space of and artifacts from the WWII childcare center.

Works Cited

URLs for works accessed in Google Books have been truncated to "books.google.com," but searching by author and title in the index at books.google.com should retrieve these works.

Abel, Mary Hinman. "Mrs. Richards and the Home Economics Movement." *The Journal of Home Economics*, vol. 3, no. 4, Oct. 1911, pp. 343–48. Cornell University Library, *HEARTH: Home Economics Archive*, hearth.library.cornell.edu/cgi/t/text/text-idx?c=hearth;cc=hearth;idno=4732504_3_004;view=toc;node=4732504_3_004%3A3.3. Accessed 2 Jan. 2018.
———. "A Peripatetic Exhibit." *Good Housekeeping*, vol. 36, no. 2, 1903, p. 194.
———. "Report to Mrs. Quincy A. Shaw, concerning the Fund Used in the New England Kitchen." *Plain Words about Food: The Rumford Kitchen Leaflets*, Home Science Publishing, 1899, pp. 134, plate. *Google Books*, books.google.com. Accessed 9 Dec. 2018.
———. "A Study in Social Economics: The Story of the New England Kitchen." *Plain Words about Food: The Rumford Kitchen Leaflets*, Home Science Publishing, 1899, pp. 135–54. *Google Books*, books.google.com. Accessed 2 Jan. 2018.
Adams, David Wallace. *Education for Extinction: American Indians and the Boarding School Experience, 1875–1928*. UP of Kansas, 1995.
Addams, Jane. *The Modern City and the Municipal Franchise for Women*, National American Suffrage Association, 1900. *Internet Archive*, archive.org/details/moderncitymunici00adda. Accessed 2 Jan. 2018.
Ahmed, Sara. *The Cultural Politics of Emotion*. Routledge, 2004.
Alcott, Louisa May. *Work: A Story of Experience*. 1873. Penguin, 1994.
Alcott, William A. "Prize Essay on the Construction of School-Houses." *Lectures Delivered before the American Institute of Instruction in Boston, August 1831*, Richardson, Lord, and Holbrook, 1832, pp. 241–59.
Allen, John. "The Whereabouts of Power: Politics, Government and Space." *Geografiska Annaler: Series B, Human Geography*, vol. 86, no. 1, 2004, pp. 19–32.

Works Cited

Allen, Polly Wynn. *Building Domestic Liberty: Charlotte Perkins Gilman's Architectural Feminism*. U of Massachusetts P, 1988.

Anthony II, Susan B. *Out of the Kitchen—Into the War: Women's Winning Role in the Nation's Drama*. Daye, 1943.

"Appeal for Men Teachers." *New York Times*, 4 Oct. 1911, p. 12. *ProQuest*. Accessed 2 Jan. 2018.

Applegarth, Risa. "Genre, Location, and Mary Austin's Ethos." *Rhetoric Society Quarterly*, vol. 41, no. 1, 2011, pp. 41–63.

———. "Personal Writing in Professional Spaces: Contesting Exceptionalism in Interwar Women's Vocational Autobiographies." *College English*, vol. 77, no. 6, 2015, pp. 530–52.

"Are There Too Many Women Teachers?" *Educational Review*, vol. 28, June 1904, pp. 98–105. *Google Books*, book.google.com. Accessed 8 Dec. 2018.

Aristotle. *Nicomachean Ethics*. Translated and edited by H. Rackham, William Heinemann Ltd., 1934. Tufts University, *Perseus Digital Library*, www.perseus.tufts.edu/hopper/text?doc=Perseus%3Atext%3A1999.01.0054%3Abook%3D2%3Achapter%3Dpos%3D17%3Asection%3D4. Accessed 8 Dec. 2018.

Auletta, Ken. "A Woman's Place." *The New Yorker*, 11 and 18 July 2011, www.newyorker.com/magazine/2011/07/11/a-womans-place-ken-auletta. Accessed 2 Jan. 2018.

Austin, John Mather. *A Voice to the Married; Being a Compendium of Social, Moral, and Religious Duties Addressed to Husbands and Wives*. A. Tompkins, 1847. *Google Books*, books.google.com. Accessed 2 Jan. 2018.

Bacon, Edmund N. "Wartime Housing." *Annals of the American Academy of Political and Social Science*, vol. 229, Sept. 1943, pp. 128–37.

Bailey, Liberty Hyde. *Woman's Place in a Scheme of Agricultural Education*. Abstract of Remarks by Dean Bailey before Girls' Club of the College of Agriculture, 11 Nov. 1910. Harvard Library, *Women Working, 1800–1930*, iiif.lib.harvard.edu/manifests/view/drs:2573685$1i. Accessed 2 Jan. 2018.

Bakhtin, M. M. *The Dialogic Imagination: Four Essays*. Edited by Michael Holquist, translated by Caryl Emerson and Holquist, U of Texas P, 1981.

Banning, Margaret Culkin. "Will They Go Back Home?" *Rotarian*, Sept. 1943, pp. 28–30. *Google Books*, books.google.com. Accessed 2 Jan. 2018.

Bardeen, C. W. "The Monopolizing Woman Teacher." *Educational Review*, Jan. 1912, pp. 17–40.

Barnard, Eunice Fuller. "Definitely Woman's Work." *Independent Woman*, vol. 21, no. 4, Apr. 1942, pp. 106–08.

Barnard, Henry. *Practical Illustrations of the Principles of School Architecture.* Tiffany, 1851. *Google Books*, books.google.com. Accessed 2 Jan. 2018.

———. *School Architecture; or, Contributions to the Improvement of School-Houses in the United States.* Barnes, 1848. *Google Books*, books.google.com. Accessed 2 Jan. 2018.

———. "School Architecture—with Illustrations." *American Journal of Education*, vol. 13, 1860, pp. 487–568. *Google Books*, books.google.com. Accessed 2 Jan. 2018.

Barnett, Scot, and Casey Boyle. "Rhetorical Ontology, or, How to Do Things with Things." Introduction. *Rhetoric through Everyday Things*, edited by Barnett and Boyle, U of Alabama P, 2016, pp. 1–16.

Barrows, Anna. *Principles of Cookery.* American School of Home Economics, 1914. *Google Books*, books.google.com. Accessed 8 Dec. 2018.

Baruch, Dorothy. "When the Need for War-Time Services for Children Is Past—What of the Future?" *Journal of Consulting Psychology*, vol. 9, 1945, pp. 45–57.

Baxandall, Rosalyn, et al. Introduction. *America's Working Women: A Documentary History, 1600 to the Present*, W. W. Norton, 1995, pp. xxi–xxvii.

Baxandall, Rosalyn, and Elizabeth Ewen. *Picture Windows: How the Suburbs Happened.* Basic Books, 2001.

Beck, Julie. "'Trouble with Girls': The Enduring Sexism in Science." *The Atlantic*, 11 June 2015, www.theatlantic.com/health/archive/2015/06/tim-hunt-resignation-science-sexism/395642/. Accessed 2 Jan. 2018.

Beecher, Catharine E. "Essay on the Education of Female Teachers for the United States." *The Family Magazine*, vol. 3, no. 2, July 1835, pp. 62–64, 102–03, 145–47. *Google Books*, books.google.com. Accessed 2 Jan. 2018.

———. *Suggestions respecting Improvements in Education.* Packard and Butler, 1829. *Google Books*, books.google.com. Accessed 2 Jan. 2018.

Beecher, Catharine E., and Harriet Beecher Stowe. *The American Woman's Home.* J. B. Ford, 1869. *Google Books*, books.google.com. Accessed 2 Jan. 2018.

Beer, Ethel S. "Help Mothers Win the War." *Trained Nurse and Hospital Review*, vol. 108, 1942, pp. 192–95.

Bernal. J. D. *Science in History.* Vol. 2, MIT P, 1971.

Berry, Riley M. Fletcher. "The Black Mammy Memorial Institute." *Good Housekeeping*, vol. 53, no. 4, Oct. 1911, pp. 562–63. Cornell University Library, *HEARTH: Home Economics Archive*, hearth.library.cornell.edu/cgi/t/text/pageviewer-idx?c=hearth;cc=hearth;ql=The Black Mammy Memorial Institute;rgn=full text;idno=6417403_1339_004;didno=6417403_1339_004;view=image;seq=0130;node=6417403_1339_004%3A3.33. Accessed 2 Jan. 2018.

Bevier, Isabel, and Susannah Usher. *The Home Economics Movement.* Vol. 1, Thomas Todd, 1906. *Google Books,* books.google.com. Accessed 2 Jan. 2018.

Blackwell, Elizabeth. *Address on the Medical Education of Women.* Baptist and Taylor, 1864. Harvard Library, *Women Working, 1830–1900,* iiif.lib.harvard.edu/manifests/view/drs:2997394$1i. Accessed 2 Jan. 2018.

Blair, Carole. "Contemporary U.S. Memorial Sites as Exemplars of Rhetoric's Materiality." *Rhetorical Bodies,* edited by Jack Selzer and Sharon Crowley, U of Wisconsin P, 1999, pp. 16–57.

Blair, Carole, et al. "Introduction: Rhetoric/Memory/Place." *Places of Public Memory: The Rhetoric of Museums and Memorials,* edited by Greg Dickinson et al., U of Alabama P, 2010, pp. 1–56.

Blandford, John B. "Wanted: 12 Million New Houses." *National Municipal Review,* Sept. 1945, pp. 376–85.

Blount, Jackie. "Spinsters, Bachelors, and Other Gender Transgressors in School Employment, 1850–1900." *Review of Educational Research,* vol. 70, no. 1, 2000, pp. 83–101.

Bolton, Sharon, and Daniel Muzio. "The Paradoxical Processes of Feminization in the Professions: The Case of Established, Aspiring and Semi-professions." *Work, Employment & Society,* vol. 22, no. 2, 2008, 281–99.

Bondi, Liz, and Joyce Davidson. "Situating Gender." *A Companion to Feminist Geography,* edited by Lise Nelson and Joni Seager, Blackwell, 2005, pp. 15–31.

Bosquet, Maurice. *Personal Hygiene.* American School of Home Economics, 1907. *Forgotten Books,* https://www.forgottenbooks.com/it/download/PersonalHygiene_10542273.pdf. Accessed 17 Nov. 2018.

Bossard, J. H. S. "Family Problems of the Immediate Future." *Journal of Home Economics,* vol. 37, no. 7, Sept. 1945, pp. 383–87, Cornell University Library, *HEARTH: Home Economics Archive,* hearth.library.cornell.edu/cgi/t/text/pageviewer-idx?c=hearth;cc=hearth;rgn=full text;idno=4732504_37_007;didno=4732504_37_007;view=image;seq=0017;node=4732504_37_007%3A7.1. Accessed 2 Jan. 2018.

Bourdieu, Pierre. *The Logic of Practice.* Translated by Richard Nice, Stanford UP, 1990.

Brown, Helen Weigel. "Uncle Sam Houses His Children." *Parents' Magazine,* Jan. 1944, pp. 39, 79–81.

Bryden, Inga, and Janet Floyd. Introduction. *Domestic Space: Reading the Nineteenth-Century Interior,* edited by Bryden and Floyd, Manchester UP, 1999, pp. 1–17.

Buchanan, Lindal. *Regendering Delivery: The Fifth Canon and Antebellum Women Rhetors.* Southern Illinois UP, 2005.

Budd, Dorothy. "While Mothers Work." *Woman's Home Companion*, vol. 69, July 1942, pp. 58–59.

Buell, Mrs. C. S. "Household Adjustment to Changing Industrial Conditions." *Proceedings of the Ninth Annual Lake Placid Conference on Home Economics*, 1–6 July 1907, pp. 93–98, *Google Books*, books.google.com. Accessed 2 Jan. 2018.

Burns, Rena. Letter. *Appendix to the Congressional Record*, vol. 921, no. 12, 1945, p. A3869.

Butler, Judith. *Bodies That Matter: On the Discursive Limits of Sex*. Routledge, 2011.

———. "Performative Acts and Gender Constitution." *Theatre Journal*, vol. 40, no. 1, 1988, pp. 519–31.

Carroll, Jane Lynott. "Raising a Baby on Shifts." *Parents' Magazine*, Oct. 1943, pp. 20, 77–78, 80.

Carson, Ruth. "Minding the Children." *Collier's*, vol. 3, 30 Jan. 1943, pp. 46–47.

Carter, Erica, et al. *Space and Place: Theories of Identity and Location*. Lawrence and Wishart, 1993.

Chadsey, Mildred. "Municipal Housekeeping." *Journal of Home Economics*, vol. 7, no. 2, 1915, pp. 53–59. *Google Books*, books.google.com. Accessed 2 Jan. 2018.

"Changes in Women's Occupations 1940–1950." Women's Bureau Bulletin 253. Government Printing Office, 1954.

Child, Lydia Maria. *The Frugal Housewife*. 1828. Carter and Hendee, 1830. Michigan State University Library, *Feeding America: The Historic American Cookbook Project*, digital.lib.msu.edu/projects/cookbooks/books/frugalhousewifechild/frch.pdf. Accessed 2 Jan. 2018.

———. *The Mother's Book*. Carter, Hendee, and Babcock, 1831. *Google Books*, books.google.com/books. Accessed 2 Jan. 2018.

Child Service Centers: Kaiser Company, Inc.—Portland Yard Oregon Shipbuilding Corporation. Kaiser Company, 1946. Booklet.

Children's Bureau. *A Children's Charter in Wartime*. Children's Bureau, 1942. Southern Methodist University, *Digital Collections*, digitalcollections.smu.edu/cdm/ref/collection/hgp/id/463. Accessed 2 Jan. 2018.

Christoph, Julie Nelson. "Reconceiving *Ethos* in Relation to the Personal: Strategies of Placement in Pioneer Women's Writing." *College English*, vol. 64, no. 6, 2002, pp. 660–79.

Clark, Clifford Edward. *The American Family Home, 1800–1960*. U of North Carolina P, 1986.

Clark, Gregory. *Rhetorical Landscapes in America: Variations on a Theme from Kenneth Burke*. U of South Carolina P, 2004.

Cleaveland, Henry William, et al. *Village and Farm Cottages: The Requirements of American Village Homes Considered and Suggested*. D. Appleton, 1856. *Google Books*, books.google.com. Accessed 2 Jan. 2018.

Cleveland, Alfred A. "The Predominance of Female Teachers." *Pedagogical Seminary*, vol. 12, no. 3, 1905, pp. 289–303. *Google Books*, books.google.com. Accessed 2 Jan. 2018.

Clifford, Geraldine J. "'Daughters into Teachers': Educational and Demographic Influences on the Transformation of Teaching into 'Women's Work' in America." *History of Education Review*, vol. 12, no. 1, 1983, pp. 15–28.

———. "'Lady Teachers' and Politics in the United States, 1850–1930." *Teachers: The Culture and Politics of Work*, edited by Martin Lawn and Gerald Grace, Falmer, 1987, pp. 3–30.

———. *Those Good Gertrudes: A Social History of Women Teachers in America*. Johns Hopkins UP, 2014.

Close, Kathryn. "After Lanham Funds—What?" *Survey Midmonthly*, 8 May 1945, pp. 131–35.

Cohen, Abby J. "A Brief History of Federal Financing for Child Care in the United States." *The Future of Children*, vol. 6, no. 2, 1996, pp. 26–40.

Cohen, Phillip N. *The Family: Diversity, Inequality, and Social Change*. W. W. Norton, 2015.

Converse, Mary. "Teaching Chemistry in Connection with Domestic Science." *Journal of Home Economics*, vol. 1, no. 2, 1909, pp. 196–98. Cornell University Library, *HEARTH: Home Economics Archive*, hearth.library.cornell.edu/cgi/t/text/pageviewer-idx?c=hearth;cc=hearth;rgn=full text;idno=4732504_1_002;didno=4732504_1_002;view=image;seq=0087;node=4732504_1_002%3A3.22. Accessed 2 Jan. 2018.

Cooley, Anna. *Domestic Art in Women's Education*. Scribner's Sons, 1911. *Google Books*, books.google.com. Accessed 2 Jan. 2018.

Corn, Wanda M., et al. *Women Building History: Public Art at the 1893 Columbian Exposition*. U of California P, 2011.

Courtney, Jennifer. "Real Men Do Housework: Ethos and Masculinity in Contemporary Domestic Advice." *Rhetoric Review*, vol. 28, no. 1, 2009, pp. 66–81.

Cott, Nancy. *The Bonds of Womanhood: "Woman's Sphere" in New England, 1780–1835*. Yale UP, 1977.

Cravens, Hamilton. "Establishing the Science of Nutrition at the USDA: Ellen Swallow Richards and Her Allies." *Agricultural History*, vol. 64, no. 2, 1990, pp. 122–33.

Crawford, Frederick. "A Three-Sided Problem." *American Women in the Postwar World: A Symposium of the Role Women Will Play in Business and Industry. Newsweek*, 1944, pp. 27–30.

Crawley, Edward J. "Should We Pay for Child Day Care?" *Cleveland News*, 18 May 1946, p. 8.

Cremin, Lawrence A. *American Education: The National Experience, 1783–1876*. Harper and Row, 1980.

"Cultivate Home Affections." *Happy Home and Parlor Magazine*, vol. 5, 1857, p. 56. *Google Books*, books.google.com. Accessed 2 Jan. 2018.

Dall, Caroline H. *"Women's Right to Labor"; or, Low Wages and Hard Work*. Walker, Wise and Co., 1860. *Google Books*, books.google.com. Accessed 2 Jan. 2018.

Davidson, Cathy, and Jessamyn Hatcher. Introduction. *No More Separate Spheres! A Next Wave in American Studies Reader*, edited by Davidson and Hatcher, Duke UP, 2002, pp. 7–26.

Davies, Margery W. *Woman's Place Is at the Typewriter: Office Work and Office Workers, 1870–1930*. Temple UP, 1982.

Davis, Almond. *The Female Preacher, or, Memoir of Salome Lincoln*. A. B. Kidder, 1843. *Google Books*, books.google.com. Accessed 2 Jan. 2018.

Dayton-Wood, Amy. "Teaching English for 'A Better America.'" *Rhetoric Review*, vol. 27, no. 4, 2008, pp. 397–414.

———. "'What the College Has Done for Me': Anzia Yezierska and the Problem of Progressive Education." *College English*, vol. 74, no. 3, 2012, pp. 215–33.

"DeafSpace." Gallaudet University, *Campus Design and Planning*, www.gallaudet.edu/campus-design-and-planning/deafspace. Accessed 4 Jan. 2018.

de Certeau, Michel. *The Practice of Everyday Life*. Translated by Steven Randall, U of California P, 1994.

"Declarations of Sentiments and Resolutions." 1848. *Available Means: An Anthology of Women's Rhetorics*, edited by Joy Ritchie and Kate Ronald, U of Pittsburgh P, 2001, pp. 138–42.

Dempsey, Mary V. "Occupational Progress of Women." *Bulletin of Women's Bureau*, no. 27, 1922. Harvard Library, *Women Working, 1800–1930*, iiif.lib.harvard.edu/manifests/view/drs:2586394$1i. Accessed 3 Jan. 2018.

"Designed for 24-Hour Child Care." *Architectural Record*, vol. 95, no. 3, Mar. 1944, pp. 84–89.

Des Jardins, Julie. *The Madame Curie Complex: The Hidden History of Women in Science*. Feminist P, 2010.

de Tocqueville, Alexis. *Democracy in America*. Vol. 2, translated by Henry Reeve, Langley, 1841. *Google Books*, books.google.com. Accessed 2 Jan. 2018.

Deutsch, Sarah. *Women and the City: Gender, Space, and Power in Boston, 1870–1940*. Oxford UP, 2000.

Dickinson, Greg. "Joe's Rhetoric: Finding Authenticity at Starbucks." *Rhetoric Society Quarterly*, vol. 32, no. 4, 2002, pp. 5–27.

Dickinson, Greg, et al. "Space of Remembering and Forgetting: The Reverent Eye/I at the Plains Indian Museum." *Communication and Critical/Cultural Studies*, vol. 3, no. 1, 2006, pp. 27–47.

"Discussion." *Lake Placid Conference on Home Economics: Proceedings of the Eighth Annual Conference*, 15–22 Sept. 1906, pp. 12–14, *Google Books*, books.google.com. Accessed 2 Jan. 2018.

Dodd, Margaret. *Chemistry of the Household*. American School of Home Economics, 1914. *Google Books*, books.google.com. Accessed 2 Jan. 2018.

Domosh, Mona, and Joni Seager. *Putting Women in Place: Feminist Geographers Make Sense of the World*. Guilford, 2001.

Downing, Andrew. *The Architecture of Country Houses: Designs for Cottages, Farm-Houses, and Villas*. D. Appleton, 1852. *Google Books*, books.google.com. Accessed 2 Jan. 2018.

Downs, Robert B. *Horace Mann: Champion of Public Schools*. Twayne P, 1974.

Dratch, Howard. "The Politics of Child Care in the 1940s." *Science and Society*, vol. 3, 1974, pp. 167–204.

Dressler, F. B. "A Sketch of Old School Houses." *Pedagogical Seminary* 2 (1892): 115–25. *Google Books*, books.google.com. Accessed 5 Oct. 2015.

Dublin, Thomas. *Transforming Women's Work: New England Lives in the Industrial Revolution*. Cornell UP, 1994.

Dudden, Faye E. *Serving Women: Household Service in Nineteenth-Century America*. Wesleyan UP, 1983.

Dufu, Tiffany. *Drop the Ball: Achieving More by Doing Less*. Flatiron, 2017.

Dumond, Annie Nelles. *Annie Nelles; or, The Life of a Book Agent*. Published by the author, 1868. *Google Books*, books.google.com. Accessed 2 Jan. 2018.

Dyer, Florence Cole. Letter to Governor Earl Warren. Los Angeles, 12 Dec. 1946. F3640: 8738–52. Proposed Legislation, Child Care Centers, 1946–1947. Earl Warren Papers. California State Archives.

Eaton, Jeannette. *Commercial Work and Training for Girls*. Macmillan, 1915. *Google Books*, books.google.com. Accessed 2 Jan. 2018.

Edwards, Janis L. "Echoes of Camelot: How Images Construct Cultural Memory through Rhetorical Framing." *Defining Visual Rhetorics*, edited by Charles A. Hill and Marguerite Helmers, Lawrence Erlbaum, 2004, pp. 179–94.

"Effect of Wartime Housing Shortages on Home Ownership." *Monthly Labor Review*, vol. 62, no. 4, 1946, pp. 560–66.

"Eight-Hour Orphans." *Saturday Evening Post*, vol. 215, no. 20, 10 Oct. 1942, pp. 20–21, 105–06.

Eliot, Charles W. "Women's Education—a Forecast." *Publications of the Association of Collegiate Alumnae*, ser. 3, no. 7, 1908, pp. 101–05. *Google Books*, books.google.com. Accessed 8 Dec. 2018.

Elliot, S. Maria. *Household Bacteriology*. American School of Home Economics, 1911. *Google Books*, books.google.com. Accessed 2 Jan. 2018.

Emerson, George B. "On the Education of Females." *The Introductory Discourse and the Lectures Delivered before the American Institute of Instruction in Boston, August, 1831*, Hilliard, Gray, Little and Wilkins, 1832, pp. 15–41. *Google Books*, books.google.com. 5 Dec. 2018.

Emerson, Joseph. *Female Education: A Discourse, Delivered at the Dedication of the Seminary Hall*. Samuel T. Armstrong and Crocker & Brewster, 1822. *Google Books*, books.google.com. 2 Jan. 2018.

"Employment in War Work of Women with Young Children." *Monthly Labor Review*, vol. 55, Dec. 1942, pp. 1184–85.

Endres, Danielle, and Samantha Senda-Cook. "Location Matters: The Rhetoric of Place in Protest." *Quarterly Journal of Speech*, vol. 97, no. 3, 2011, pp. 257–82.

Enoch, Jessica. *Refiguring Rhetorical Education: Women Teaching African American, Native American, and Chicano/a Students, 1865–1911*. Southern Illinois UP, 2008.

Evans, Mary Elizabeth. "Nursery School Lessons Learned in Wartime." *Journal of Home Economics*, vol. 38, no. 5, May 1946, pp. 257–60.

"Exhibits and Prizes." *Journal of Home Economics*, vol. 3, no. 4, 1911, pp. 397–99. Cornell University Library, *HEARTH: Home Economics Archive*, hearth.library.cornell.edu/cgi/t/text/pageviewer-idx?c=hearth;cc=hearth;rgn=full text;idno=4732504_3_004;didno=4732504_3_004;view=image;seq=0077;node=4732504_3_004%3A3.18. Accessed 2 Jan. 2018.

"Extended School Services: Information Activities." *Education for Victory*, vol. 2, no. 12, Dec. 1943, pp. 3–4.

Fern, Fanny. "The Working Girls of New York." 1868. *The Oxford Book of Women's Writing in the United States*, edited by Linda Wagner-Martin and Cathy Davidson, Oxford UP, 1995, pp. 321–23.

Field, Jessie. *The Corn Lady: The Story of a Country Teacher's Work*. A. Flanagan, 1911. *Google Books*, books.google.com. Accessed 2 Jan. 2018.

Filene, Catherine, editor. *Careers for Women*. Houghton Mifflin, 1920. *Google Books*, books.google.com. Accessed 2 Jan. 2018.

Finck, Barbara. "Cooperation on the Home Front." *Parents' Magazine*, vol. 20, 1945, pp. 24–25, 60, 62, 64, 66.

Finnegan, Cara. "Doing Rhetorical History of the Visual: The Photograph and the Archive." *Defining Visual Rhetorics*, edited by Charles A. Hill and Marguerite Helmers, Lawrence Erlbaum, 2004, pp. 195–214.

Fleischman, Doris. *An Outline of Careers for Women: A Practical Guide to Achievement.* Doubleday, Doran and Co., 1928. Harvard Library, *Women Working, 1800–1930,* iiif.lib.harvard.edu/manifests/view/drs:3552133$1i. Accessed 3 Jan. 2018.

Fleming, David. *City of Rhetoric: Revitalizing the Public Sphere in Metropolitan America.* SUNY P, 2008.

Fordham, Signithia, and John U. Ogbu. "Black Students' School Success: Coping with the Burden of 'Acting White.'" *The Urban Review,* vol. 18 no. 3, 1986, pp. 1–31.

Foucault, Michel. *Power/Knowledge: Selected Interviews and Other Writings, 1972–1977.* Edited by Colin Gordon, translated by Gordon et al., Pantheon, 1980.

Friedan, Betty. *The Feminine Mystique.* 1963. W. W. Norton, 2001.

Garbus, Julie. "Service-Learning, 1902." *College English,* vol. 64, no. 5, 2002, pp. 547–65.

Garrett, Elizabeth Donaghy. *At Home: The American Family, 1750–1870.* Harry N. Abrams P, 1990.

Gerard, Margaret. "Psychological Effects of War on the Small Child and Mother." *American Journal of Orthopsychiatry,* vol. 13, July 1945, pp. 493–96.

Gilman, Charlotte Perkins. *The Home: Its Work and Influence.* 1903. U of Illinois P, 1973.

Glenn, Cheryl. *Rhetoric Retold: Regendering the Rhetorical Tradition from Antiquity to the Renaissance.* Southern Illinois UP, 1997.

Glover, Katherine. "Women at Work in Wartime." Public Affairs Committee, 1943.

Goggin, Maureen Daly, and Beth Fowkes Tobin, editors. *Women and Things, 1750–1950: Gendered Material Strategies.* Routledge, 2016.

Gold, David and Jessica Enoch, editors. *Women at Work: Rhetorics of Gender and Labor.* U of Pittsburgh P, 2019.

Goodrich, Henrietta. "Suggestions for a Professional School of Home Economics and Social Economics." *Lake Placid Conference on Home Economics Proceedings,* 1st, 2nd, and 3rd Annual Conferences, 1899, 1900, 1901, pp. 26–40. *Google Books,* books.google.com. Accessed 3 Jan. 2018.

Goodrich, Samuel. *Fireside Education.* New York: F. J. Huntington, 1838. *Google Books,* books.google.com. Accessed 3 Jan. 2018.

Gottlieb, Agnes Hooper. "Beyond Muckraking." *American Journalism,* vol. 14, no. 3–4, 1997, pp. 330–32.

Green, Emma. "America's Profound Gender Anxiety." *The Atlantic,* 31 May 2016, www.theatlantic.com/politics/archive/2016/05/americas-profound-gender-anxiety/484856/. Accessed 3 Jan. 2018.

Gregg, Melissa, editor. *The Affect Theory Reader*. Duke UP, 2010.
Gries, Laurie. *Still Life with Rhetoric: A New Materialist Approach to Visual Rhetorics*. Utah State UP, 2015.
Gross, Daniel M. "Introduction: A New Rhetoric of Passions." *The Secret History of Emotion: From Aristotle's* Rhetoric *to Modern Brain Science*, U of Chicago P, 2006, pp. 1–20.
Gullett, Gayle. "'Our Great Opportunity': Organized Women Advance Women's Work at the World's Columbian Exposition of 1893." *Illinois Historical Journal*, vol. 87, no. 4, 1994, pp. 259–76.
Halberstam, Judith. *Female Masculinity*. Duke UP, 1998.
Hale, Sarah Josepha. "Female Education." *American Ladies Magazine*, vol. 7, 1834, pp. 499–502. *Google Books*, books.google.com. Accessed 3 Jan. 2018.
———. *Manners: Happy Homes and Good Society All the Year Round*. J. E. Tilton, 1867. *HathiTrust*, babel.hathitrust.org/cgi/pt?id=hvd.hw22xg;view=1up;seq=7. Accessed 3 Jan. 2018.
Hall, G. Stanley. *Adolescence: Its Psychology and Its Relationship to Physiology, Anthropology, Sociology, Sex, Crime, Religion, and Education*. Vol. 2, D. Appleton, 1905. *HathiTrust*, babel.hathitrust.org/cgi/pt?id=cool.ark:/13960/t99603x6c;view=1up;seq=7. Accessed 17 Nov. 2018.
Hallenbeck, Sarah. "Toward a Posthuman Perspective: Feminist Rhetorical Methodologies and Everyday Practices." *Advances in the History of Rhetoric*, vol. 15, 2012, pp. 9–27.
Hallenbeck, Sarah, and Michelle Smith. "Mapping Topoi in the Rhetorical Gendering of Work." *Peitho*, vol. 17, no. 2, 2015, pp. 200–25, peitho.cwshrc.org/files/2015/09/17HallenbeckSmith.pdf. Accessed 3 Jan. 2018.
Halloran, S. Michael. "Aristotle's Concept of Ethos, or If Not His, Someone Else's." *Rhetoric Review*, vol. 1, no. 1, 1982, pp. 58–63.
Halttunen, Karen. "Groundwork: American Studies in Place. Presidential Address to the American Studies Association, November 4, 2005." *American Quarterly*, vol. 58, no. 1, 2006, pp. 1–15.
Haraway, Donna. "Situated Knowledge: The Science Question in Feminism and the Privilege of Partial Perspective." *Feminist Studies*, vol. 14, no. 3, 1988, pp. 575–99.
Hariman, Robert, and John Louis Lucaites. "Dissent and Emotional Management in a Liberal Democratic Society: The Kent State Iconic Photograph." *Rhetoric Society Quarterly*, vol. 31, no. 3, 2001, pp. 5–31.
Harper, Ida Husted. "Women Ought to Work." *The Independent*, vol. 53, 1901, pp. 1123–27. *Google Books*, books.google.com. Accessed 3 Jan. 2018.
Harris, Diane Suzette. *Little White Houses: How the Postwar Home Constructed Race in America*. U of Minnesota P, 2013.

Harvey, David. "Between Space and Time: Reflections on the Geographical Imagination." *Annals of the Association of American Geographers*, vol. 80, no. 3, 1990, pp. 418–34.

———. *Spaces of Hope*. U of California P, 2000.

Hawhee, Debra. "Rhetoric's Sensorium." *Quarterly Journal of Speech*, vol. 101, no. 1, 2015, pp. 2–17.

Hayden, Dolores. *Building Suburbia: Green Fields and Urban Growth, 1820–2000*. Pantheon, 2003.

———. *The Grand Domestic Revolution: A History of Feminist Designs for American Homes, Neighborhoods, and Cities*. MIT P, 1981.

———. *Power of Place: Urban Landscapes as Public History*. MIT P, 1995.

———. *Redesigning the American Dream. The Future of Housing, Work, and Family Life*. Norton, 2002.

Healy. "Continuance of Child-Care Program." *Congressional Record—House*, vol. 91, no. 7, 1945, p. 8657.

Herman, Barbara. "#DistractinglySexy Twitter Meme Takes Off after Scientist Tim Hunt Resigns over Sexist Remarks." *IBT*, 11 June 2015, www.ibtimes.com/distractinglysexy-twitter-meme-takes-after-scientist-tim-hunt-resigns-over-sexist-1963006. Accessed 3 Jan. 2018.

Hill, Catherine, et al. "Why So Few? Women in Science, Technology, Engineering, and Math." American Association of University Women, 2010, www.aauw.org/files/2013/02/Why-So-Few-Women-in-Science-Technology-Engineering-and-Mathematics.pdf. Accessed 3 Jan. 2018.

Hill, Charles A. "The Psychology of Rhetorical Images." *Defining Visual Rhetorics*, edited by Hill and Marguerite Helmers, Lawrence Erlbaum, 2004, pp. 25–40.

"Historic American Buildings Survey: Maritime Child Development Center." HABS Nos. CA-2718. 2001. City of Richmond, California, *Document Center*, www.ci.richmond.ca.us/DocumentCenter/View/2126. Accessed 3 Jan. 2018.

"History & Culture." *Rosie the Riveter WWII Home Front: National Historic Park, California*, National Park Service, https://www.nps.gov/rori/learn/historyculture/index.htm. Accessed 4 Feb. 2019.

Hochschild, Arlie, and Anne Machung. *The Second Shift: Working Families and the Revolution at Home*. Penguin, 2012.

Hoffman, Nancy. Introduction. *Woman's "True" Profession: Voices from the History of Teaching*. 2nd ed., Harvard Education P, 2003, pp. 1–22.

Hogg, Charlotte. "Including Conservative Women's Rhetorics in an Ethics of Hope and Care." *Rhetoric Review*, vol. 34, no. 4, 2015, pp. 391–408.

Honey, Maureen. *Creating Rosie the Riveter: Class, Gender, and Propaganda during World War II*. U of Massachusetts P, 1984.

———. Introduction. *Bitter Fruit: African American Women in World War II*, edited by Honey, U of Missouri P, 1999, pp. 1–34.

hooks, bell. "Homeplace (as a site of resistance)." *Yearning: Race, Gender, and Cultural Politics*, South End P, 1990, pp. 41–50.

Hoover, Herbert. "Address to the White House Conference on Child Health and Protection." 19 Nov. 1930. *The American Presidency Project*, www.presidency.ucsb.edu/ws/?pid=22442. Accessed 3 Jan. 2018.

"The Household Workers' Association." National Women's Trade Union League of America Records, 1910–1934; B-16, folders 24, 30, 58 and 63. Harvard Library, *Women Working, 1800–1930*, iiif.lib.harvard.edu/manifests/view/drs:2581382$1i. Accessed 3 Jan. 2018.

Howe, Julia Ward. Introduction. *Women's Work in America*, edited by Annie Nathan Meyer, Henry Holt, 1891, pp. 1–2. *Google Books*, books.google.com. Accessed 3 Jan. 2018.

Hubbard, Phil, et al., editors. *Key Thinkers on Space and Place*. Sage, 2004.

Huling, Caroline A. *Letters of a Business Woman to Her Niece*. Feno, 1906. Harvard Library, *Women Working, 1800–1930*, iiif.lib.harvard.edu/manifests/view/drs:2574301$1i. Accessed 3 Jan. 2018.

Hunt, Caroline L. *The Life of Ellen H. Richards*. Whitcomb and Barrows, 1918. *Google Books*, books.google.com. Accessed 3 Jan. 2018.

———. "Woman's Public Work for the Home." *Ninth Lake Placid Conference Proceedings*, 1–6 July 1907. *Google Books*, books.google.com. Accessed 3 Jan. 2018.

Hunt, Sylvia. "'Throw Aside the Veil of Helplessness': A Southern Feminist at the 1893 World's Fair." *The Southwestern Historical Quarterly*, vol. 100, 1996, pp. 48–62.

Hyde, Michael J. "Rhetorically, We Dwell." Introduction. *The Ethos of Rhetoric*, edited by Hyde, U of South Carolina P, 2004, pp. xiii–xxviii.

Hymes, James L. "Child Care Problems of the Night Shift Mother." *Journal of Consulting Psychology*, vol. 8, no. 4, 1944, pp. 225–28.

Irving, Washington. "The Legend of Sleepy Hollow." *The Life and Works of Washington Irving*, edited by Richard Henry Stoddard, Pollard and Moss, 1880. *Google Books*, books.google.com. Accessed 3 Jan. 2018.

Jack, Jordynn. "Acts of Institution: Embodying Feminist Rhetorical Methodologies in Space and Time." *Rhetoric Review*, vol. 28, no. 3, 2009, pp. 285–303.

———. *Science on the Home Front: American Women Scientists in World War II*. U of Illinois P, 2009.

Johnson, Jenell. "'A Man's Mouth Is His Castle': The Midcentury Fluoridation Controversy and the Visceral Public." *Quarterly Journal of Speech*, vol. 102, no. 1, 2016, pp. 1–20.

Johnson, Nan. *Gender and Rhetorical Space in American Life, 1866–1910*. Southern Illinois UP, 2002.

———. "History." *Peitho*, vol. 18, no. 1, 2015, pp. 15–18, peitho.cwshrc.org/files/2015/10/18.1Johnson.pdf. Accessed 3 Jan. 2018.

Johnston, Eric. "Aprons or Overalls." *American Women in the Postwar World: A Symposium of the Role Women Will Play in Business and Industry*, Weekly P, 1944, pp. 14–16.

Jones, Jacqueline. *Labor of Love, Labor of Sorrow: Black Women, Work, and the Family from Slavery to the Present*. Basic Books, 2010.

———. *Soldiers of Light and Love: Northern Teachers and Georgia Blacks, 1865–1871*. U of Georgia P, 1992.

Judah, Uriah M. "The Village School." *The Republic* vol. 3, no. 5, 1852, pp. 227–29. *HathiTrust*, babel.hathitrust.org/cgi/pt?id=mdp.39015035103707;view=1up;seq=854. Accessed 3 Jan. 2018.

Keating, AnnLouise. "Interrogating "Whiteness," (De)Constructing "Race."" *College English*, vol. 57, no. 8, 1995, pp. 901–18.

Kellogg, Rhoda. "Extended School Services—An 'Accepted Part' of the School Program." *Education for Victory*, vol. 3, no. 15, 3 Feb. 1945, pp. 9–10.

Kennedy, Tammie M., Krista Ratcliffe, and Joyce Irene Middleton. "Oxymoronic Whiteness—from the White House to Ferguson." Introduction. *Rhetorics of Whiteness: Postracial Hauntings in Popular Culture, Social Media, and Education*, edited by Kennedy, Ratcliffe, and Middleton. Southern Illinois UP, 2017, pp. 1–18.

Kerber, Linda W. "Separate Spheres, Female Worlds, Woman's Place: The Rhetoric of Women's History." *Journal of American History*, vol. 75, no. 1, 1988, pp. 9–39.

Kerr, Virginia. "One Step Forward—Two Steps Back: Child Care's Long American History." *Child Care, Who Cares? Foreign and Domestic Infant and Early Childhood Developmental Politics*, edited by Pamela Ruby, Basic Books, 1973, pp. 157–71.

Kessler-Harris, Alice. *Gendering Labor History*. U of Illinois P, 2007.

Kimble, James J., and Lester C. Olson, "Visual Rhetoric Representing Rosie the Riveter: Myth and Misconception in J. Howard Miller's 'We Can Do It!' Poster." *Rhetoric and Public Affairs*, vol. 9, no. 4, 2006, pp. 533–69.

Kimmel, Michael. *The Gendered Society*. 3rd ed., Oxford UP, 2008.

Kirsch, Gesa. "Being on Location: Serendipity, Place, and Archival Research." *Beyond the Archives: Research as a Lived Process*, edited by Kirsch and Liz Rohan, Southern Illinois UP, 2008, pp. 20–28.

Kiskaddon, Louise, et al. "Creative Activity in Nursery School." *School Arts*, vol. 43, 1943, p. 291.

"'The Kitchen'—Women's Big Post-War Goal." *Bo's'n's Whistle*, 11 May 1945, p. 7.

Kohlstedt, Sally Gregory. "Parlors, Primers, and Public Schooling: Education for Science in Nineteenth-Century America." *Isis*, vol. 81, 1990, pp. 425–45.

Kraditor, Aileen. *Up from the Pedestal: Selected Writings in the History of American Feminism*. Quadrangle, 1968.

Kushner, David. *Levittown: Two Families, One Tycoon, and the Fight for Civil Rights in America's Legendary Suburb*. Walker, 2009.

Ladd-Taylor, Molly. *Mother-Work: Women, Child Welfare, and the State, 1890–1930*. U of Illinois P, 1994.

Larned, Linda Hull. "Club Women and Home Economics." *Lake Placid Conference on Home Economics: Proceedings of the Fourth Conference*, 1909, pp. 85–91. *Google Books*, books.google.com. Accessed 17 Nov. 2018.

Leach, Abby. "The Ideal Curriculum for a Woman's College." *Publications of the Association of Collegiate Alumnae*, vol. 3, no. 1, 1898, pp. 16–21. *Google Books*, books.google.com. Accessed 3 Jan. 2018.

Leavitt, Sarah H. *From Catharine Beecher to Martha Stewart: A Cultural History of Domestic Advice*. U of North Carolina P, 2002.

Lenroot, Katharine F. "Needed: Daytime Mothers." *New York Times Magazine*, 13 Dec. 1942, pp. 18–19, 25.

Leonard, D. L. "Women as Educators." *The Chicago Schoolmaster*, vol. 5, no. 53, 1872, 271–77. *HathiTrust*, babel.hathitrust.org/cgi/pt?id=uiuo.ark:/13960/t2j67qr50;view=1up;seq=284. Accessed 3 Jan. 2018.

L'Eplattenier, Barbara. "An Argument for Archival Research Methods: Thinking beyond Methodology." *College English*, vol. 72, no. 1, 2009, pp. 67–79.

Levenstein, Harvey. "The New England Kitchen and the Origins of Modern American Food Habits." *American Quarterly*, vol. 32, 1980, pp. 369–86.

Lewis, Agnes. "Day-Care Centers Called Imitation of Soviet Union." *Philadelphia Sunday Bulletin*, 13 June 1948, p. 13.

Lewis, Tiffany. "Municipal Housekeeping in the American West: Bertha Knight Landes's Entrance into Politics." *Rhetoric and Public Affairs*, vol. 14, no. 3, 2011, pp. 465–91.

Lindsay, Malvina. "American Home Life." *Washington Post*, 31 Jan. 1946, p. 6.

Lippincott, Gail. "Experimenting at Home: Writing for the Nineteenth-Century Domestic Workplace." *Technical Communication Quarterly*, vol. 6, no. 4, 1997, pp. 365–80.

Logan, Shirley Wilson. "'What Are We Worth': Anna Julia Cooper Defines Black Women's Work at the Dawn of the Twentieth Century." *Sister Circle: Black Women and Work*, edited by Sharon Harley and the Black Women and Work Collective, Rutgers UP, 2002, pp. 146–63.

———. "'When and Where I Enter': Race, Gender, and Composition Studies." *Feminism and Composition Studies: In Other Words*, edited by Susan Jarratt and Lynn Worsham. Modern Language Association of America, 1998, pp. 45–57.

Lomawaima, K. Tsianina. "Domesticity in the Federal Indian Schools: The Power of Authority over Mind and Body." *American Ethnologist*, vol. 20, no. 2, 1993, pp. 227–40.

Lundberg, Emma O. "Our Concern—Every Child: State and Community Planning for Wartime and Post-War Security for Children." Bureau Publication 303. United States Department of Labor, 1944. *Internet Archive*, archive.org/details/ourconcerneveryc00lund_0. Accessed 3 Jan. 2018.

Lyon, Mary. "Principles and Design of the Mount Holyoke Female Seminary." 1837. *Pioneers of Women's Education in the United States: Emma Willard, Catharine Beecher, Mary Lyon*, edited by Willystine Goodsell, McGraw-Hill, 1931, pp. 278–303.

MacDonald, Walter. "Reds Howled for Child Care Funds." *New York World-Telegram*, 26 Feb. 1948, p. P4.

———. "Rich Parents Chiseling City on Child Care." *New York World-Telegram*, 28 Feb. 1947, pp. P1–P2.

Maddux, Kristy. *Practicing Citizenship: Women's Rhetoric at the 1893 Chicago World's Fair*. Penn State P, 2019.

———. "Without Touching upon Suffrage: Gender and Economic Citizenship at the World's Columbian Exposition." *Rhetoric Society Quarterly*, vol. 47, no. 2, 2017, pp. 105–30.

Malin, Brent. "Communication with Feeling: Emotion, Publicness, and Embodiment." *Quarterly Journal of Speech*, vol. 87, no. 2, 2001, pp. 216–30.

Mallett, Shelley. "Understanding Home: A Critical Review of the Literature." *Sociological Review*, vol. 52, no. 1, 2004, pp. 62–89.

Mann, Horace. *A Few Thoughts on the Powers and Duties of Woman: Two Lectures*. Hall, Mills, 1853. *Google Books*, books.google.com. Accessed 3 Jan. 2018.

———. *Lecture on Education*. Marsh, Capen, Lyon and Webb. 1840. *Google Books*, books.google.com. Accessed 3 Jan. 2018.

———. *Lectures and Annual Reports on Education*. Mary Mann, 1867. *Google Books*, books.google.com Accessed 3 Jan. 2018.

———. "Report of the Secretary of the Board of Education on the Subject of Schoolhouses, Supplementary to His First Annual Report." *Common School Journal*, vol. 1, no. 19, Oct. 1839, pp. 289–97. *Google Books*, books.google.com/books. Accessed 3 Jan. 2018.

———. *School Houses: The Form and Arrangement Best Adapted for Promoting the Health, Comfort, and Improvement of Children*. Hodson, 1839. *Google Books*, books.google.com. Accessed 3 Jan. 2018.

Martin, George H. "Boston Schools One Hundred Years Ago." *New England Magazine*, vol. 26, 1902, pp. 628–42.

"Mary Lowell Stone Home Economics Exhibit." *Lake Placid Conference on Home Economics Proceedings*, 1st, 2nd, and 3rd Annual Conferences. 1899, 1900, 1901, pp. 58–59. *Google Books*, books.google.com. Accessed 3 Jan. 2018.

Massey, Doreen. *Space, Place, and Gender*. U of Minnesota P, 1994.

Massumi, Brian. *Parables for the Virtual: Movement, Affect, Sensation*. Duke UP, 2002.

Matthews, Glenna. *The Rise of Public Woman: Woman's Power and Woman's Place in the United States, 1630–1970*. Oxford UP, 1992.

May, S. J. "An Address Delivered by S. J. May, at the Opening of a New and Highly-Improved District Schoolhouse in Hanover, Mass. June 20, 1839." *Common School Journal*, vol. 2, no. 14, 15 July 1840, pp. 218–24. *Google Books*, books.google.com. Accessed 3 Jan. 2018.

McAlister, Joan Faber. "Figural Materialism: Renovating Marriage through the American Family Home." *Southern Communication Journal*, vol. 76, no. 4, 2011, pp. 279–304.

———. "Ten Propositions for Communications Scholars Studying Space and Place." *Women's Studies in Communication*, vol. 39, no. 2, 2016, pp. 113–21.

McDowell, Linda. *Gender, Identity, and Place: Understanding Feminist Geographies*. U of Minnesota P, 1999.

McGinnis, Esther. "Broadening Family Horizons." *Journal of Home Economics*, vol. 37, no. 4, 1945, pp. 193–96. Cornell University Library, *HEARTH: Home Economics Archive*, hearth.library.cornell.edu/cgi/t/text/pageviewer-idx?c=hearth;cc=hearth;rgn=full text;idno=4732504_37_004;didno=4732504_37_004;view=image;seq=0013;node=4732504_37_004%3A6.1. Accessed 3 Jan. 2018.

Mead, Margaret. "The Women in the War." *While You Were Gone: A Report on Wartime Life in the United States*, edited by Jack Goodman, Simon and Schuster, 1946, pp. 274–89.

"Meeting of the Teaching Section of the Lake Placid Conference." *Journal of Home Economics*, vol. 1, no. 1, Feb. 1909, pp. 10–22.

Meyer, Agnes. "War Orphans, U.S.A." *Reader's Digest*, vol. 43, Aug. 1943, pp. 98–102.

———. "Women Aren't Men." *Atlantic Monthly*, vol. 186, 1950, pp. 32–36.

Meyer, Annie Nathan, editor. *Women's Work in America*. Henry Holt, 1891. *Google Books*, books.google.com/books?id=aPTNIE12b0kC&pg=PP7#v=onepage&q&f=false. Accessed 3 Jan. 2018.

Meyerowitz, Joanne J. *Women Adrift: Independent Wage Earners in Chicago, 1880–1930*. U of Chicago P, 1988.

Mezerik, A. G. "Getting Rid of the Women." *Atlantic Monthly*, vol. 175, no. 6, June 1945, pp. 79–83.

Micciche, Laura R. *Doing Emotion: Rhetoric, Writing, Teaching*. Boynton/Cook, 2007.

Middleton, Joyce Irene. "Talking about Race and Whiteness in *Crash*." *College English*, vol. 69, no. 4, 2007, pp. 321–34.

Milbourne, Chelsea Redecker, and Sarah Hallenbach. "Gender, Material Chronotopes, and the Emergence of the Eighteenth-Century Microscope." *Rhetoric Society Quarterly*, vol. 43, no. 5, 2013, pp. 401–24.

Milkman, Ruth. *Gender at Work: The Dynamics of Job Segregation by Sex during World War II*. U of Illinois P, 1987.

Miller, Susan. "The Feminization of Composition." *The Politics of Writing Instruction: Postsecondary*, edited by Richard Bullock and John Trimbur. Boynton/Cook, 1991, pp. 39–53.

Minns, George. "Reminiscences of Boston Schools—Forty Five Years Ago." *Massachusetts Teacher*, vol. 26, Oct. 1873, pp. 373–75. *Google Books*, books.google.com. Accessed 3 Jan. 2018.

"Model Cottage." *Godey's Lady's Book*, vol. 45, July–Dec. 1852, pp. 172–73. *HathiTrust*, babel.hathitrust.org/cgi/pt?id=nyp.33433081675559;view=1up;seq=755. Accessed 3 Jan. 2018.

Moisio, Risto, and Mariam Beruchashvili. "Mancaves and Masculinity." *Journal of Consumer Culture*, vol. 16, no. 3, 2016, pp. 656–76.

Moje, Elizabeth Birr. "Powerful Spaces: Tracing the Out-of-School Literacy Spaces of Latino/a Youth." *Spatializing Literacy Research and Practice*, edited by Kevin M. Leander and Margaret Sheehy, Peter Lang, 2004, pp. 15–38.

Morton, Rosalie Slaughter. *A Woman Surgeon: The Life and Work of Rosalie Slaughter Morton*. Frederick A. Stokes, 1937.

Mossell, Mrs. N. F. *The Work of the African American Woman*. Geo. S. Ferguson, 1908.

"Most Common Occupations for Women." Women's Bureau, United States Department of Labor, 2014, www.dol.gov/wb/stats/most_common_occupations_for_women.htm. Accessed 3 Jan. 2018.

Mountford, Roxanne. *The Gendered Pulpit: Preaching in American Protestant Spaces*. Southern Illinois UP, 2003.

Mullenbach, Cheryl. *Double Victory: How African American Women Broke Race and Gender Barriers to Help Win World War II*. Chicago River P, 2013.

National Association of Day Nurseries. *When Mother's Away: A Guide to the Development of Children's Day Care Units in Wartime*. Child Welfare League of America, 1943.

"News from Institutions." *Journal of Home Economics*, vol. 1, no. 1, 1909, 92–94. Cornell University Library, *HEARTH: Home Economics Archive*, hearth.library.cornell.edu/cgi/t/text/pageviewer-idx?c=hearth;cc=hearth;rgn=full text;idno=4732504_1_001;didno=4732504_1_001;view=image;seq=0094;node=4732504_1_001%3A4.17. Accessed 3 Jan. 2018.

Noddings, Nell. "Feminist Critiques of the Professions." *Review of Research in Education*, vol. 16, 1990, pp. 393–424.

Norton, Alice P. *Food and Dietetics.* American School of Home Economics, 1907. *Google Books*, books.google.com. Accessed 3 Jan. 2018.

———. "Home Economics." *The Elementary School Teacher and Course of Study*, vol. 2, no. 1, 1901, pp. 39–40. *Google Books*, books.google.com. Accessed 3 Jan. 2018.

"Nurseries Solving Big Problem for Mothers in Kaiser Shipyard." *New York Times*, 17 Nov. 1944, p. 16L.

Office of Civilian Defense. *Services for Children of Working Mothers in War Time.* Office of Civilian Defense, June 1943. *HathiTrust*, https://babel.hathitrust.org/cgi/pt?id=uiug.30112062316085;view=1up;seq=5. Accessed 9 Dec. 2018.

Operatives' Magazine: Containing Articles upon Literary and Religious Subjects, Written by Manufacturing Operatives. Harvard Library, *Women Working, 1800–1930*, iiif.lib.harvard.edu/manifests/view/drs:2868487$1i. Accessed 3 Jan. 2018.

Orvell, Miles. *The Death and Life of Main Street: Small Towns in American Memory, Space, and Community.* U of North Carolina P, 2014.

"Our History." Women's Bureau, United States Department of Labor, www.dol.gov/wb/info_about_wb/interwb.htm. Accessed 3 Jan. 2018.

Patton, June O., et al. "Moonlight and Magnolias in Southern Education: The Black Mammy Memorial Institute." *The Journal of Negro History*, vol. 65, no. 2, 1980, 149–55.

Penny, Virginia. *The Employments of Women: A Cyclopaedia of Woman's Work.* Walker, Wise, & Co., 1863. *Google Books*, books.google.com. Accessed 3 Jan. 2018.

Perelman, Chaim, and Lucia Olbrechts-Tyteca. *The New Rhetoric: A Treatise on Argumentation.* U of Notre Dame P, 1969.

Perlmann, Joel, et al. "Literacy, Schooling, and Teaching among New England Women, 1730–1820." *History of Education Quarterly*, vol. 7, no. 2, 1997, pp. 117–39.

Perlmann, Joel, and Robert A. Margo. *Women's Work? American Schoolteachers, 1650–1920.* U of Chicago P, 2001.

Pfister, Elta. "The Case for Child Care Centers." *Journal of Consulting Psychology*, vol. 8, no. 4, 1944, pp. 199–205.

Phelps, Almira Lincoln. *Lectures to Young Ladies: Comprising Outlines and Applications of the Different Branches of Female Education*. Carter, Hendee, 1833. *Internet Archive*, archive.org/details/lecturestoyoung100phelrich/page/n5. Accessed 17 Nov. 2018.

Phelps, Elizabeth Stuart. *The Silent Partner*. 1871. Feminist P, 1983.

Pittman, Coretta. "Black Women Writers and the Trouble with *Ethos*: Harriet Jacobs, Billie Holiday, and Sister Souljah." *Rhetoric Society Quarterly*, vol. 37, no. 1, 2007, pp. 43–70.

Plain Talk and Friendly Advice to Domestics. Phillips, Sampson, 1855. *Google Books*, books.google.com. Accessed 22 Jan. 2018.

Poirot, Kristan, and Shevaun E. Watson. "Memories of Freedom and White Resilience: Place, Tourism, and Urban Slavery." *Rhetoric Society Quarterly*, vol. 45, no. 2, 2015, pp. 91–116.

Portales, Patricia. "Tejanas on the Home Front: Women, Bombs, and the (Re)Gendering of War in Mexican American World War II Literature." *Latina/os and World War II: Mobility, Agency, and Ideology*, edited by Maggie Rivas-Rodriguez and B. V. Olguín, U of Texas P, 2014, pp. 175–96.

Porter, James. *The Operative's Friend, and Defence; or, Hints to Young Ladies Who Are Dependent on Their Own Exertions*. C. H. Peirce, 1850. *Google Books*, books.google.com. Accessed 3 Jan. 2018.

Potter, Alonzo, and George B. Emerson. *The School and Schoolmaster*. William B. Towle and N. Capen, 1848.

Powell, Malea. "Stories Take Place: A Performance in One Act." *College Composition and Communication*, vol. 64, no. 2, 2012, pp. 383–406.

Prelli, Lawrence. "Rhetorics of Display: An Introduction." *Rhetorics of Display*, edited by Prelli, U of South Carolina P, 2006, pp. 1–40.

Prentice, Allison L., and Marjorie R. Theobald. "The Historiography of Women Teachers: A Retrospect." *Women Who Taught: Perspectives on the History of Women and Teaching*, edited by Prentice and Theobald, U of Toronto P, 1991, pp. 3–33.

"President Obama at the University of Kansas." C-Span, 22 Jan. 2015, *YouTube*, www.youtube.com/watch?v=j-Rh_lHNU_w. Accessed 3 Jan. 2018.

Proceedings of Conference on Day Care of Children of Working Mothers with Special Reference to Defense Areas. Held in Washington, DC, 31 July–1 Aug. 1941. United States Department of Labor, Bureau Publication no. 281. Government Printing Office, 1942. *Internet Archive*, archive.org/details/proceedingsofcon42conf. Accessed 3 Jan. 2018.

Proceedings of the Conference on the Care of Dependent Children. Held in Washington, DC. Government Printing Office, 1909.

The Profession of Home Making: A Condensed Home-Study Course. American School of Home Economics, 1911. *HathiTrust*, catalog.hathitrust.org/Record/006602227. Accessed 13 Feb. 2019.

Quiñonez, Naomi. "Rosita the Riveter: Welding Tradition with Wartime Transformation." *Mexican Americans & World War II*, edited by Maggie Rivas-Rodriguez, U of Texas P, 2005, pp. 245–68.

Ratcliffe, Krista. *Rhetorical Listening: Identification, Gender, Whiteness*. Southern Illinois UP, 2005.

Reynolds, Nedra. "*Ethos* as Location: New Sites for Understanding Discursive Authority." *Rhetoric Review*, vol. 11, no. 2, 1993, pp. 325–38.

———. *Geographies of Writing: Inhabiting Places and Encountering Difference*. Southern Illinois UP, 2007.

Rice, Jenny Edbauer. "The New 'New': Making a Case for Critical Affect Studies." *Quarterly Journal of Speech*, vol. 94, no. 2, 2008, pp. 200–12.

Rich, Adrienne. "Notes toward a Politics of Location." *Blood, Bread, and Poetry: Selected Prose 1979–1985*. W. W. Norton, 1994.

Richards, Ellen. "Count Rumford, and His Work for Humanity." *Plain Words about Food: The Rumford Kitchen Leaflets*. Home Science Publishing, 1899, 19–27. *Google Books*, books.google.com. Accessed 4 Jan. 2018.

———. *Euthenics, the Science of Controllable Environment: A Plea for Better Living Conditions as a First Step toward Higher Human Efficiency*. 2nd ed., Whitcomb & Barrows, 1912. *Google Books*, books.google.com. Accessed 4 Jan. 2018.

———. "The Housekeeper's Laboratory." *The New England Kitchen Magazine*, vol. 3, no. 1, Apr. 1895, pp. 5–6. *Google Books*, books.google.com. Accessed 4 Jan. 2018.

———. Letter to the Massachusetts Board of World's Fair Managers. 27 Dec. 1893. *MIT Archives*, libraries.mit.edu/archives/exhibits/esr/esr-rumford.html. Accessed 4 Jan. 2018.

———. "The Place of Science in Woman's Education." *The American Kitchen Magazine*, vol. 7, no. 6, Sept. 1897, pp. 224–27. *Google Books*, books.google.com. Accessed 4 Jan. 2018.

———. "Preface to Part I." *Plain Words about Food: The Rumford Kitchen Leaflets*. Home Science Publishing, 1899, pp. 132–33. *Google Books*, books.google.com. Accessed 4 Jan. 2018.

———. "The Relation of College Women to Progress in Domestic Science." Paper presented to the Association of Collegiate Alumnae, 24 Oct. 1890. Series 2, no. 27, pp. 1–10.

———. "Scientific Cooking in the New England Kitchen." *Forum*, vol. 15, May 1859, pp. 355–61. *Google Books*, books.google.com. Accessed 4 Jan. 2018.

———. "Wanted: A Test for Manpower." *Clarkson Bulletin*, vol. 3, no. 3, 1906, pp. 3–11. *MIT Archives*, web.mit.edu/hartman/public/digital/manpower/index.htm. Accessed 4 Jan. 2018.

Rickert, Thomas. *Ambient Rhetoric: The Attunements of Rhetorical Being*. U of Pittsburgh P, 2013.

Rivers, Nathaniel A., and Ryan P. Weber. "Ecological, Pedagogical, Public Rhetoric." *College Composition and Communication*, vol. 63, no. 2, 2011, 187–218.

Rohan, Liz. "Reveal Codes: A New Lens for Examining and Historicizing the Work of Secretaries." *Computers and Composition*, vol. 20, 2003, pp. 237–53.

Rose, Elizabeth. *A Mother's Job: The History of Day Care, 1890–1960*. Oxford UP, 1999.

Rose, Gillian. *Feminism & Geography: The Limits of Geographical Knowledge*. U of Minnesota P, 1993.

Rothery, Agnes Edwards. "The Successful Mother." *Home Progress*, vol. 2, no. 3, Nov. 1912, pp. 31–34. *Google Books*, books.google.com. Accessed 4 Jan. 2018.

Rothstein, Edward. "Assessing a Future from 120 Years Ago: Field Museum Looks Back at the Chicago World's Fair." *New York Times*, 1 Nov. 2013, www.nytimes.com/2013/11/02/arts/design/field-museum-looks-back-at-chicagos-worlds-fair.html. Accessed 4 Jan. 2018.

Rottenberg, Catherine. "Happiness and the Liberal Imagination: How Superwoman Became Balanced." *Feminist Studies*, vol. 40, no. 1, 2014, pp. 144–68.

Royce, Josiah. "Present Ideals of American University Life." *Scribner's Magazine*, vol. 10, 1891, pp. 376–88.

"The Rumford Kitchen at the World's Fair." *The New England Kitchen Magazine: A Domestic Science Monthly*, vol. 1, 1894, pp. 11–12. *Google Books*, books.google.com. Accessed 4 Jan. 2018.

Russell, Anna U., and William Russell. *Introduction to the Young Ladies' Elocutionary Reader*, James Munroe and Company, 1845. HathiTrust, https://babel.hathitrust.org/cgi/pt?id=loc.ark:/13960/t7mp69t0z;view=1up;seq=9. Accessed 5 Dec. 2018.

Ryan, Kathleen, et al. "Identifying Feminist Ecological Ethē." Introduction. *Rethinking Ethos: A Feminist Ecological Approach to Rhetoric*, edited by Ryan et al., Southern Illinois UP, 2016, pp. 1–22.

Ryan, Mary. *Womanhood in America: From Colonial Times to the Present*. New Viewpoints, 1975.

———. *Women in Public: Between Banners and Ballots, 1825–1880*. Johns Hopkins UP, 1992.

Sandberg, Sheryl. *Lean In: Women, Work, and the Will to Lead.* Knopf, 2013.

Schiappa, Edward. *Defining Reality: Definitions and the Politics of Meaning.* Southern Illinois UP, 2003.

Schroeder, Rilla. "Housing in the Battle for Production." *Independent Woman,* vol. 21, no. 21, 1942, pp. 4–6, 27.

Schuyler, Joseph B. "Women at Work." *The Catholic World,* Apr. 1943, pp. 26–30.

Scott, Joan Wallach. *The Fantasy of Feminist History.* Duke UP, 2011.

Selzer, Jack. "Habeas Corpus: An Introduction." *Rhetorical Bodies,* edited by Selzer and Sharon Crowley. U of Wisconsin P, 1999, pp. 3–15.

Shapiro, Laura. *Perfection Salad: Women and Cooking at the Turn of the Century.* Farrar, Straus, and Giroux, 1986.

Sharer, Wendy B. *Vote and Voice: Women's Organizations and Political Literacy, 1915–1930.* Southern Illinois UP, 2004.

Sharpless, Rebecca. *Cooking in Other Women's Kitchens: Domestic Workers in the South, 1865–1960.* U of North Carolina P, 2010.

Sharpling, Gerard Paul. "Towards a Rhetoric of Experience: The Role of *Enargeia* in the Essays of Montaigne." *Rhetorica,* vol. 10, no. 2, 2002, pp. 173–92.

Shaver, Lisa. *Beyond the Pulpit: Women's Rhetorical Roles in the Antebellum Religious Press.* U of Pittsburgh P, 2012.

———. "'No Cross, No Crown': An Ethos of Presence in Margaret Prior's *Walks of Usefulness.*" *College English,* vol. 75, no. 1, 2012, pp. 61–78.

Shaw, Stephanie. *What a Woman Ought to Be and Do: Black Professional Women Workers during the Jim Crow Era.* U of Chicago P, 1996.

Sigourney, Lydia. "Perceptions of the Beautiful." *Godey's Lady's Book,* vol. 20, 1840, p. 9.

———. "Superficial Attainments." *Godey's Lady's Book,* vol. 21, July 1840, pp. 29–31.

"Sisters in a Circle." Preface. *Sister Circle: Black Women and Work,* edited by Sharon Harley and The Black Women and Work Collective, Rutgers UP, 2002, pp. xv–xix.

Skinner, Carolyn. *Women Physicians and Professional Ethos in Nineteenth-Century America.* Southern Illinois UP, 2014.

Slaughter, Anne Marie. *Unfinished Business: Women, Men, Work, Family.* Random House, 2015.

Sloan, Samuel. *American Houses: A Variety of Original Designs for Rural Buildings.* Samuel Sloan, 1861. *Google Books,* books.google.com. Accessed 4 Jan. 2018.

Small, Walter Herbert. *Early New England Schools.* Arno P, 1969.

Smith, A. Lapthorn. "Higher Education of Women and Race Suicide." *Popular Science Monthly,* vol. 65, Mar. 1905, pp. 467–73.

Smith, Craig R. "*Ethos* Dwells Pervasively: A Hermeneutic Reading of Aristotle on Credibility." *The* Ethos *of Rhetoric*, edited by Michael J. Hyde, U of South Carolina P, 2004, pp. 1–19.

Smith, Mary Roberts. "Report of Committee on Courses of Study in Home Economics in Colleges and Universities." *Lake Placid Conference on Home Economics: Proceedings of the Fourth Annual Conference*, 1902, pp. 17–25. *Google Books,* books.google.com. Accessed 17 Nov. 2018.

———. "Shall the College Curriculum Be Modified for Women?" *Publications of the Association of Collegiate Alumnae*, ser. 3, no. 1, 1989, pp. 1–15. *Google Books,* books.google.com. Accessed 17 Nov. 2018.

Soja, Edward W. *Postmodern Geographies: The Reassertion of Space in Critical Social Theory*. Verso, 1989.

———. *Seeking Social Justice*. U of Minnesota P, 2010.

Soper, Sarah Clatterbuck. "What It's Like as a 'Girl' in the Lab." *New York Times*, 18 June 2015, www.nytimes.com/2015/06/18/opinion/what-its-like-as-a-girl-in-the-lab.html. Accessed 4 Jan. 2018.

Spack, Ruth. *America's Second Tongue: American Indian Education and the Ownership of English, 1860–1900*. U of Nebraska P, 2002.

Spain, Daphne. *Gendered Spaces*. U of North Carolina P, 1992.

"The Sphere of Woman," *Godey's Lady's Book*, vol. 40, Mar. 1850, p. 209. *Google Books*, books.google.com. Accessed 4 Jan. 2018.

Spock, Benjamin. *The Common Sense Book of Baby and Child Care*. Duell, Sloan, and Pearce, 1946.

Stage, Sarah. "Ellen Richards and the Social Significance of the Home Economics Movement." *Rethinking Home Economics: Women and the History of the Profession*, edited by Stage and Virginia Vincenti, Cornell UP, 1997, pp. 17–33.

———. "Home Economics: What's in a Name?" *Rethinking Home Economics: Women and the History of the Profession*, edited by Stage and Virginia Vincenti, Cornell UP, 1997, pp. 1–13.

Starr, Penny. "Gloria Steinem: In U.S., Home Is 'Single Most Dangerous Place for a Woman.'" *CNSNews.com*, www.cnsnews.com/news/article/gloria-steinem-us-home-single-most-dangerous-place-woman. Accessed 4 Jan. 2018.

"A Startling Question." *Happy Home and Parlor Magazine*, vol. 5, 1857, pp. xxi–xxii. *Google Books*, books.google.com. Accessed 2 Jan. 2018.

Steelman, Ruth. "The First Year of Extended School Services in Greensboro." *Education for Victory*, vol. 3, no. 17, 3 Mar. 1943, pp. 12–13.

Stevenson, Betsy. "An 'Experiment in Universal Child Care in the United States: Lessons from the Lanham Act." *The White House Blog*, 22 Jan. 2015, obamawhitehouse.archives.gov/blog/2015/01/22

/experiment-universal-child-care-united-states-lessons-lanham-act. Accessed 4 Jan. 2018.

Stoddard, George D. "Emergency Nursery Schools and Child Health." *Child Health Bulletin*, vol. 10, 1934, pp. 193–201.

Stoltzfus, Emilie. *Citizen, Mother, Worker: Debating Public Responsibility for Child Care after the Second World War*. U of North Carolina P, 2003.

Stone, Lucy. "Progress of Fifty Years." *The Congress of Women, Held in the Woman's Building, World's Columbian Exposition*. Vol. 1, edited by Mary Kavanaugh Oldham Eagle, International Publishing, 1894, pp. 58–61. *Google Books*, books.google.com. Accessed 4 Jan. 2018.

Stone, Pamela. *Opting Out? Why Women Really Quit Careers and Head Home*. U of California P, 2007.

Suggs, Redding S. *Mother-Teacher: The Feminization of American Education*. U of Virginia P, 1978.

Sugrue, Thomas J. "Jim Crow's Last Stand: The Struggle to Integrate Levittown." *Second Suburb: Levittown, Pennsylvania*, edited by Dianne Harris, U of Pittsburgh P, 2010, pp. 175–99.

Sumner, Margaret. *Chats on Garment Salesmanship: Written for the Benefit and Instruction of Saleswomen throughout America Who Appreciate Their Positions and Are Endeavoring to Develop Their Sales Ability*. Printz-Biederman, 1917. *Google Books*, books.google.com. Accessed 4 Jan. 2018.

Swartz, Lora. "Child Service Centers." *Journal of Home Economics*, vol. 37, no. 2, Feb. 1945, pp. 76–79. Cornell University Library, *HEARTH: Home Economics Archive*, hearth.library.cornell.edu/cgi/t/text/pageviewer-idx?c=hearth;cc=hearth;rgn=full text;idno=4732504_37_002;didno=4732504_37_002;view=image;seq=0020;node=4732504_37_002%3A6.4. Accessed 4 Jan. 2018.

Sykes, G. "Teaching and Professionalism: A Cautionary Perspective." Michigan State University, Apr. 1987. Paper Presentation.

Terrill, Bertha. *Household Management*. American School of Home Economics, 1907. *Internet Archive*, https://archive.org/details/householdmanage01econgoog. Accessed 4 Jan. 2018.

"30 Shocking Domestic Violence Statistics That Remind Us It's an Epidemic." *Huffpost*, 6 Dec. 2017, www.huffingtonpost.com/2014/10/23/domestic-violence-statistics_n_5959776.html. Accessed 2 Jan 2018.

Thomas, M. Carey. "Present Tendencies in Women's College and University Education." *Educational Review*, Jan. 1908, pp. 64–85.

Thomas, W. I. "Woman and the Occupations." *Selected Articles on the Employment of Women*, edited by Edna Dean Bullock, H. W. Wilson Co., 1911, pp. 28–40. *Google Books*, books.google.com. Accessed 4 Jan. 2018.

Tuan, Yi-Fu. *Space and Place: The Perspective of Experience.* U of Minnesota P, 1977.

———. *Topophilia: A Study of Environmental Perceptions, Attitudes, and Values.* Prentice Hall, 1974.

Tuthill, Louisa. *The Young Lady's Home.* Lindsay and Blakiston, 1848. *Google Books*, books.google.com. Accessed 4 Jan. 2018.

VanHaitsma, Pamela. "Anna Wood, Irene Leache, and the 'Opulent Friendships' of Women Teachers." *Women at Work: Rhetorics of Gender and Labor*, edited by David Gold and Jessica Enoch, U of Pittsburgh P, 2019.

Vapnek, Lara. *Breadwinners: Working Women and Economic Independence: 1865–1920.* U of Illinois P, 2009.

Veysey, Lawrence. *The Emergence of the American University.* U of Chicago P, 1965.

Vorhies, Heather Blain. "Women and Corporate Communication in the Early American Republic." *Peitho*, vol. 19, no. 1, 2016, pp. 5–27, peitho.cwshrc.org/files/2017/01/19.1_Blain-Vorhies_FINAL.pdf. Accessed 4 Jan. 2018.

Walker, Francis A. "Guide to the Rumford Kitchen. *Plain Words about Food: The Rumford Kitchen Leaflets.* Home Science Publishing, 1899, pp. 11–14. *Google Books*, books.google.com. Accessed 4 Jan. 2018.

Walker, Lynne. "Home Making: An Architectural Perspective." *Signs*, vol. 27, no. 3, 2002, pp. 823–35.

Walsh, Edwina. *Schoolmarms: Women in America's Schools.* Caddo Gap, 1995.

"Wartime Care and Protection of Children of Employed Mothers." Hearing before the Committee on Education and Labor, United States Senate, 78th Congress, 8 June 1943. Government Printing Office, 1943.

Waxman, Olivia B. "#DistractinglySexy Trends in Response to Nobel Scientist's Sexist Remarks." *Time*, 12 June 2015, time.com/3918909/distractingly-sexy-tim-hunt/. Accessed 4 Jan. 2018.

Weimann, Jeanne Madeline. *The Fair Women.* Academy Chicago, 1981.

Weiner, Lynn Y. *From Working Girl to Working Mother: The Female Labor Force in the United States, 1820–1980.* U of North Carolina P, 1985.

Wells, Susan. *Out of the Dead House: Nineteenth-Century Women Physicians and the Writing of History.* U of Wisconsin P, 2001.

Welter, Barbara. "The Cult of True Womanhood: 1820–1860." *American Quarterly*, vol. 18, 1966, pp. 151–74.

Wetherill, G. G. "Health Problems in Child Care Centers." *Hygeia*, vol. 21, Sept. 1943, pp. 634–35.

West, Candace, and Don H. Zimmerman. "Doing Gender." *Gender and Society*, vol. 1, no. 2, 1987, pp. 125–51.

Wheelock, David C. "The Federal Response to Home Mortgage Distress: Lessons from the Great Depression." *Federal Reserve Bank of St. Louis Review*, May/June 2008, pp. 133–48.

"While Mothers Work." *The Bo's'n's Whistle*, 7 Oct. 1943, pp. 12–13.

"While Their Parents Build Planes." *Women's Home Companion*, vol. 70, March 1943, pp. 6, 8, 10.

White, Mimi. "Gender Territories: House Hunting on American Real Estate TV." *Television & New Media*, vol. 14, no. 3, 2013, pp. 228–43.

White, Sallie Joy. *Housekeepers and Home-Makers*. Jordan, Marsh & Co., 1888. *Google Books*, books.google.com. Accessed 4 Jan. 2018.

Whitman, Walt. "Death in the School-Room—a Fact." *The Ladies' Garland*, vol. 5, no. 3, Sept. 1841, pp. 73–75. *Google Books*, books.google.com. Accessed 4 Jan. 2018.

Whitney, Miss M. W. "Scientific Study and Work for Women." *Education*, Sept. 1882, pp. 58–69.

Willard, Frances. *Occupations for Women: A Book of Practical Suggestions for the Material Advancement, the Mental and Physical Development, and the Moral and Spiritual Uplift of Women*. Success, 1897. *Google Books*, books.google.com. Accessed 4 Jan. 2018.

Williams, Mary E. "Domestic Science in New York City Schools." *The Journal of Home Economics*, vol. 1, no. 1, 1909, pp. 77–80.

Woman's Work: A Journal Devoted to the Employments of Women, vol. 1, no. 6, May 1885. Harvard Library, *Women Working, 1800–1930*, iiif.lib.harvard.edu/manifests/view/drs:3836061$1i. Accessed 4 Jan. 2018.

"Women and the Township." *Harper's Bazaar*, vol. 29, no. 2, 11 Jan. 1896, p. 22.

Women's Bureau. "Fourteenth Report of the Director of the Women's Bureau for the Fiscal Year Ended June 30, 1932." Government Printing Office, 1932. *Google Books*, books.google.com. Accessed 4 Jan. 2018.

———. *Handbook of Facts on Women Workers*. Bulletin 225. Government Printing Office, 1948.

———. "Mothers and Families." United States Department of Labor, Aug. 2014, www.dol.gov/wb/stats/mother_families.htm. Accessed 4 Jan. 2018.

———. "Second Annual Report of the Director of the Women's Bureau for the Fiscal Year Ended June 30, 1920." *Annual Report of the Director of the Women's Bureau*. Government Printing Office, 1920. *Google Books*, books.google.com. Accessed 4 Jan. 2018.

———. "Third Annual Report of the Director of the Women's Bureau for the Fiscal Year Ended June 30, 1921." Government Printing Office, 1921. *Google Books*, books.google.com. Accessed 4 Jan. 2018.

———. "Women Workers in Their Family Environment." Bulletin No. 183. Government Printing Office, 1941. *Google Books*, books.google.com. Accessed 4 Feb. 2019.

"Women's Institutes in North Carolina." *Journal of Home Economics*, vol. 1, no. 2, 1909, pp. 161–3. Cornell University Library, *HEARTH: Home*

Economics Archive, hearth.library.cornell.edu/cgi/t/text/pageviewer -idx?c=hearth;cc=hearth;rgn=full text;idno=4732504_1_002;didno =4732504_1_002;view=image;seq=0052;node=4732504_1_002%3A3.9. Accessed 4 Jan. 2018.

"Woman's Sphere in Modern Life." *Godey's Lady's Book,* vol. 45, July–Dec. 1852, pp. 171–72. *HathiTrust,* babel.hathitrust.org/cgi/pt?id=nyp .33433081675559;view=1up;seq=755. Accessed 4 Jan. 2018.

Wood, Andrew F. "Managing the Lady Managers: The Shaping of Heterotopian Spaces in the 1893 Chicago Exposition's Woman's Building." *Southern Communication Journal,* vol. 69, no. 4, 2004, pp. 289–302.

Woolman, Mary Schenck. "The Home Scientific: What the College Course May Contribute." *New York Tribune,* Sunday Magazine, 11 June 1905, p. 7. Library of Congress, *Chronicling America,* chroniclingamerica.loc .gov/lccn/sn83030214/1905-06-11/ed-1/seq-31/. Accessed 8 Dec. 2018.

"World's Food Fair." *New England Kitchen Magazine,* vol. 2, no. 2, 1894, pp. 3–9. *Google Books,* books.google.com. Accessed 4 Jan. 2018.

Wright, Gwendolyn. *Building the Dream: A Social History of Housing in America.* Pantheon, 1981.

Yellin, Emily. *Our Mothers' War: American Women at Home and at the Front during World War II.* Free P, 2004.

Yergeau, Melanie, et al. "Multimodality in Motion: Disability and Kairotic Spaces." *Kairos,* vol. 18, no. 1, 2013, kairos.technorhetoric.net/18.1 /coverweb/yergeau-et-al/. Accessed 4 Jan. 2018.

Young, John H. *Our Deportment, or The Manners, Conduct and Dress of the Most Refined Society,* F. B. Dickerson & Co., 1880. *Google Books,* books. google.com. Accessed 5 Dec. 2018.

Zucker, Henry L. "Working Parents and Latchkey Children." *The Annals of the American Academy of Political and Social Science,* vol. 236, Nov. 1944, pp. 43–50.

Index

Page numbers in italics denote illustrations.

Abel, Mary Hinman, 98, 99–103
Adams. W. J., 46
Addams, Jane, 100, 112
advice manuals, 1–2, 20–21; architectural, 36–38, *38*; career literature/vocational autobiography, 16, 180; domestic, 77–78, 94; domestic science literature, 86, 91, 93, 96–97, 107; for men, twenty-first century, 179; visuals, *38, 39*
African American women: domestic science and, 117–18; in domestic service, 14–17, 86, 118, 177; home as site of resistance, 177–78, 199n1; housing, 164; teachers, 28, 67–68; in workforce, 14–18, 22, 86, 125–26, 168–69, 177, 182, 198n5. *See also* marginalized women's experiences; race issues; segregation
"After Lanham Funds-What?" (Close), 152
agency, 10–11
Ahmed, Sara, 151–52, 154, 157
Alcott, William, 46–47
Allen, J., 12
Allen, Polly Wynn, 178
American Association of University Women (AAUW), 85, 89

American Home Economics Association (AHEA), 85, 115
American Institute of Instruction, 46, 47
American Woman's Home (Beecher and Stowe), 1–2, *3, 4,* 38
American Women in the Postwar World, 160
"America's Profound Gender Anxiety" (Green), 175
Anthony, Susan B., II, 185
Aoki, Eric, 173
"Appeal for Men Teachers" (*New York Times*), 64
Applegarth, Risa, 16, 74, 99
"Aprons or Overalls" (Johnston), 150
architectural plans, 1–3, 36–39; childcare centers, 134–36; DeafSpace, 174–75; feminist critiques of, 23, 178; model house designs, *3, 4,* 39, *41*; schools, 46–51, *50,* 54–57, *55, 56,* 59, 65; vines, emotional impact of, 37, *38,* 40–42. *See also* home
Architecture of Country Houses: Designs for Cottages, Farm-Houses, and Villas (Downing), 37–42, *38*
architecture of gender, 163
Aristotelian ethos, 74, 97, 115

229

artifacts, 24–25, 189–90
Association of Collegiate Alumnae, 85, 89, 100, 109
audience: childcare center visuals and, 139, 145–46; enthymematic argument, 105–6, 109, 197n13; ethos and, 74, 88–89, 98–103, 111, 124
autobiography, vocational, 16, 180

back-to-the-home movement, 155–64, 168
Backus, Samuel, 37
Backus, William, 37
Bacon, Edmund, 131–32
Bakhtin, M. M., 10
Banning, Margaret Culkin, 153–54
Barnard, Eunice, 147, 148, 195n5
Barnard, Henry, 46–51, 53–54; *Practical Illustrations of the Principles of School Architecture*, 56; *School Architecture; or, Contributions to the Improvement of School-Houses in the United States*, 47–51, *50*, *56*, 56–57, 59
Barnett, Scot, 13
Barrows, Anna, 92
Baruch, Dorothy, 137, 149, 152–53
Baxandall, Rosalyn, 14, 162
Beecher, Catharine E., 39, 42, 70; *American Woman's Home* (Beecher and Stowe), 1–2, *3*, *4*, 38; *Suggestions respecting Improvements in Education*, 59–60
Beer, Ethel S., 137, 145
Berry, Riley M. Fletcher, 118
Bevier, Isabel, 83, 84, 90, 91
birthrate, postwar, 163
Bitter Fruit: African American Women in World War II (Honey), 168
Black Mammy Memorial Institute, 118

Blair, Carole, 8, 136, 173–74
bodies, 12–13, 32–33, 62, 166, 174
Bolton, Sharon, 183
Bondi, Liz, 33, 58
Bossard, J. H. S., 160–61
"Boston Schools One Hundred Years Ago" (Martin), 44
Bourdieu, Pierre, 95
Boyle, Casey, 13
Brown, Helen Weigel, 131
Bryden, Inga, 21
Bryn Mawr College, 73, 86, 89
Budd, Dorothy, 144
Buell, Mrs. C. S., 92, 113–14
Burke, Kenneth, 105, 173
Butler, Judith, 32, 52–53, 154

Calvinist theology in teaching practices, 44, 53
cardinal virtues, 21
career options, 70; professionalization, 73. *See also* teaching profession
Carlisle Indian Industrial School, 65–66
Carroll, Jane, 120
Carson, Ruth, 139–40
Carter, Erica, 9
Chadsey, Mildred, 112–13
The Chemistry of Cooking and Cleaning: A Manual for House-keepers (Richards), 85
Chemistry of the Household (Dodd), 96–97, 186
Chicago World's Fair (Columbian Exposition, 1893), 99, 103–5
Child, Lydia Maria, 46, 78, 97
childcare centers, 27, 120–70; activists, 151–55, 159; back-to-the-home movement, 155–64, 168; communism fears and, 159, 162, 166, 172;

community responsibility and, 152–53; domestic assistance for mothers, 148; exigency of, 152–53; funding for, 121–24, 134, 151, 155, 164; government decision-making, 138, 151, 164, 175; as homelike space, 5, 122–24, 137, 138–46, 153–54; location of, 134–36; love and care in, 143; mothers' concerns about, 136–39; patriotism and, 143–46, *145*; postwar debate, 122, 150–55; private, 164; racial prejudice and, 135, 144, 153, 163–64, 168, 198n5; safety and security, 141–43; as secondary domestic space, 5, 149–50; spatial rhetorics of, 7, 122–24, 130–47, 152–54; as superhomes, 137–38, 146–50, 154; "victory home" rhetoric and, 122, 155; visual depictions of, 139–41, *140, 141, 142, 144, 145*; as "war nursery," 121–22, 125, 137, 157, 164; white middle-class assumptions about, 125–26; worker credentials, 148. *See also* "motherless home"

A Children's Charter in Wartime, 130
Child Service Centers booklet, 134
Christoph, Julie Nelson, 99
cities: "anti-urban sentiment," 22, 37; municipal housekeeping movement, 76, 111–13
Clark, Clifford, 162–63
Cleaveland, Henry William, 37
Cleveland, Alfred, 62, 64–65
Clifford, Geraldine, 66, 67
Close, Kathryn, 152
colleges and universities: criticisms of effect on women, 83, 87–88; elective system, 80–83; German university, 81; historically black, 117–18; knowledge as locatable, 118–19;

laboratories, 82–88, 182; land-grant universities, 86, 116–17; Massachusetts Institute of Technology, 84–85, 87; professionalization, 73, 77, 80–88, 93; Richards and, 84–88; women's colleges, 73, 80, 86, 89. *See also* domestic science; domestic scientists

Common Sense Book of Baby and Child Care (Spock), 157–58
communism, fears of, 159, 162, 166, 172
Conference on Day Care of Children of Working Mothers with Special Reference to Defense Areas (1941), 132
Congressional Hearings on Wartime Care and Protection of Children of Employed Mothers, 135
Converse, Mary, 90
Cooley, Anna, 113
Cooper, Anna Julia, 16
"Cooperation on the Home Front" (Finck), 146–47, *147*
corporal punishment in school, 44–45, 51, *52*
Cott, Nancy, 35, 43, 195nn2, 3
Courtney, Jennifer, 179
Cravens, Hamilton, 100, 102
Crawford, Frederick, 160
Crawley, Edward, 158
credibility, 27, 74–75
Cremin, Lawrence, 44
cult of domesticity, 21, 36
The Cultural Politics of Emotion (Ahmed), 151–52

Daniell, Maria, 103–9
Davidson, Cathy, 21
Davidson, Joyce, 33, 58
DeafSpace, 174–75

de Certeau, Michel, 9–10, 11
"Declaration of Sentiments," 17
Defense Housing and Community Facilities and Services Act of 1940 (Lanham Act), 134
deiktikos (exhibit), 98
democratic principles, 20, 137, 143–44, 159, 162, 168, 185. *See also* patriotism
Dempsey, Mary V., 14
Deutsch, Sarah, 22
Dickinson, Greg, 8, 173, 174
disability studies perspective, 174–75
display, as spatio-rhetorical strategy, 76, 98–110; epideictic character, 104–6, 109; negative reactions of customers, 102–3; peripatetic tradition, 110; purposeful crafting of, 98–99
#distractinglysexy hashtag movement, 182
"The District School Teacher" (*Harper's Weekly*), 62, 63
Dodd, Margaret, 96–97, 186
domestic science, 5, 13, 72–119, 172, 184; absence of children and emotion, 186–87; African American women and, 117–18; beyond the home, 76, 110–14, 198n16; contemporary unfamiliarity with, 114–15; display, spatio-rhetorical strategy of, 76, 98–110; elitism of, 76, 99, 102–3; enthymematic argument, 105–6; ethos and spatial rhetorics, 73–74, 77–80, 84, 88–97, 118–19; exhibits, 76, 85, 91, 99–103, 109–10, 114, 116; experiments, 94–97; extracurricular efforts, 86; home economics, 85–87, 98–110, 114–18, 197n7; idyllic home, contestation of, 76–77, 91–93, 177; kitchen as laboratory, 94–97, *95*; laboratories, 82–88, 182; Lake Placid Conferences, 85, 92, 97, 114; Mary Lowell Stone Home Economics exhibit, 109–10; men's contributions to, 105–6; motherhood and, 76–77, 88, 92–93; municipal housekeeping movement, 76, 111–13; New England Kitchen, 76, 99–103, 114, 116; Rumford Kitchen, 76, 99, 103–9, 110; scientific expertise of women, 72, 74–76, 86, 90–91, 106–7, 110–14, 198n16
domestic scientists, 6–7, 18, 27, 72–119, 174; academic positions, 114; as conservative, 74, 87, 115–16; display of knowledge, 100–102; ethos, collective construction of, 74–75; public sphere and, 76; scientist, as title, 73; spatio-rhetorical tactics, 84, 94
domestic service, 14–17, 86, 118, 177
domestic violence, 178–79
dominant discourses: childcare during wartime, 125, 150, 157, 175; northeastern United States, 34–35; of professionalization, 84; teaching and, 35–36, 42–43, 51, 67; of white middle-class home, 7–10, 13, 18–20, 25–26, 76–79
Downing, Andrew, 36–37, *38*, 39–42, 54, 186
Dratch, Howard, 164
Dressler, F. B., 48
drudgery, white middle-class home as site of, 76–77, 79, 89–91, 96
Dublin, Thomas, 17
Durant, Sarah, 182
dwelling, ethos as, 74

Edwards, Janis L., 139
"Eight-Hour Orphans," 133
Eliot, Charles, 82

elitism, of domestic science, 76, 99, 102–3
Elliot, S. Maria, 91
Emerson, George B., 39
Emerson, Joseph, 1, 28–29, 181
emotions: collective dimension, 123–24, 134; movement and "sliding," 157; narrativized context, 123; repetition, 154–55; rhetorical nature of, 123–24, 129; spatial rhetorics of, 7, 11, 27, 122–25, 129–34, 159, 164–65, 186–88; "sticky," 129, 151–52, 154–57; structural influences on, 187
The Employments of Women: A Cyclopaedia of Woman's Work I (Penny), 181
enargeia (vivid textual description), 139
Endres, Danielle, 8, 9
engendering space, 26, 32–33, 36, 43, 48, 179, 182–84
enthymematic argument, 105–6, 109, 197n13
epideictic strategy, 104–6, 109
"Essay on the Construction of School-Houses" (Alcott), 46
ethos: Aristotelian trifecta, 74, 97, 115; audience, 74, 88–89, 98–103, 111, 124; authority and, 74–75, 111; collective construction of, 74–75, 79–80, 106, 109; of domestic science, 73–74, 77–80, 84, 88–97, 118–19; as dwelling, 74; good sense as criterion, 92; higher education and construction of, 81; as negotiation, 99; precedes actor, 77, 88–89; professional, 6, 13, 27, 74–76, 88–89, 172; space connected to, 2, 74–75, 118–19
Evans, Mary Elizabeth, 143
extracurricular education, 81, 86, 110

fantasy echo, 30
Federal Housing Administration, 162, 164
Female Education (Emerson), 1, 28–29
Female Education (Phelps), 42
"Female Education" (Hale), 45
femininity, spatial discourse of, 36
feminism: architectural plans, critiques of, 23, 178; materialist/maternalist strand, 17–18, 178; women's work and, 184–86
feminist scholarship, 5–12, 116, 171–77, 180; emotive spatial rhetorics and working motherhood, 186–88
A Few Thoughts on the Powers and Duties of Woman (Mann), 60
"Figural Materialism: Renovating Marriage through the American Family Home" (McAlister), 179
Finck, Barbara, 146–47, *147*
Finnegan, Cara, 146
Fleming, David, 10
Floyd, Janet, 21
Food and Dietetics, 91
Foucault, Michel, 27, 175
Frugal Housewife (Child), 78, 97

Gallaudet University, 174–75
gender geography, 22, 42, 60, 184
Gerard, Margaret, 128–29
GI Bill, 162
Gilman, Charlotte Perkins, 79, 196n2
Glenn, Cheryl, 23
Glover, Katherine, 133, 135, 148
Godey's Lady's Book, 39, *40*, *41*, 56, 62
Goodrich, Henrietta, 114
Gordon, Linda, 14
Great Depression, 125–30, *126*, *127*, 136
Green, Emma, 175
Gross, Daniel, 27

Hale, Sarah Josepha, 45
Hall, G. Stanley, 83
Hallenbeck, Sarah, 19, 34, 180
Halloran, S. Michael, 74, 79, 81
Halttunen, Karen, 8
Happy Home and Parlor Magazine, 36
Hariman, Robert, 123–24
Harris, Samuel F., 118
Harvey, David, 12, 175
Hatcher, Jessamyn, 21
hauntings, 176
Hayden, Dolores, 17–18, 23, 36, 163, 165, 178
"Health Problems in Child Care Centers" (Wetherill), 120, *121*
Heidegger, Martin, 74
"Help Mothers Win the War" (Beer), 137, 145
Hoffman, Nancy, 71
Hogg, Charlotte, 116
home: childcare centers equated with, 5, 122, 124, 137, 138–46; as economic unit of production, 35–36, 78–79; emotional spatial rhetorics of, 37–39, 124–25; ideological component, 38–39; intersectional understanding of, 177–78; lack of housing, 131–32, 161–62; lived experiences of, 130–32; master bedroom, 179; physical and decorative features, 33, 42, 179; school as, 6, 31–32, 52–57, 60–62, 66; as scientific site, 73–75, 90–91; soldiers, investment in, 127; spatial rhetorics of, 6, 176–80, 182; spatial rhetorics of, turn of nineteenth century, 35–43; wartime effects on, 130–32; working mothers and, 126–29. *See also* architectural plans; domestic science; white middle-class home

home economics, 85–87, 114–15, 196–97n4, 197nn6, 7. *See also* domestic science
"Homeplace (a site of resistance)" (hooks), 177–78, 199n1
Honey, Maureen, 125, 168
hooks, bell, 177–78, 199n1
Hoover, Herbert, 128
Household Bacteriology (Elliot), 91
Household Management (Terrill), 78–79
housing, 131–33; anti-urban sentiment, 37; "victory home," 39, 122, 155, 161–64
Howe, Julia Ward, 17
Hubbard, Phil, 9
Hull-House, 100
Hunt, Caroline, 103, 104–5, 109, 196n1
Hunt, Tim, 182
Hyde, Michael, 74, 115
Hygeia article, 120, *121*
Hymes, James, 138, 143

identities: intersectional, 4–7, 14–15, 75–76, 177–78; professional, 35, 73–75, 81–82, 85, 87, 90; property of, 95–96; regendered, 32–33, 57–62, 176
idios (private domain), 23
Industrial Revolution, 78–79, 89
innocence of spatiality, 12
intersectionality of race, class, and culture, 5, 7, 14–15, 75–76, 166–68; childcare centers and, 157; homemaking by nonwhite people, 177–78

Jack, Jordynn, 128
Jim Crow ideology, 135
Johnson, Jenell, 134
Johnson, Nan, 174
Johnson, Thomasina, 135

Johnston, Eric, 150
Jones, Jacqueline, 67–68
Jones, Rebecca, 75
Journal of Home Economics, 89, 93, 98, 110, 112
journals and newspapers, 17, 36; childcare center promotion, 138; domestic science, 85, 89, 93, 98, 105, 109, 112; education profession, 47; World War II period, 120–21, *121*

Kaiser Child Service Centers, 134–36, 138, 140, *141, 142,* 143, 149–50; postwar "back-to-home" rhetoric, 155–56, *156*
Keating, AnnLouise, 26
Kellogg, Rhoda, 154
Kennedy, Tammie, 176
Kerber, Linda, 21–22
Kerr, Virginia, 129
Kessler-Harris, Alice, 15
Kimble, James J., 166
Kirsch, Gesa, 189
Kitchin, Rob, 9

laboratories, 82, 102; in home, 94–97, *95*; Women's Laboratory (MIT), 84–85, 87–88, 182
Lake Placid Conferences on Home Economics, 85, 92, 97, 114
Lancasterian system, 65
Langdon, Dr., 132–33
Lanham Act, 134
Larned, Linda Hull, 92
"latchkey children," 121, 133
Leach, Abby, 82
Lean In: Women, Work, and the Will to Lead (Sandberg), 169
Leavitt, Sarah, 78
Lefebvre, Henri, 175–76
Lenroot, Katharine, 129, 133

Leonard, D. L., 64–65
L'Eplattenier, Barbara, 188
Levenstein, Harvey, 100
Lewis, Agnes, 159
Lewis, Tiffany, 111
Library of Home Economics series (Richards et al.), 86, 91, 93, 96
Lindsay, Malvina, 155
Lippincott, Gail, 91
literacy, women's, 45–46
location, politics of, 28
Logan, Shirley Wilson, 68
Lomawaima, K. Tsianina, 65
Loudon, J. C., 57
Lucaites, John, 123–24
Lundberg, Emma, 133
Lyon, Mary, 58, 60, 80

MacDonald, Walter, 158–59
Magazine War Guide, 138
Male Teachers' Association of New York City, 62
Malin, Brent, 123, 166
Mallett, Shelley, 178
Mann, Horace, 46–47, 51, 53–54, 57, 60–61, 66, 195n5
Manpower Commission, 128–29
"Mapping Topoi in the Rhetorical Regendering of Work" (Hallenbeck and Smith), 19
marginalized women's experiences, 7–8, 26, 76, 125–26. See also African American women; race issues; segregation
marriage, 15, 67, 80, 179
Martin, George H., 44–45
Mary Lowell Stone Home Economics exhibit, 109–10
Massachusetts Institute of Technology (MIT), 84–85, 87–88
Massey, Doreen, 36

materiality: feminist movements, 17–18, 23, 178; material renovations, 10, 59; of metaphors, 191; of objects, 12–13; topophilia, 11, 38, 123, 130, 149, 157, 166, 186
Matthews, Glenna, 36, 42
McAlister, Joan Faber, 9, 179
McDowell, Linda, 25, 48, 52
McGinnis, Esther, 161
Mead, Margaret, 150–51, 155
meaning-making, space and, 6–12, 21, 27–29, 33, 70–71, 95, 188
memorial sites, 173–74
Mexican American women, 167–68
Meyer, Agnes, 121, 160
Meyerowitz, Joanne, 14, 18
Micciche, Laura, 129
middle class, growth in, 163–64
Middleton, Joyce Irene, 176
"Minding the Children" (Carson), 139–40
Minns, George, 45
"The Modern City and the Municipal Franchise for Women" (Addams), 112
Morgan, Robin, 115, 184
Morrill Act (1862), 86, 116–17
Mossell, Mrs. N. F., 16
motherhood: domestic science and, 76–77, 88, 92–93; emotional spatial rhetorics and working, 160, 186–87; poverty and, 168–69; republican, 21, 37, 43, 45–46, 61, 80; service to state, 127–28; teaching as similar to, 31, 61, 68–69. *See also* childcare centers; war plants; working mothers
"motherless home," 7, 27, 121–70, 165; lack of housing and, 131–33; spatio-rhetorical anxiety and, 129–34. *See also* childcare centers; war plants

mother's pensions, 23, 127
Mountford, Roxanne, 23
Mount Holyoke Female Seminary, 60, 80
multimodal historiographic research, 24, 123–24, 189–90
"Multimodality in Motion" (Yergeau et al.), 174
mundane spaces, 174–76
municipal housekeeping movement, 76, 111–13
museum, 16, 173
Muzio, Daniel, 183
Myers, Nancy, 75

National Housing Agency, 161–62
nation-state, 35
Native American students, 65–66
New Deal, 131
New England, 35, 44–46; new schoolhouses built, 57–58
New England Kitchen, 76, 99–103, *101*, 111, 114, 116, 197n10
New England Kitchen Magazine, 94, 105, 109
Noddings, Nell, 183
No More Separate Spheres (Davidson and Hatcher), 21
nondeliberate rhetorics, 34, 53, 57–58, 61
Norton, Alice, 90

Obama, Barack, 169
Oberlin, 80
objects, 12–13, 47
occupation, 10–12, 18–19; double meaning of, 8, 180; as source of authority, 74–75; spatial, 10, 18–19, 74–75, 175–76
Occupations for Women: A Book of Practical Suggestions for the

Material Advancement, the Mental and Physical Development, and the Moral and Spiritual Uplift of Women (Willard), 2, 16
Office of Civilian Defense, 150
Office of War Information, 138
oikos (household), 23
Olbrechts-Tyteca, Lucia, 137
Olson, Lester, 166
"On School Houses and School Apparatus" (Adams), 46
Orvell, Miles, 163
Ossing Center, 135, 144
Ott, Brian, 8, 173
Out of the Kitchen-Into the War: Women's Winning Role in the Nation's Drama (Anthony), 185

parlor, school as, 56–57
patriotism: at childcare centers, 143–46, *145*; homeownership as, 162; of working mothers, 125, 128, 129
Penny, Virginia, 181
Perelman, Chaim, 137
performance of space, 32–33, 52–53, 99, 110, 123, 238
Personal Hygiene, 91
Pfister, Elta, 142–43
Phelps, Almira Lincoln, 42
philanthropic work, 113–14, 116
photographs, 139–41, 146
Pittman, Coretta, 88
place, 8–9, 12. *See also* space; woman's place
poverty, working mothers and, 168–69
power, 11–12, 15, 24–28, 33–34, 165–66, 169–70
Practical Illustrations of the Principles of School Architecture (Barnard), 56
Pratt, Richard Henry, 65–66

"The Predominance of Female Teachers" (Cleveland), 62, 64–65
Prelli, Lawrence, 98, 104, 105, 108
Prentice, Allison, 69
presence, 119, 137
private sphere, 20, 60–61, 98. *See also* home; white middle-class home
privatism, 37, 54
professional ethos, 6, 13, 27, 74–76, 88–89, 172
professionalization: of childcare workers, 148; colleges and universities, 73, 77, 80–88, 93
The Profession of Home Making: A Condensed Home-Study Course, 93
professions, feminization of, 183–84
public sphere, 7; homelike spaces, 76, 110–14; as masculine, 6, 36, 42–43, 47–48; municipal housekeeping movement, 76, 111–13; negative understandings of, 47–48; rhetorical spaces, 23–24; women's infiltration of, 22–23
"public woman," epithet of, 43, 51–52, 60
purity, 42–43

Quiñonez, Naomi, 167–68

race issues: child care, 135; homemaking, alternative to white, 177–78; intersectionality of race, class, and culture, 5, 7, 14–15, 75–76, 157, 177–78; teaching and, 34–35, 66–68. *See also* African American women; marginalized women's experiences
"Raising a Baby on Shifts" (Carroll), 120
Ratcliffe, Krista, 176
Refiguring Rhetorical Education (Enoch), 69

regendering: of home, 172–73; of school, 6, 26–27, 32–34, 52–57, 66–69, 172; of space, 26, 32; of teacher identity, 32–33, 57–62, 176; of work, 6, 19, 172
"Reminiscences of Boston Schools-Forty-Five Years Ago" (Minns), 45
"Report of the Secretary of the Board of Education on the Subject of Schoolhouses" (Mann), 46–47
republican motherhood/womanhood, 21, 37, 43, 45–46, 61, 80
reputation, 119
Reverby, Susan, 14
Reynolds, Nedra, 10, 12, 27, 61, 70–71, 191
Rhetorics of Whiteness: Postracial Hauntings in Popular Culture, Social Media, and Education (Kennedy, Middleton, and Ratcliffe), 176
Rice, Jenny, 123
Rich, Adrienne, 28
Richards, Ellen Swallow, 72–74, 77, 84–88, 172, 182, 184, 198n16; displays as public outreach, 98; on drudgery, 89–90; maternal role, 87–88; New England Kitchen and, 99–103; Works: *The Chemistry of Cooking and Cleaning: A Manual for House-keepers* (Richards), 85; "The Housekeeper's Laboratory," 94; *Library of Home Economics* series (Richards et al.), 86, 91, 93, 96; "The Place of Science in Woman's Education," 92
Richmond, California, 131
Richter, Henry, 51, *52*, 62, 196n7
Rivers, Nathaniel A., 191
Roosevelt, Franklin D., 131, 162
Rose, Gillian, 9
Rosie the Riveter, *121*, 125, 166, *167*

Rothery, Agnes Edwards, 127–28
Rottenberg, Catherine, 168–69
Ruiz, Vicki, 167
Rumford, Count, 105–6
Rumford Kitchen, 76, 99, 103–9, *107*, *108*, 110
"Rumford Leaflets," 107
Ryan, Kathleen, 75
Ryan, Mary, 22, 42, 175–76

Sandberg, Sheryl, 5, 19, 169
Schiappa, Edward, 190–91
School Architecture; or, Contributions to the Improvement of School-Houses in the United States (Barnard), 47–51, *50*, *56*, 56–57, 59
Schoolmarms: Women in America's Schools (Walsh), 69–70
schoolmaster, 33, 44
schools: Calvinist theology in, 44, 53; complaints about condition of, 47–52; corporal punishment, 44–45, 51, *52*; early American, 44–46; education at home, 45–46; gendered space of, 28–29; gendered turf wars, 33–34, 62–65; as home, 6, 31–32, 52–57, 60–62, 66; location, 49–50, 54; as masculine, 31–34, 42–48, 51–52, *52*; as palimpsest, 70–71; as parlor, 56–57; physical site, 34, 46–52; as prison, 6, 31–32, 50–62, 172, 173; as private, domestic arena, 60–61; regendering of, 6, 26–27, 32–34, 52–57, 66–69, 172; renovation of, 54–58; shift from masculine to feminine, 6, 31–35, 57–62; as white middle-class space, 34–35. *See also* colleges and universities; teaching profession
Schuyler, Joseph, 160
scientific method, 72, 74, 81, 101, 104

Scott, Joan Wallach, 30, 171, 192
Second Bill of Rights (1944), 162
segregation: childcare centers, 135, 168, 198n5; housing, 157, 163–64, 198n4; in laboratories, 87, 182; schools, 67–68, 135; workplaces, 168, 182, 198n5
Selzer, Jack, 13
Senda-Cook, Samantha, 8, 9
"Separate Spheres, Female Worlds, Woman's Place" (Kerber), 21–22
separate spheres ideology, 20–24, 33, 36, 57; gender geography, 22, 42, 60, 184
Services for Children of Working Mothers in War Time (Office of Civilian Defense), 150
Shapiro, Laura, 79, 85, 86–87
Share Your Home campaign, 131
Sharpless, Rebecca, 15, 117
Sharpling, Gerard, 139
Shaver, Lisa, 75, 119
Shaw, Stephanie, 117
Sigourney, Lydia, 31, 56, 62
Silva, Ines Varela, 182
Skinner, Carolyn, 75
Smith, A. Lapthorn, 83
Smith, Craig, 74, 77
Smith, Mary Roberts, 91, 197n6
Smith, Michelle, 19, 180
social media, 182
Soja, Edward, 12, 165
Sorosis (women's club), 17
space: (re)construction of, 10–11; engendering, 26, 32–33, 36, 43, 48, 179, 182–84; haunted by whiteness, 176; instability of, 9–10, 32; meaning-making and, 6–12, 21, 27–29, 33, 70–71, 95, 188; rhetoricity of, 10, 23–24
Spaces of Hope (Harvey), 175

"Spaces of Remembering and Forgetting: The Reverent Eye/I at the Plains Indian Museum" (Dickinson, Ott, and Aoki), 173
Spain, Daphne, 23, 36, 184
spatial injustice, 165
spatiality: control of, 43; innocence of, 12, 165; theories of, 24–25
spatial parallels, 29, 56, 112, 177, 181
spatial rhetorics, 8–13; of childcare centers, 7, 122–24, 130–47, 152–54; defined, 6–9; domestic science ethos and, 75, 88–97; domestic science experiments, 94–97; domestic violence and, 178–79; emotive, 7, 11, 27, 122–25, 129–34, 159, 164–65, 186–88; feminization of professions, 183–84; gendered debate, 33–34; of home, 6, 176–80, 182; of knowledge, 118–19; nondeliberate, 34, 53, 57–58, 61; of school's physical state, 47–48; selection, 105–7; three premises, 10–11; at turn of nineteenth century, 35–43. *See also* separate spheres ideology
spatial silencing, 164
spatial turn in humanities, 8
spatio-rhetorical analytical method, 9–13, 25, 36, 183, 188–92; artifacts, 189–91; spatial debate, 190–91
sphere, as domain, 21–22
"The Sphere of Woman" (*Godey's Lady's Book*), 39, *40*, 62
Spitzer, Danielle, 182
Spock, Benjamin, 157–58
Stage, Sarah, 84, 85–86, 114–15
Steelman, Ruth, 140, 149–50
Steinem, Gloria, 179
"sticky" emotions, 129, 151–52, 154–57
Stoltzfus, Emilie, 125, 136, 151
Stowe, Harriet Beecher, 1–2, *3, 4,* 39

suburban neighborhoods, 157, 162–64
"The Successful Mother" (Rothery), 127–28
Suggestions respecting Improvements in Education (Beecher), 59–60
Sugrue, Thomas J., 163–64

"Teaching Chemistry in Connection with Domestic Science" (Converse), 90
teaching profession, 5, 13, 18, 31–71; devaluing of, 33, 69–70; diversity in, 66–68; embodied presence, 64–65; feminization and maternalization of, 26–27, 29, 33; indirect influence of woman teacher, 60–61; male students and, 64–65; marginalized women in, 28, 66–68; mother figures, teachers as, 61–62, 66–69; as "overchosen," 66; regendered identity of, 32–33, 57–62, 176; "schoolmarm" figure, 67, 69–70; as way to avoid marriage, 67, 80; women as more fit for, 58–60; women's movement into field, 34–35, 61–62, 172. *See also* schools
temporality, 34
terministic screens, 105
Terrill, Betha, 78–79, 196–97n4
Thomas, M. Carey, 73, 82, 89, 184
Tocqueville, Alexis de, 20
topophilia, 11; for childcare center, 149, 166; for traditional home, 38, 123, 130, 157, 166, 186
transgender people, 175
Tuan, Yi-Fu, 9, 11, 38, 123, 186
Tuthill, Louisa, 20–21

"Uncle Sam Houses His Children" (Brown), 131
unions, 17, 114, 185

Usher, Susannah, 83, 84, 90, 91
Utica Normal and Industrial Institute (Mississippi), 117

Valentine, Gill, 9
Vassar College, 84
veterans, 122, 150, 162
Veysey, Laurence, 80–81
Village and Farm Cottages (Cleaveland, Backus, and Backus), 37
The Village School in an Uproar (Richter), 51, *52*, 62, 196n7
virtue, 21, 42–43
visuals: of childcare centers, 139–41, *140, 141, 142, 144, 145*; in instruction literature, *38*, 39; photographs, 139–41, 146; social media, 182. *See also* display, as spatio-rhetorical strategy
Vocation Office for Girls (Boston), 17
von Pettenkofer, Max, 102
von Voit, Carl, 102

wages, 15–18, 66, 70, 126–27
Walker, Lynne, 23
Walsh, Edwina, 69–70
"War Orphans, U.S.A." (Meyer), 121
war plants, 4–5, 7, 13, 18, 128–38, 157, 184–85; anxieties about women working in, 129–34; boomtowns, 131–32; concerns with efficiency, 134; domestic assistance for mothers, 148; proximity of childcare centers, 134–36. *See also* childcare centers
"Wartime Housing" (Bacon), 131–32
Weber, Ryan P., 191
"We Can Do It" poster (Miller), 166, *167*
Weiner, Lynn, 18, 126
Welter, Barbara, 21, 36
West, Candace, 43

Wetherill, G. G., 120, *121*
When Mother's Away pamphlet, 145
"While Their Parents Build Planes," 143–44, *144*
White House Conference on Child Health and Protection (1930), 129
White House Conference on Children and Youth (1909), 127
white middle-class home, 1–5, 26; African American women as workers in, 14–17, 86, 118, 177; American-ness of, 37; childcare center debates and, 157–58; domestic science focused on, 72–76; dominant notions of, 7–10, 13, 18–20, 25–26, 76–79; idyllic site, contestation of, 76–77, 91–93, 177; Industrial Revolution's effect on, 78–79, 89; marginalized women's experience omitted, 7–8, 26; as national mission, 36–37; as postwar "victory home," 39, 122, 155, 161–64; as sacred place, 160–61; school as, 56; as site of drudgery, 76–77, 79, 89–91, 96; women's role in creating and maintaining, 42. *See also* home
white middle-class women: anxieties about, 18–19, 22, 42, 129–34; policing of, 22, 43, 52. *See also* domestic science; teaching profession; war plants
whiteness, rhetorics of, 18, 68–69; hauntings, 176; nonpresence, 26
Whitney, M. W., 82–83, 93, 94
Willard, Frances, 2, 16
Williams, Fannie Barrier, 16
Williams, Mary, 90–91, 93
"Will They Go Back Home?" (Banning), 153–54
woman's place, 185; home as, 1–2, 20–25, 77; school as, 57–62

women: barriers to access and work, 14–16, 174, 180–81; indirect influence of, 43, 60–61; intersectional identities, 4–7, 14–15, 75–76, 177–78
"Women as Educators" (Leonard), 64
"Women at Work in Wartime" (Glover), 133, 135, 148
"The Women in the War" (Mead), 150–51
Women's Bureau (Department of Labor), 17, 126–27, 150
women's clubs, 17, 110
Women's Laboratory (MIT), 84–85, 87–88, 182
women's rights activists, 79, 87
Women's "True" Profession: Voices from the History of Teaching (Hoffman), 71
women's work, 13–20; African American women and, 14–18, 22, 86, 125–26, 168–69, 177, 182, 198n5; feminism and, 184–86; shifts in, 13–14, 61–62, 172; wages, 15–16, 66, 70, 126–27. *See also* domestic science; teaching profession; war plants
Woolman, Mary Schenck, 83, 94
working class, 37; domestic science and, 99–100, 102–3, 113–14; higher education opportunities, 116–17; resistance to elitism, 102–3; teachers, 67
working mothers, 124–25, 163, 166–70; conditions for, 126–27; demographics, 125; home and, 126–29; marginalized groups, 125–26; national childcare conversations, 132–34; patriotism, 125, 128, 129; resistance to returning home, 150–51; spatio-rhetorical anxiety and, 129–34;

working mothers (*continued*)
white, as social problem, 126. See *also* childcare centers; motherhood; war plants

The Work of the African American Woman (Mossell), 16

World's Congress of Representative Women (1893), 104

World's Fair in St. Louis (Louisiana Purchase Exposition), 110

World War I, 126, 127

World War II period, 5, 7, 18, 120–70; housing, 131–32, 161–63; increase in women's labor force participation, 128–29; mixed signals to women, 128–29; Rosie the Riveter, *121*, 125, 166, *167*; veterans, 122, 150, 162. See *also* childcare centers; war plants

Wright, Gwendolyn, 36

Wulff, Norma, 158

Yergeau, Melanie, 174

Young, John H., 42

The Young Lady's Home (Tuthill), 20–21

Zimmerman, Don H., 43

Zucker, Henry, 133

Jessica Enoch, an associate professor of English at the University of Maryland, is the author of *Refiguring Rhetorical Education: Women Teaching African American, Native American, and Chicano/a Students, 1865–1911* (SIU Press, 2008). She is a coeditor of *Burke in the Archives: Using the Past to Transform the Future of Burkean Studies* (with Dana Anderson), *Women at Work: Rhetorics of Gender and Labor* (with David Gold), and *Mestiza Rhetorics: An Anthology of Mexicana Activism in the Spanish-Language Press, 1887–1922* (with Cristina Devereaux Ramirez).

Studies in Rhetorics and Feminisms

Studies in Rhetorics and Feminisms seeks to address the interdisciplinarity that rhetorics and feminisms represent. Rhetorical and feminist scholars connect rhetorical inquiry with contemporary academic and social concerns, exploring rhetoric's relevance to current issues of opportunity and diversity. This interdisciplinarity is transforming the rhetorical tradition as we have known it (upper-class, agonistic, public, and male) into regendered, inclusionary rhetorics (democratic, dialogic, collaborative, cultural, and private). Our intellectual advancements depend on such ongoing transformation.

Rhetoric, whether ancient, contemporary, or futuristic, always inscribes the relation of language and power at a particular moment, indicating who may speak, who may listen, and what can be said. The only way we can displace the traditional rhetoric of masculine-only, public performance is to replace it with rhetorics that are recognized as being better suited to our present needs. We must understand more fully the rhetorics of the non-Western tradition, of women, of a variety of cultural and ethnic groups. Therefore, Studies in Rhetorics and Feminisms espouses a theoretical position of openness and expansion, a place for rhetorics to grow and thrive in a symbiotic relationship with all that feminisms have to offer, particularly when these two fields intersect with philosophical, sociological, religious, psychological, pedagogical, and literary issues.

The series seeks scholarly works that both examine and extend rhetoric, works that span the sexes, disciplines, cultures, ethnicities, and sociocultural practices as they intersect with the rhetorical tradition. After all, the recent resurgence of rhetorical studies has been not so much a discovery of new rhetorics as a recognition of existing rhetorical activities and practices, of our newfound ability and willingness to listen to previously untold stories.

The series editors seek both high-quality traditional and cutting-edge scholarly work that extends the significant relationship between rhetoric and feminism within various genres, cultural contexts, historical periods, methodologies, theoretical positions, and methods of delivery (e.g., film and hypertext to elocution and preaching).

Queries and submissions:

Professor Emerita Shirley Wilson Logan
University of Maryland
Email: slogan@umd.edu

Cheryl Glenn
Department of English
402 Burrowes Bldg.
Penn State University
University Park, PA 16802-6200
Email: cjg6@psu.edu

Other Books in the Studies in Rhetorics and Feminisms Series

*Retroactivism in the Lesbian Archives:
Composing Pasts and Futures*
Jean Bessette

*Feminist Rhetorical Science Studies:
Human Bodies, Posthumanist Worlds*
Edited by Amanda K.
Booher and Julie Jung

*A Feminist Legacy:
The Rhetoric and Pedagogy
of Gertrude Buck*
Suzanne Bordelon

*Regendering Delivery:
The Fifth Canon and
Antebellum Women Rhetors*
Lindal Buchanan

Rhetorics of Motherhood
Lindal Buchanan

*Conversational Rhetoric:
The Rise and Fall of a Women's
Tradition, 1600–1900*
Jane Donawerth

*Mestiza Rhetorics:
An Anthology of Mexicana Activism in
the Spanish-Language Press, 1887–1922*
Edited by Jessica Enoch and
Cristina Devereaux Ramírez

Feminism beyond Modernism
Elizabeth A. Flynn

Women and Rhetoric between the Wars
Edited by Ann George, M. Elizabeth
Weiser, and Janet Zepernick

*Rhetorical Feminism and
This Thing Called Hope*
Cheryl Glenn

*Educating the New Southern Woman:
Speech, Writing, and Race at the
Public Women's Colleges, 1884–1945*
David Gold and Catherine L. Hobbs

Food, Feminisms, Rhetorics
Edited by Melissa A. Goldthwaite

*Women's Irony:
Rewriting Feminist Rhetorical Histories*
Tarez Samra Graban

*Claiming the Bicycle:
Women, Rhetoric, and Technology
in Nineteenth-Century America*
Sarah Hallenbeck

*The Rhetoric of Rebel Women:
Civil War Diaries and
Confederate Persuasion*
Kimberly Harrison

*Evolutionary Rhetoric:
Sex, Science, and Free Love in
Nineteenth-Century Feminism*
Wendy Hayden

*Liberating Voices:
Writing at the Bryn Mawr Summer
School for Women Workers*
Karyn L. Hollis

*Gender and Rhetorical Space
in American Life, 1866–1910*
Nan Johnson

*Antebellum American Women's Poetry:
A Rhetoric of Sentiment*
Wendy Dasler Johnson

*Appropriate[ing] Dress:
Women's Rhetorical Style in
Nineteenth-Century America*
Carol Mattingly

*The Gendered Pulpit
Preaching in American
Protestant Spaces*
Roxanne Mountford

*Writing Childbirth:
Women's Rhetorical Agency
in Labor and Online*
Kim Hensley Owens

*Rhetorical Listening:
Identification, Gender, Whiteness*
Krista Ratcliffe

*Feminist Rhetorical Practices:
New Horizons for Rhetoric,
Composition, and Literacy Studies*
Jacqueline J. Royster and
Gesa E. Kirsch

*Rethinking Ethos:
A Feminist Ecological
Approach to Rhetoric*
Edited by Kathleen J. Ryan, Nancy
Myers, and Rebecca Jones

*Vote and Voice:
Women's Organizations and
Political Literacy, 1915–1930*
Wendy B. Sharer

*Women Physicians and Professional
Ethos in Nineteenth-Century America*
Carolyn Skinner

*Praising Girls:
The Rhetoric of Young
Women, 1895–1930*
Henrietta Rix Wood